MEDIA, DEMOCRACY AND SOCIAL CHANGE

MEDIA, DEMOCRACY AND SOCIAL CHANGE

RE-IMAGINING POLITICAL COMMUNICATIONS

AERON DAVIS
NATALIE FENTON
DES FREEDMAN
GHOLAM KHIABANY

Los Angeles | London | New Delhi
Singapore | Washington DC | Melbourne

Los Angeles | London | New Delhi
Singapore | Washington DC | Melbourne

SAGE Publications Ltd
1 Oliver's Yard
55 City Road
London EC1Y 1SP

SAGE Publications Inc.
2455 Teller Road
Thousand Oaks, California 91320

SAGE Publications India Pvt Ltd
B 1/I 1 Mohan Cooperative Industrial Area
Mathura Road
New Delhi 110 044

SAGE Publications Asia-Pacific Pte Ltd
3 Church Street
#10-04 Samsung Hub
Singapore 049483

© Aeron Davis, Natalie Fenton, Des Freedman and Gholam Khiabany 2020

First published 2020

Editor: Michael Ainsley
Editorial assistant: Amber Turner-Flanders
Production editor: Imogen Roome
Copyeditor: Aud Scriven
Proofreader: Leigh C. Smithson
Indexer: Adam Pozner
Marketing manager: Susheel Gokarakonda
Cover design: Lisa Harper-Wells
Typeset by: Cenveo Publisher Services

Library of Congress Control Number: 2020940586

British Library Cataloguing in Publication data

A catalogue record for this book is available from the British Library

ISBN 978-1-5264-5695-3
ISBN 978-1-5264-5696-0 (pbk)

CONTENTS

ACKNOWLEDGEMENTS

For the last decade each of the authors of this book has been involved in the running and teaching of a Master of Arts (MA) programme in Political Communications at Goldsmiths, University of London where we all work. It has been a joy. Students come to us from all over the world and from many different political persuasions, but they all share one thing – a passion for politics. We would like to thank wholeheartedly each and every one of them. They have helped us to see things differently, interrogate political communications anew and better understand our own relationships to the field. And many have joined us along the way in campaigning to create change in the world. Thank you all – you have been a constant source of inspiration.

The MA in Political Communications was designed on the premise of bringing critical perspectives to the fore. Being critical means getting political. The questions we ask in this course are the same ones that prompted us to write this book: How do we live our politics on a daily basis as academics and as activists? Who holds the power to influence the political decisions that structure our lives? How might democracy be done better? What is the relationship between politics, the individual, institutions and the media? And crucially, where can we find political hope in times of crisis? Very many friends and colleagues have, perhaps unwittingly, offered their insight, direction, support, solidarity and a fair bit of political solace in meetings, at pubs, at conferences, on marches, on picket lines and demonstrations, as we have struggled to find answers to these questions. We want to extend a heartfelt thank you to everyone, but in particular to Sarah Banet-Weiser, Veronica Barassi, Lance Bennett, Mike Berry, Clea Bourne, Andrew Calabrese, Bart Cammaerts, Paula Chakravartty, James Curran, Stephen Cushion, Will Davies, Lina Dencik, Lee Edwards, Greg Elmer, Myria Georgiou, Jeremy Gilbert, Peter Golding, Deborah Grayson, David Hesmondhalgh, Dan Jackson, Jo Littler, Mirca Madianou, Angela McRobbie, Tom Mills, Liz Moor, Graham Murdock, Kaarina Nikunen, Angela Phillips, Victor Pickard, Joanna Redden, Anamik Saha, Heather Savigny, Bev Skeggs, Annabelle Sreberny, Gavan Titley, Emiliano Trere, Hilary Wainwright, Andy Williams, Milly Williamson, Kate Wright, Barbie Zelizer.

We also want to thank the Department of Media, Communications and Cultural Studies at Goldsmiths for continuing against all the odds to be a place in the university sector where politics is still welcomed and encouraged as a crucial part of what we do and who we are as academics. Long may it last. And to all the academic and professional support staff, the technicians, the porters, the cleaners and the catering staff at Goldsmiths who have played a vital part in enabling us to think, write, teach and do what we do, the best we can. In this atmosphere of collegiality and contestation the ideas and debates behind this book have grown and developed together. To acknowledge this we are keen for it to be read as a collaborative undertaking, although each of us have taken prime responsibility for the main writing of two chapters: Chapter 1: Natalie Fenton; Chapter 2: Des Freedman; Chapter 3: Des Freedman; Chapter 4: Aeron Davis; Chapter 5: Aeron Davis; Chapter 6: Gholam Khiabany; Chapter 7: Natalie Fenton; Chapter 8: Gholam Khiabany.

Thank you to Michael Ainsley at Sage who encouraged us to do it in the first place, was good humoured and supportive throughout, and didn't get fed up when we were campaigning instead of writing.

The biggest thank you of all of course goes to our partners and families who bear the brunt of academic lives lived in political turmoil.

A CORONAVIRUS FOREWORD

It is April 2020. We are copyediting this volume while in lockdown, from our different homes. We wrote this book in the knowledge that media, democracy and society were being radically reconfigured by globalisation, new technologies and neoliberalism. The great financial crash, platform capitalism, legacy media collapses and the rise of right-wing populist leaders were some of the challenging by-products of these shifts. We felt the fields of political communication, journalism and media studies needed to critically engage with such developments more than they had done.

Six months after handing over the completed manuscript, it is now apparent that we were writing just prior to an unforeseen global disaster; one whose consequences are set to change the world around us. COVID-19, which soon spread from mainland China to every part of the world in a matter of months, now threatens nations on multiple levels. At the time of writing, over three million people have been infected and over 211,000 people have died. It is likely that these figures will grow manyfold as the virus continues to mutate and spread, having a devastating impact on poorer nations with fewer economic and health resources to call on. Most countries are in a state of protracted lockdown. Economies have simply stopped functioning. Vaccines and other possible health solutions are months if not years away. No nation has a clear exit strategy for or any idea of when or how we will return to business as normal.

It is very difficult to predict where this is all leading. Such is the level of shock to socio-economic and political systems, and such is the potential for multiple domino effects to occur, that any serious forecasts can become redundant in a matter of days. The big question is whether this worldwide event will lead to new paradigm shifts and the kind of grand transformations of societies that took place after the Second World War. Or, will the same trends, highlighted and critiqued in this volume, continue as before, as they tended to do after the great financial crash of 2007–8?

At this point, we can only briefly speculate on what seems fairly apparent in the medium term and attempt to outline some key questions to think about. One such outcome is that four decades of mainstream economic thinking has been turned on its head. Stock markets are pogoing up and down. Months of lockdown of non-essential employment is proving disastrous to many sectors, from manufacturing to retail, international airlines to Hollywood. Millions are being made unemployed every day. Treasury departments and central banks in wealthier economies are scrambling to keep companies afloat, boost benefit schemes and maintain capital flowing through their economies. In order to do so, they are borrowing or inventing quantities of capital at levels they previously said were impossible.

The economic impact is clearly not being felt evenly. The ability of poorer economies to lockdown their peoples, borrow to stay afloat and prevent mass infections is far more limited. Precarious workers, on zero hours or temporary contracts, are the first to be let go. Large numbers of people have little or no savings to keep them going and minimal spaces to relocate to for extended periods of lockdown. Debts – whether personal, corporate or public – are skyrocketing.

Whenever the dust eventually clears, it will be extremely hard to go back to neoliberal economic norms. Debts, including sovereign debt, will be unserviceable. Many companies and whole industries will either be bust, have crippling debts or be nationalised. As in wartime, much larger parts of the economy will have to be state-managed. Governments will have to decide what parts of the economy to save and what to let go. So much for the once dominant logics of free markets, privatisation, austerity economics and 'magic money trees'. But if they are gone, what alternative schools of economic thought might take their place?

Globalisation is rapidly moving into reverse. It was already slowing in the wake of the financial crisis, rising trade barriers and with a new cohort of nationalist-populist leaders. But now, many international flows and exchanges have come to an abrupt halt. More than 90% of flights have stopped. Borders have been solidly closed. Powerful states are competing ever more viciously for precious health equipment on international markets. Economic unions, such as the European Union, are coming under increasing strain as nations, of necessity, seek alternative social and economic solutions. International investment has stopped and international bodies, such as the United Nations (UN), the World Health Organization (WHO) and the Organisation for Economic Co-operation and Development (OECD), pinball between opposing national agendas. What vision of globalisation will emerge from the crisis and which states are likely to be more dominant in any new world order?

While neoliberal economic norms may be crumbling before our eyes, governments around the globe are desperately trying to assert command and control policies with dramatic consequences for democratic rights. The difference between government responses lies not in a better healthcare provision in countries with less casualties, but in their governments' repressive measures and serious restrictions in circulation of information. The bourgeoisie, which according to the *Communist Manifesto* had drawn 'even the most barbarian nations into civilisation' by rapid improvement of instruments of production and the means of communication, is increasingly using barbarian means and policies to roll back the most civilised gains of people everywhere. The evidence is undeniable. In the UK reports of domestic violence have increased by 50% in recent weeks; and abortion rights are under attack in the United States, Britain and Poland (Marty, 2020; Sowemimo, 2020; Walker, 2020). The Modi government in India suspended the ban on prenatal sex testing and disclosure of the sex of foetuses which had been introduced to stop selective abortion of female foetuses (Bose, 2020). Women represent 70% of the health and social sector workforce globally and carry the significant burden of caring for elderly relatives and children, and yet they have become one of the main targets of assorted government responses in the current crisis. A large number of employed women work parttime and under the most uncaring and uncertain working conditions, and these are precisely the kinds of jobs that are at risk. Pandemics affect women and men differently (Lewis, 2020).

Contrary to government propaganda everywhere, COVID-19 discriminates. African-American people represent 13% of the United States, population but over one-third of the victims of COVID-19 have been black. In Britain, according to a black health activist, 'whilst BME communities account for 14% of the UK population, they make up 44% of NHS doctors and 24% of nurses. But 70% of front-line workers who have died are BME' (Farah, 2020). In Britain black and Asian people are more than twice as likely to be affected than white people (Fekete, 2020) and we see similar pictures in other countries. Indigenous people in Brazil and other Latin American nations as well as aboriginal people in Australia are at a much higher risk. The link with racism is also apparent in the rapid rise of racial abuse and violence in general and towards Chinese communities in particular. The death toll in refugee camps is also on the rise and the overcrowding, lack of medical facilities and basic provisions represent a frightening scenario.

As governments begin to contemplate the date of resuming 'business as normal', the normal business of repression and war of many communities and countries has not been suspended. Kashmir remains under permanent lockdown, and repression and restriction has intensified with Modi's decision to extend the high-speed internet ban in the region; Israel's bombing and the siege of Gaza has continued as the world diverts its gaze elsewhere; Saudi Arabia might have restricted air travel, but not for the fighter jets that bomb Yemen; the tragedy of Syria continues; the failed state of Libya is failing even more; and the United States continues to pursue its aggressive and inhuman sanctions against a number of countries. Yet all our mainstream news channels are dominated by one thing: COVID-19.

The coronavirus crisis, which has highlighted the devastating impact of the erosion of democratic processes and institutions, is being used to introduce and implement new restrictions. In March 2020, research by openDemocracy revealed that parliaments in thirteen countries were partially or fully suspended, leaving more than 500 million people unrepresented (Provost et al., 2020). Around the world, addressing the current crisis is managed not through investment in health care but through punishment. In Kenya the police are beating and killing people. In India migrant workers are beaten and sprayed with chemicals and thousands of workers – old, young and children – are forced to walk hundreds of miles to return home to self-isolate. In the Philippines, poor people who have violated the curfew are put in dog cages; and in Paraguay people are beaten and threatened with tasers. A new policy passed by Hungary's parliament is allowing Prime Minister Orban to rule by decree and in the Philippines and Thailand a state of emergency has been declared (Ratcliffe, 2020). It is not just that the lockdown has temporarily stopped the wave of pro-democracy/anti-neo-liberal protests and revolts which had dominated the political landscapes in Iraq, Iran, Lebanon, Argentina, Chile, Ecuador, France, and many more countries. Governments are preparing for the protests that are surely to come when the devastating impact of job losses and poverty become even more visible. Such assaults on the democratic rights of citizens, carried out in the name of protecting them, is already part of the strategy of political establishments around the world for tackling the crisis. The 'herd' has no immunity under Covid Capitalism. In the calmer political climate of Britain, the human rights organisation Liberty has labelled new emergency laws introduced as part of the government's response to COVID-19 as the 'biggest restriction of our freedom in a generation' (Liberty, 2020). Fekete has rightly warned us that history 'teaches us that inhumane police practices are quick to establish but hard to dismantle with long-term consequences for policing by consent within a democratic order' (2020).

Meanwhile, political parties and the recent resurgence of populist right-wing politicians continues along with the drive towards nationalism. Tub-beating, 'strong' leaders are looked to in times of national crisis. Experts remain conflicted as those in health, business and politics are confronted with new problems they have no immediate answers for. Public support for leaders like Donald Trump, Boris Johnson and Jair Bolsonaro remained fairly robust in the early months of the crisis. However, it is also likely that the relatively slow responses of these regimes will also lead to some of the highest death tolls too. Months if not years of economic crisis are also likely to dent their poll ratings. Will the hardships endured on the ground – the loss of jobs, the demise of democratic rights and the death of thousands of people – lead to a new rise in radical left-wing parties or a return to technocratic centrist politics? In the UK, a raft of activism has emerged over sick pay, police powers, protection and rights for care-workers and nurses, food supplies and universal basic income, all of which highlight the fundamental social inequalities that a pandemic exposes and that we refer to throughout this book. Alongside the protest, local mutual aid groups are emerging, often organising online in an attempt to respond to the daily consequences of a lockdown for the sick and the vulnerable and highlighting the cracks of a decimated welfare system.

The pandemic has certainly intensified some of the trends that we highlight in the rest of this book. The state is now forced into playing an interventionist role in national life – co-ordinating bailouts, presiding over lockdowns, and disseminating propaganda and public relations – that many theorists deemed to be impossible with the alleged hollowing out of the state under neoliberalism. Coronavirus has provided the authorities with an opportunity to ramp up surveillance under the guise of mass testing, tracing and identification, but also, as in the cases of Hungary and South Africa, to weaken press freedom by introducing new laws on the publication of 'false information' that increases states' oversight over the right to free expression. It is also the case that with newspapers facing economic meltdown due to the collapse in advertising revenue, the state is now being asked by the news industry to step in and underwrite the journalism that is now defined as an 'essential service'. In the case of the UK, this is particularly ironic given that the press campaigned long and hard against effective regulation on the basis that it would lead to unwarranted state 'intrusion' into the industry.

Another preoccupation of this book concerns the extent to which the balance of power in the political communications landscape is tilting away from traditional news media and towards digital intermediaries. It is certainly true that the digital giants will be the ones to benefit: Amazon is flourishing amid the pandemic, with Jeff Bezos adding over £19bn to his fortune in the first quarter of 2020. Google and Facebook have joined forces to develop a contact tracing app that could see private industry partnering with public agencies in an almighty data grab with huge commercial advantage for Big Tech.

Concerns over 'fake news' have also come to the fore once more. However, preliminary reports into the scale of misinformation suggests that, despite the World Health Organization's claims of an 'infodemic', a majority of misleading reports consist of repurposing existing claims about, for example, remedies, rather than outright fabrication (Brennen et al., 2020). Ofcom, the UK's communications regulator, found that nearly half of all respondents had encountered some false or misleading information but that, to the extent they came across this misinformation in closed groups or social media, these were also the least trusted platforms (Ofcom, 2020). This does not fully compensate for the harm done by populist leaders, such as those in Italy, Brazil, Hungary and the US, who have used their own channels to propagate racist conspiracy theories and to challenge emerging scientific consensus on COVID-19, but it does suggest some limits to the impact of deliberate misinformation.

Perhaps a more significant issue – and one that we deal with throughout this volume – is the residual political impact of the mainstream news media precisely because it tends to trade less in outright distortion than in more subtle agenda-setting that promotes elite frames. Many established news organisations saw huge increases in traffic and ratings as publics desperately tried to make sense of the pandemic. The European Broadcasting Union reported a 20% increase in audiences for news bulletins of public service broadcasters, while in the UK, 27 million people (around 40% of the entire population) viewed the prime minister's announcement of lockdown on television with a further 24 million tuning in to watch the Queen's 'broadcast to the nation'. Meanwhile the *Guardian*, *Financial Times* and *Telegraph* all recorded record figures for their online content, evidence that legacy outlets were particularly well placed to benefit from this spike in interest given the global scale of the pandemic. Furthermore, predictions of the inexorable decline of the BBC (under pressure from commercial rivals like Netflix together with changing patterns of media consumption) would appear to be a little premature, when Ofcom figures show that 82% of the online population regularly turned to the BBC for news and information about COVID-19, with 36% of them identifying the BBC as their *main* source of information, far above any other platform (Ofcom, 2020). Mainstream media are playing a hugely significant role in how the crisis is narrated and, crucially, in framing the debate about what kind of changes societies will need to make following the pandemic.

Yet despite some impressive examples of comprehensive and critical reporting, fact-checking and scrutinising, there have been repeated examples across different environments of a failure systematically to interrogate government responses. Instead there is a propensity to amplify official statements in endless bland press briefings and to reproduce the slogan that 'we're all in this together'. Of course, even a global pandemic does not magically transcend pre-existing political loyalties, so there was far more criticism on liberal US cable news networks of, for example, Donald Trump's haphazard steering of the crisis than there was of the UK government's actions concerning testing and tracing across the majority of the British press.

Two consequences flow from this. First, that those welcome examples of hard-hitting journalism do not signify a durable or profound radicalisation of our political communications systems, but instead simply illustrate the depth of the social and economic crisis today – a classic example of 'indexing'. Second, that even the increased audiences and occasional outburst of truth-telling have failed to revive the public's trust in a media contaminated by too many years of accommodation with elite power and corporate priorities. While traditional outlets are certainly trusted more than social media platforms, a series of polls carried out after the outbreak of the pandemic found that journalists were among the least credible sources of information and that, according to a 10-country survey carried out by Edelman (2020), employers were trusted far more than governments and media, with officials and journalists 'at the bottom of the rank'. A poll for Kekst CNC in April 2020 found that there had been a significant decline in public confidence in the media in Germany, the US, the UK and Sweden and that the media were, across the board, the worst performing sector (Kekst CNC, 2020). It seems that even a crisis as serious as the coronavirus is not going to restore the credibility of our dominant political communications actors.

Instead, what we need more than ever is a fiercely independent and critical media that truly 'comforts the afflicted and afflicts the comfortable' – neither the risk-averse stenography of much public service broadcasting nor the click-bait of online media. We do not know how life will change after coronavirus but, just as huge questions are being asked about our political priorities and economic norms, we must make sure that our political communications systems do not return to 'normal' service.

1

PUTTING POLITICS BACK INTO POLITICAL COMMUNICATIONS

INTRODUCTION

We are writing this book in 2019. Donald Trump has been President of the United States of America for two years. The UK is (endlessly) on the verge of leaving the European Union (EU). Established political parties have been shaken as new political parties have emerged and won power in France and Italy. Neo-fascist political groups are gaining in popularity across the US and Europe; Brazil, once a beacon of hope for new democratic practices, has elected the far-right president Jair Bolsonaro. The political landscape is febrile and unstable; uncertainty abounds. In these circumstances, political communications has never been more relevant as a discipline, just as the practices and institutions that it interrogates have never been more central to the conduct of politics and public affairs. Trends, so readily tossed around by commentators, policymakers and politicians, from the emergence of 'post-truth' to the circulation of 'fake news', and from the ubiquity of political marketing to the importance of data mining, are seen to shape political landscapes as never before. Political life is ever more thoroughly infused with symbolic practices and communicative dynamics; the idea and practice of politics is endlessly *narrated*, *mediated*, *affected*, *imagined* and *technologised*. Political communications, once a fringe specialism that occupied the borderlands of political science and media studies, has moved into the limelight of academic research and scholarly output.

Yet there is a problem. On the one hand, there is a danger that the lure of technology seduces the reach of our analyses into political communications such that they are entranced by the platforms, actors and rituals that we seek to evaluate; that, as we are part of the social order we are studying, so we too become mesmerised by the passion and rage of social media exchanges and the unfettered power of algorithms to shape public debate and knowledge; that we elevate media logics above often more fundamental (and less visible) conflicts concerning resource distribution, and end up defining power in relation to the management of symbolic spaces and the use of rhetorical flourishes rather than broader political economic systems. Perversely, this focus on media logics also serves to shift an emphasis away from politics itself. What types of politics communicated in what sorts of ways are able to address the current crises we face, are undoubtedly key questions for the field. But by prioritising the communicative we have too often relegated the political to a secondary order, only relevant in relation to the forms of communication it is manifest in rather than being a construct of the social, economic and cultural context it is part of. And so we begin this book with the contention that political communications runs the risk of diminishing the political and fetishising the communicative. And this is something we should be ever mindful of.

On the other hand, the context we seek to situate our analyses within needs to free itself from the straitjacket of taken-for-granted Western/liberal/secular assumptions of relative homogeneity as divergent voices emerge and demand recognition. As distinctions of left and right politics are challenged, as political elites from established parties are increasingly distrusted and rejected in elections, as citizens search for alternative political solutions to ever-increasing problems, the old recourse to liberal democratic political framing has been drawn into question and found wanting. Yet much work in political communications still takes Western concepts and practices of liberal democracy as its starting point, organising premise and ultimate aim. This is despite its many shifting configurations and failures: increased levels of inequality between and within nation-states, the change in the nature of the state at a national and global level, rejection of mainstream political parties too often seen as self-serving and non-representative, and the hollowing out of institutions in which publics have traditionally sought to engage in political activities. And so, as we engage with a critical political analysis, we also need to consider how we think beyond the confines of liberal democracy to what democracy could become, and the type of political visions that may be required to take us there.

At a time when established political norms are increasingly fragile, there are huge opportunities for a renewal not simply of political communications but of politics itself. When struggles for democracy in democratic societies and elsewhere have intensified, there is a need to go beyond the defence and recovery of hard-earned democratic rights within a liberal democratic framework that threatens to return us to the very politics that got us into these difficulties in the first place. This is particularly true for political communications that often begins and ends with the entirely understandable yet sadly misplaced defence of communicative plurality devoid of a critique of power and politics and the social and economic inequalities of unjust social structures. Liberal democracy reduced to a diversity politics of communicative abundance is where so much scholarship in political communications returns to and is most comfortable (Fenton and Titley, 2015). It is an approach that has become so normalised, so expected, so much part of a certain academic common sense, that it refuses to acknowledge its own assumptions and recognise that it too is operating from a particular political premise located often in a Western colonial past where liberal democracy is couched as a benevolent saviour. Or from a place where meritocratic, market-friendly understandings of equality and freedom feel most at home.

This book is an attempt to remind ourselves that at the heart of the political/communications nexus sits the unfulfilled promises of modern capitalism in this particular neoliberal moment: a heart that bleeds from a degenerative democracy, that aches from an exasperated citizenry, that is under attack from massive and increasing inequality, a weakened establishment and a degraded public sphere. Our objective is to assess how recent structural developments concerning neoliberal economics, state power and political engagement have affected the political communications environment, and to identify the ways in which media and communications can play a role in the radical critique of neoliberal democratic frames and the regeneration of democracy done differently.

So it should be clear from the outset that in its critique of political communications this book itself has a politics – just as all others do but so rarely acknowledge or care to reflect on what that politics might mean. Bringing politics to the forefront of political communications means recognising its genealogy in particular canons of thought as well as in particular political contexts and histories. And in doing so, it also allows the reimagining of what a democratic politics might mean in the digital age.

Wearing our political hearts on our sleeves means that our critique begins from a different starting place that does not prioritise the communicative realm, but rather seeks to take account of the social order of institutionalised capitalism (Fraser and Jaeggi, 2018) of which the communicative realm is a part. This then directs us towards an analysis of structural inequality, technological change, political realignment and the possibilities for *social transformation* (that are too often left out because they require a politics to be recognised and made relevant). In doing so, we hope to go beyond an analysis of the current moment to imagine how things could be otherwise.

This is where this book takes its leave. It is an argument for engaging with the political; an argument for the imperative of *critical theory*. Horkheimer (1982) once said that critical theory is adequate only if it meets three criteria: it must be *explanatory*, *practical*, and *normative*. Most of us get stuck on the first – how many of us ever do all three? Critical analysis must be empirical social enquiry and be framed by normative philosophical argument so that it can explain what is wrong with current social reality, identify the actors to change it and, in so doing, provide both clear norms for criticism and achievable practical goals for social and political transformation. To be explanatory, practical and normative requires interrogating 'the political' including our own political values and assumptions. Without it, we cannot understand what is going on or assess where we want to be and we cannot begin to determine how to get there. And so we are attempting to restore the centrality of politics – struggles over the reproduction of everyday social relations – to our scholarship, as we also attempt to understand how technologies and systems of communication are themselves shaped by and interact with these struggles.

There are many ways to refocus forms of critical analysis in political communications, but whichever way you do so requires the structures and consequences of capitalism and liberal democracy to be front and centre of our analyses. Such an analysis will include the formations and practices of the state as one means of unpicking the many ways in which capitalism and liberal democracy are entangled. But it also requires a deeper understanding of the imbricated relations between structural and cultural factors, including the history, legacies and contemporary lived experiences of colonialism outlined below. Crucially, a critical analysis must also include the identification of an emancipatory political vision.

THE STRUCTURES AND CONSEQUENCES OF CAPITALISM

Our media systems are indelibly connected to the political and economic systems of which they are a part. The brutal form of capitalism that many of us now exist within has massively increased inequality, with the accumulation of wealth in ever fewer hands (Cribb et al., 2018; Dorling, 2014; Oxfam, 2019), and has led to increasingly precarious and insecure labour (Armstrong, 2018), with increases in poverty (Armstrong, 2018; Piketty, 2014), and massive environmental degradation as a result of extractive relations to nature (Intergovernmental Panel on Climate Change [IPCC],

2018; McKie, 2017), alongside the hollowing out of democracy by market forces (Brown, 2015). And as Fraser notes, this has involved 'the corporate capture of political parties and public institutions at the level of the territorial state…[and]…the usurpation of political decision making power at the transnational level by global finance' (Fraser and Jaeggi, 2018: 3). These contemporary characteristics of advanced capitalism form the social, political and economic relations that our media systems exist within. They are part of our social order, of our capitalist social formation and the practices and consequences that this social formation results in – from who owns what, to the forms of labour, the nature of production, the means of exchange, the operation of the markets, and the various stresses and injuries these exert on daily lives lived in debt, insecurity and fear. From the global digital giants channelling our desires for social connection and extracting our data to sell for vast profit to the now almost quaint, old-fashioned moguls of legacy media, capitalism is the vessel they travel in and the politics of neoliberalism creates the conditions for the journey.

If we think back to the Frankfurt School, or to early writings by Habermas, capitalism as a political economic system was central to their analysis. This was the school of critical theory that attempted to explain our social totality through an interdisciplinary project with an historical and material normative foundation and an emancipatory intention. The desire to understand capitalism was an attempt to reveal its deep structures, expose its contradictions and tensions and expound any emancipatory possibilities. When the desire shifted focus to wanting to understand media or technology at a more granular level, then the deep structures and economic systems too frequently became a 'given'. Once capitalism as a political economic system with social and cultural consequences was no longer holding our critical gaze, an acceptance that we need not bother ourselves with alternatives to capitalism seemed to seep into every critical crevice. The digital age was upon us and we became blindsided by its infinite capabilities and potentials. Tools, gadgets, apps; mapping, describing and plotting networks took over. This was communication *science* and it looked so pretty, was so measurable and appeared to be so objective. While understandable as a means to get to grips with a technological revolution, it also left us with solutions stuck largely in a technological bind.

The 'tech for good' brigade

Examples of the technological bind can be found in the 'tech for good' brigade – look how crowdsourcing platforms can be used for gathering and sharing information to foster accountability in the workplace (Arora and Thompson, 2018); look how social media can link communities together and enable them to share resources (Tully and Ekdale, 2014); look how governments and parties can communicate with citizens so much better (Chadwick and Howard, 2009; Delaney, 2019; Gibson, 2015; Kreiss, 2016; Price and Cappella, 2002); look how it can empower citizens and connect family in far-flung places (Oreglia, 2014); look how data mining, contact tracing and machine learning can predict the likelihood of disease outbreaks and control their spread (Mayer-Schonberger and Cukier, 2013) – all of which may well be true of course, but in promising good things to come, our gaze is averted from bigger, broader and deeper concerns about the systemic harms that remain. The 'tech for good' brigade cannot be simplistically written off as the 'cyber-utopians' of yore hell-bent on fervent proclamations of the glorious wonders of technological revolution. Rather, this is a more tempered optimism that frequently recognises the many problems of the internet age (surveillance, data privacy, misinformation, trolling, loneliness, etc.) yet rarely seeks to interrogate why these problems exist. The solution therefore remains in better technology or regulatory reform of the ways technology firms operate. Being seduced by technology then blind-sides us to focus on solutions bound to liberal democratic systems with the permanent offer of what *could be* without a keen critical analysis of *what is*. The 'tech for good' brigade promise just enough commitment to the public interest within this new form of platform commerce and just enough tinkering around the edges with minor reforms to hold technological raptures in check to ensure that capitalism is left unhindered. And so the link between social analysis and normative critique is severed.

The 'tech for good brigade' are a hangover from the naïve utopianism of the 1990s dot-com bubble. The unbridled enthusiasm claiming an epochal technological transforma-tion of all the world's ills may have dampened, but the deep furrows of this ideology are still very much with us and can be found in many areas of media and communications, and particularly in areas focused on social and developmental change. In information and communication technology (ICT) for social change and ICT and development literature there is a strong tendency to look to 'the digital' as a means of removing barriers, building wealth and creating sustainability (Elder et al., 2013) when much of the evidence suggests otherwise, or at least problematises simplistic understandings that tend to disregard or under-emphasise power relations (Madianou, 2015, Madianou et al., 2016; Mansell, 2010; Silva and Westrup, 2009; Thompson, 2008; Unwin, 2009). The notion that expanding internet access is the path to deliverance from poverty, inequality and precarity assumes that a lack of integration into global capitalism is the main cause of these problems rather than the reverse. It supposes that worldwide economic divides can be overcome simply by improving digital literacy, rather than tackling the massive digital corporate dominance of the likes of Google, Facebook and Amazon that seek to turn the world and all our data into a massive advertising and marketing enterprise. The 'tech for good' ideology supports a raft of government and non-profit initiatives to expand internet access and make non-gov-ernmental organisations (NGOs) more tech savvy. In turn, these also provide a convenient public relations (PR) gloss for platform capitalists keen to extend their reach and expand their consumer markets (Arora, 2018).

The 'tech for good' approach also refuses, or at least is very rarely willing, to recognise that they too have a politics. If you believe the internet (more or less in its current form) can solve inequality then you believe that ultimately you can align the desire for social good with profit-driven greed – in other words, that advanced global capitalism can work for the good of everyone despite all the evidence to the contrary. This politics is also associated with what Zuboff (2019) calls 'instrumentarianism': an approach based on the logic of and power that comes from recording and anticipating human behaviour, while refusing to tackle the fact that this data harvesting is also part of a system of capitalism that is using that data to sell to advertisers. In other words, faith in computation replaces politics as a basis for governance.

The 'tech as resistance' posse

It is not only the 'tech for good' brigade that is captured by capitalism, but also those who see the path to resistance of the tech giant takeover as being through disrupting technology in order to unsettle the systems that exist rather than offering broader political economic visions of emancipation. Here we find the hackers and the pirates who may arrive with a revolutionary impulse, but are quickly swallowed up by the geeks' desire to believe in the power of technology as an unruly force that can undermine dominant power and challenge authority. Often the politics of these disruptive interventions align with an anarchist tradition.

Anonymous is a social movement that stems from the online image board 4Chan and originally circulated via subcultural memes across the web, before also spreading offline with the distinctive Guy Fawkes masks visible at many protests around the world. Anonymous 'rejects morality or constraints and features call for absolute freedoms, especially freedom of speech' (McQuillan, 2015: 1372). Lulzsec, a spin-off from Anonymous, specialised in hacking private security firms and state surveillance agencies and then releasing their data to the public. Anonymous caused disruption by launching Distributed Denial of Service Attacks to overload websites of organisations they believed were complicit with corporate and government control. This chimes with Castells' argument that the internet offers multiple prospects for intervention and manipulation, coming from myriad social nodes that can combine to create a new symbolic counter-force capable of shifting dominant power relations and empowering sovereign audiences through the creative autonomy bestowed upon them. Ultimately, Castells suggests this could provide 'the material and cultural basis for the anarchist utopia of networked self-management to become a social practice' (Castells, 2009: 346), such that 'significant political change will result, in due time, from the actions of networked social movements ... Minds that are being opened up by the winds of free communication and inspire practices of empowerment enacted by fearless youth' (Castells, 2015: 312). Such accounts depend on the implicit assumptions about the consequential relations between networked communications and political demands that will result in social and political change. This is a leap of faith that is hard to reconcile with the enduring realities of poverty and the burgeoning wealth of the 1%.

Crucially, this also leaves us with the increasing incorporation of the political into the symbolic and an underlying techno-determinism in approaches to social change. Political participation is construed via the role of the individual subject that develops new techniques of the self as autonomous acts of resistance in a networked world. These acts of resistance will form multitudes that will become social movements, and enlightened capitalists can do the rest by doing their best. But the networks we function within are deeply commodified. While they may be conducive to sociality – and indeed to political mobilisation – they are also a major resource for capitalism that enables the exploitation of labour through constant access to the worker and the erosion of social conditions such as stable contexts for the affiliation, co-operation and organisation that are necessary for alternative discourses to emerge (Fenton, 2016). Politics and political organisation emerge from histories that do not evaporate in the face of technology. The 'tech as resistance' posse prioritise personal autonomy based on the freedom of self-will that all too quickly collapses into individualistic autonomy that is more conducive to the capitalist order rather than destructive of it. Such an approach may enable respect for diversity, but it can never offer a means of breaking free of capitalism to discover ways of living together better through radically democratised political systems.

Media logics undone

There are of course many scholars wanting to understand in deeper sociological ways what a world seeped in media technologies is like. But often, here too, capitalism is more of an inconvenient distraction than a critical starting point and media logics are seen to exert an overarching influence on other areas of social reproduction. Theories of mediatisation have attempted to describe what a world dominated by media is (e.g. Couldry and Hepp, 2013; Hjarvard, 2011). As Lunt and Livingstone (2016) note, theories of mediatisation are suggestive of a 'metaprocess' within the larger analysis of modernity alongside the likes of 'globalisation' (Corner, 2018) and refer to the many ways in which media shape social and cultural transformation. But as many have noted (e.g. Corner, 2018; Deacon and Stanyer, 2014; Ekstrom et al., 2016), mediatisation theory often lacks a sense of history and neglects deep institutional analyses. As Murdock (2017: 119) argues:

> [w]hile shifts in the organisation of economic activity are referenced, mediatisation research has not so far developed a comprehensive analysis of the central role played by the resurgence of market fundamentalist models of capitalism in reorganising the relations between media and social and cultural life it seeks to address, despite claims of being holistic and contextual.

Murdock refers to this as 'the elephant in the room' in mediatisation research, and suggests that in their efforts to provide a 'more complete account of the elephant they have neglected to ask who owns it and trains it and what it is doing in the room' (2017: 120) in the first place. Even when such research has progressed to considerations of 'deep mediatisation – in which the very elements and building blocks from which the social is constructed are based in processes of mediatisation, accompanied by automated data processing' (Couldry and Hepp, 2017: 1) that is corporately controlled and profit-driven – we are left without a deep analysis of the ways in which market fundamentalism has reordered social life in the interests of capital.

In these circumstances the complexity of institutional formations is underinterrogated. Or worse, they become so reified that they are impervious to change and once more our vision of a better world becomes captured by capitalism. So we do politically useful stuff – for example, we empirically document the decay, crises and democratic demise we see, we show how political rhetoric is at odds with reality and how media, technologies and systems of communication are shaped by and interact with these struggles – but we come to a standstill when we get to a vision of how the world could be otherwise. Unless of course we go straight back to the defence and recovery of liberal democratic rights that have failed in their ability to stand up to the worse vagaries of life under capitalism. So the answer to increasing concentration of media ownership becomes the further liberalisation of digital markets, that becomes neo-liberal translations of freedom into market freedom and equality into digital access while 'systematically denying the social prerequisites for realising deeper, more adequate interpretations' (Fraser and Jaeggi, 2018:17) that are truly emancipatory.

Capitalism writ large

The predominance of media logics in our field is even more surprising when currently the kings of capitalism are the digital giants – Facebook, Alphabet (the parent company of Google), Amazon and Apple. If we add Microsoft to this list, together they have a combined annual revenue larger than the gross domestic product (GDP) of 90% of the world's countries (Lawrence and Laybourn-Langton, 2019). Apple is the first trillion-dollar company in history. Jeff Bezos, the founder and owner of Amazon, is the richest person in history, with his net wealth increasing by $400 million a day in 2018. These corporations form the largest oligopolies the world has ever seen. They are resistant to traditional forms of regulation and are largely out of reach of democratically organised political will-formation. In other words, they are mostly unaccountable. Hence Mark Zuckerberg, founder and CEO of Facebook, persistently refuses requests to appear before a Parliamentary Committee in the UK in relation to the Facebook–Cambridge Analytica data breach that is claimed to have influenced the outcome of the European referendum that will have a dramatic impact on the political future of the UK (Cadwalladr and Graham-Harrison, 2018).

The Cambridge Analytica scandal has put data-driven political campaigning in the spotlight. Cambridge Analytica were driven ultimately by a commercial imperative and the immense possibilities of harnessing the financial worth of billions of people's data to better target their insecurities and fear and channel their voting responses (a politics of capital accumulation). They distorted democratic processes through illegally scraping people's data from the likes of Facebook, psychologically profiling their identities, and then bombarding the 'persuadables' with unattributable memes and messages to shift their voting behaviour in the direction of their clients' political will and ambition (Moore, 2018). They have been accused of hacking democracy and impacting directly on the election of Donald Trump and the European Referendum in the UK. This sort of digital political campaigning is possible because of the vast global archive of personal data created from what are, in essence, global monopolistic advertising platforms. Tambini (2018) shows how Facebook advertising was crucial to the UK 2016 Referendum on Europe and the UK 2017 General Election – the platform became a one-stop shop for fundraising, recruitment, profiling, segmentation, message targeting and delivery. But there remains no publicly available data on what parties' money was spent on, what the actual content was, or who this digital campaigning was targeted at. The scale and dominance of the tech giants enables highly targeted, relatively invisible and totally unaccountable political campaigning. And this should really come as no surprise since the entire premise of these platforms has been built on the principle of ensuring that advertising (of any sort) sells better than it ever has before.

In the UK the Electoral Commission (2018) and Information Commissioner (2018) have both issued reports about recent digital campaigning trends, raising concerns about whether political parties and other campaigning organisations and companies are complying with electoral and data protection law. Both make recommendations for greater transparency in political campaigning and reflect a growing consensus that the regulation of online campaigning needs to change. They note that the move to targeted messaging, and the inability for all citizens to see and adjudicate between information in a targeted online campaigning environment, raise questions about equality of information, open debate and transparency. But it is unclear whether proposed changes really deal with the problem, how they could be enforced and who should be responsible for regulation.

Perhaps more importantly, none of the recommendations challenge the underlying premise of the current commercial, advertising-first, data-driven system. While they may be concerned to address issues of transparency, accountability and privacy they do this in relation to already existing systems that exploit personal data for the purposes of personalised targeting for ad sales. Consequently, all of them fall short of providing a long-term solution that can be fully trusted to support democracy. In this example we see how commercial systems of data capture are intricately entangled with state power and the institutionalised order of capitalism.

Meanwhile Facebook is fast becoming the dominant digital platform for news. Google has some 90% of global desktop search and Google and Facebook together account for around two-thirds of all digital advertising in the US (eMarketer, 2019). According to the *Wall Street Journal*, 85 cents of every dollar spent on digital advertising in America goes to Google and Facebook, evidence of a concentration of market power in two companies that not only own the playing field but are also able to set the rules of the game as well (*Wall Street Journal*, 2017). And in 2019 they soaked up 67% of the world's digital ad spend (eMarketer, 2019). These companies are not only the most concentrated forms of media ownership we have ever seen, they are also key to the contemporary condition of advanced capitalism. The bewildering market power wielded by the likes of Google and Facebook has not come at the expense of the influence of mainstream press and broadcasters. Google, Facebook and Twitter are, if anything, *reinforcing* the agenda-setting power of the mainstream news brands by facilitating their increased circulation through algorithms. The gatekeeping power of Google and Facebook works *in tandem* with that of mainstream news providers, mutually reinforcing each other around what they consider to be real, legitimate and authoritative news (Media Reform Coalition, 2018).

More recently, arguments around 'platform capitalism' (Srnicek, 2017), 'cognitive capitalism' (Boutang, 2011), 'communicative capitalism' (Dean, 2009) and 'surveillance capitalism' (Zuboff, 2019) are at least bringing capitalism back into focus. Zuboff painstakingly outlines how the current economic system online, driven by advanced forms of advertising typified by Facebook, Google and Twitter, seduces us onto their platforms, monitors our behaviour, and then sells that information back to advertisers so they can target their goods ever more precisely. Zuboff (2019) explains just how relentless, intrusive and exploitative this form of surveillance is. If industrial capitalism works by generating surpluses, surveillance capitalism gains these surpluses from our own behaviour – the more data it can extract about us the more surplus it gathers, because the better it can sell its predictions about who we are and what we might buy. In this manner surveillance capitalism is also deeply but subtly coercive – subtle because it is highly individualised and difficult to know when and how it is happening as it happens constantly, and coercive because it preys upon our innate human need to be connected and to communicate with friends and family. As Chun (2017) has argued, digital networks have been central to the emergence of neoliberalism, replacing 'society' with connectable individuals habitually captured in a cycle of 'update' and 'refresh' that feeds the inversion of privacy and publicity that drives neoliberalism and networks. It is surveillance capitalism's one-way mirror into the finest details of our most intimate and everyday lives – a veritable matrix of prediction and control. And it is a form of marketisation that feeds from the very necessity of non-marketised social relations that drives social media creating social surplus.

In the digital age, the search for connectedness with humanity and our environment leads to an ever-increasing disconnectedness from them as the relations of dependency between people, institutions and corporations are rendered invisible. Our data inputs are accorded no economic value and those corporations who endlessly reproduce them do not pay. This is capitalism perceived through the lens of consumption rooted in the commercial purpose and exploitative revenue model of the major platforms. Zuboff (2019: 17) warns that as industrial capitalism flourished at the expense of nature and now threatens to cost us the earth, 'so an information civilisation shaped by surveillance capitalism and its new instrumentarian power will thrive at the expense of human nature and will threaten to cost us our humanity'.

Zuboff's analysis of the various types of technological surveillance and data extraction is compelling, but despite the book's title she is far more quiet on matters of capitalism (Morozov, 2019). This is largely because Zuboff is in fact a reformist who seeks to humanise capitalism in the interests of the sovereign consumer rather than overthrow it. Consequently, she says little about how the tech giants relate to and interact with businesses, governments and financial agencies, how they leverage political power, and how these aspects are related to their enduring need for long-term profitability. Surveillance is her focus rather than how the practices of surveillance serve capitalism. Her concept of value and hence of surplus value hinges on the emancipated consumer rather than the liberated worker. So as long as there is no behavioural surplus – i.e. tech companies do not extract our data for purposes of advertising – then we are free:

> The struggle for power and control in society is no longer associated with the hidden facts of class and its relationship to production but rather by the hidden facts of automated [sic] engineered behaviour modification. (Zuboff, 2019, cited in Morozov, 2019: npn)

Once more this fails to address how market fundamentalism, deregulation and non-regulation of global capitalism has vastly increased inequality within and between nations and left the majority of the world's population more impoverished. Since the 2008 financial crash, the wealth of the richest 1% in the world has grown at an average of 6% per year compared to 3% for the rest. If this rate continues, the world's richest 1% will own two-thirds of the world's wealth by 2030 (House of Commons Library, 2018). Stiglitz shows how political and economic forces have combined in the interest 'of the 1%, for the 1% by the 1%' (2013: xxxix). With concentrations of wealth come concentrations of power. In the UK, the Institute for Public Policy Research (IPPR, 2018) Commission on Economic Justice reveals how the financial health of the UK is brutally divided along lines of income, geography, gender, ethnicity and age. It ranks the UK as the fifth most unequal country in Europe. And there are plentiful analyses of how inequality damages our societies, our economies and our democratic systems (Dorling, 2014; Piketty, 2014; Wilkinson and Pickett, 2009, 2018). There is a direct relationship between the practices of unequal capital accumulation and the politics of data, metrics and social media. The business model of these digital oligopolies concentrates economic and technological power, contributes to rising inequality, undermines privacy, largely ignores democratic principles and norms, increases work insecurity (through the gig economy) and renders virtually everyone who is part of it unaccountable. Yet the sovereign consumer asserting their individual rights for more and better consumption is where Zuboff's analysis lands – and so once more we are left with an approach that is ultimately captured by capitalism.

Focusing on individual consumer rights rather than citizens and their need for collective ownership and control also resists a critical analysis of the role of state institutions and their entanglement with capitalism. Reconsidering the formations and practices of the state (see Chapter 3) also turns our gaze to the politics of exclusion and misrecognition such as the politics of race and gender that is made explicit in any discussion of inequality and is addressed in part below and throughout this book.

Formations and practices of the state

The state and capitalist economy are intimately entwined. Capitalism requires a particular legal framework for the functioning of private enterprise and market exchange. Deregulation of the market has enabled the amassing of global corporate capital. The likes of the World Trade Organization (WTO) aim to maximise the flow of international trade uninhibited by national policies that may seek to protect the national interest and the public good to the advantage of mega global corporations (including media and tech corporations). And so capitalist states also operate at a transnational level of governance, creating particular geopolitical hegemonies. Most recently we have seen this in the form of financialised capitalism that involves a new layer of governance through global financial institutions – the International Monetary Fund (IMF), the World Bank, the WTO, the European Central Bank and bond rating agencies – that set the rules around free trade, are entirely unaccountable and remain largely untouched by political action at the state level, yet set strict limits on what states can and cannot do. This was made alarmingly clear in the aftermath of the financial crisis of 2008 when these organisations instructed national governments how to order their economies so that banks and financial agencies could recoup the finance they had lent to governments, in order to solve the problems they had brought about in the first place through irresponsibly and recklessly encouraging individual debt. Streeck (2011: 29) notes how this makes explicit the balance between two sovereign bodies – the people and the international markets – and how it has been drastically skewed in one direction leading to the 'dialectic of democracy and capitalism … unfolding at breathtaking speed'.

On one level, state institutions have seen their economic power weakened in this process. Yet they must also exert power through the requirement to deal with the subsequent fallout of increasing inequality and poverty as less money is recouped through taxation and less money is available for redistribution through social welfare. As globalisation of capital and financialisation increase, governments and bureaucrats lose the ability to control economic, environmental and other policy areas (Davis, 2019). As Davis (2019: 47) notes, '[t]he largest transnational corporations and financial institutions now control more funds than most of our largest economies'. While nation-states are losing control of things such as environmental degradation, climate change, food distribution and energy resources, so they are left having to cope with the consequences of reduced corporate taxation, deregulation and a weakened welfare state leading to more crime, more homelessness, more ill-health and more protest. Citizens experience this variously as a loss of sovereignty, being overlooked and left behind or simply as feeling irrelevant (CSF, 2018). It is clear then that state institutions are deeply embroiled in the capitalist economy and we cannot understand capitalism without understanding the role of the state institutions within it.

The precise configuration of capitalism at any one time is reliant upon the dynamic between economic power and political power, with citizens having virtually no influence over the former and increasingly being squeezed out of the latter. But this does not mean that economic power is totalising or that the capitalist state has a single and unified political character. Struggles take place constantly within capitalism and in relation to the state whether they come from climate activists, anarchists, horizontalists or feminists, whether they refer to different forms of economy – a citizens' economy, the solidarity economy to participatory or radical democracy (see Chapter 7) – all seek to influence the particular configurations of capitalism and the state as each of them in turn responds and adapts to each other. Understanding where the balance of power lies in capitalist economies and state institutions, and how we are formed and constrained by them, is vital if we seek to change them.

Considering the structures and consequences of capitalism provides a meta-analysis for political communications. Whilst a focus on capitalism encourages us to take economic factors seriously, this does not mean that our analyses will be economically reductive. While a consideration of global capitalism is concerned with the corporate capture of institutions of the state and the hijacking of political decision making power at the transnational level by global finance, it also brings to the fore a politics of inequality and maldistribution of wealth that forces an explanation not only of social class but also of race, gender, sexuality and disability along with other markers of difference that reveal ingrained, historical status hierarchies, injuries of misrecognition and harms of discrimination. Power and wealth are differentially distributed not only at the level of corporations, states and citizens but also at the level of the social and the cultural and must be understood in these ways too. People from black and minority ethnic communities, women, disabled people and LGBTQ+ people experience multiple, differential and intersectional forms of socio-economic disadvantage. It is not enough to insist on a political economic critique of capitalism without also attending to the numerous ways in which the likes of feminist thought, cultural theory and postcolonial theory have also deepened this analysis to take account of political culture and history that is tied to differential subject production. Paying attention to the history, legacies and lived experiences of colonialism makes this abundantly clear.

History, legacies and lived experiences of colonialism

Capitalism exploits culturally and socially constructed differences and is lived through the uneven formations of race, gender, class, region and nationality (Lowe, 2015). As Danewid (2019: npn) has argued, 'race-making practices are intrinsic to processes of capital accumulation because racism supplies the precarious and exploitable lives that capitalism needs to extract land and labour'. Melamed (2015: 77) also notes that:

> Capital can only be capital when it is accumulating, and it can only accumulate by producing and moving through relations of severe inequality among human groups — capitalists with the means of production/workers without the means of subsistence, creditors/debtors, conquerors of land made property/the dispossessed and removed. These antinomies of accumulation require loss, disposability, and the unequal differentiation of human value, and racism enshrines the inequalities that capitalism requires.

As capitalism is nurtured by the state, so the state, confers political powers that are differential and distinguish between rights-bearing individuals and dependent members of subordinate groups. The state inscribes freedoms and subjection – who gets access to political protection and who does not:

> Status differential is forged politically. The paradigmatic agencies that afford or deny protection are states. And it is largely states too, that continue to perform the work of political subjectivation. They codify the status hierarchies that distinguish citizens from subjects, nationals from aliens, entitled workers from dependent scroungers – all categories that invite racialization. (Fraser and Jaeggi, 2018: 42)

Territorial states declare who can and cannot be considered citizens within their borders. This has been made alarmingly clear in the bitter battles over migration and asylum, and the likes of the Windrush scandal in the UK when the Home Office classified thousands of long-term British residents as illegal immigrants, forcing many of them out of their jobs and homes and in some cases resulting in detention and deportation. The

Windrush scandal was one part of the 'hostile environment' legislation introduced by Theresa May when she was Home Secretary to bring down immigration figures, and it is legislation that remains active today. Donald Trump came to power on the promise of building a wall on the US border with Mexico. Both responses relate back to the financial crash of 2008 and the consequences of the austerity policies that followed, punishing the poor rather than regulating the banks, and feeding feelings of social and economic insecurity that turned the blame onto welfare scrounging, job-stealing immigrants and minorities or others deemed 'external' and unworthy or simply dangerous, from Muslims to refugees.

Other discriminatory policies directed at migrants have been enacted in the name of national security. One week after his inauguration, President Donald Trump issued an Executive Order titled 'Protecting the Nation from Foreign Terrorist Entry into the United States', which became known as the Muslim ban. In 2018 the US State Department refused more than 37,000 visa applications compared to only 1,000 the year before when the ban had not been fully implemented (Aljazeera, 2019). The US has intervened militarily or otherwise in Muslim-majority countries that are listed in the ban, and has been accused of contributing to conditions that have led to violence and political instability in these countries (Iran, Iraq, Libya, Somalia, Sudan, Syria and Yemen). Capitalism's political order is geopolitical. These extant expressions of state power invite racial discrimination and entitlement that is predicated on a colonial history. The manner in which the many forms of exclusion and dispossession are carried out today cannot be understood outside the 'legacies of colonial expropriation' (Chakravartty and Da Silva, 2012: 369, 374). It is racialised populations who suffer most from a lack of political protection in capitalist societies.

The mass media have also played their part in framing and fanning debates around asylum and migration. In an analysis of media coverage in five EU states, Berry et al. (2016) found that refugees and migrants have been consistently framed negatively as a problem rather than a benefit to societies. In the UK, the majority of the press were found to have consistently campaigned aggressively against refugees and migrants. In other research on public reactions to the 2008 financial crisis, Berry (2019) notes how many respondents thought that the deficit had been created by immigrants sponging off the welfare state and bleeding the NHS dry. He also points to the fact that research reveals Britons to be more in favour of restrictive asylum policies than Germans, Spaniards or Swedes (who had more favourable press coverage). While these attitudes cannot be attributed to media reporting alone, the 'repetitive, negative, narrow and derogatory' (Berry et al., 2016: npn) reporting of the British tabloid press plays its part.

States order and manage varying levels of structures and infrastructures of governance, including those that relate directly to the media. In the UK, where market freedom and the expansion of a capitalist economy are the mantra of the right, the mainstream commercial newspaper industry is able to resist any meaningful form of independent regulation within or across media markets (Fenton, 2018). After refusing the form of independent regulation recommended by the 18 month-long Leveson Inquiry into the ethics and standards of the press (Leveson, 2012), the majority of national newspapers signed up to the non-Leveson compliant regulator called the Independent Press Standards Organisation (IPSO) – except IPSO is anything but independent and is run largely by the industry for the industry with a newly appointed chair, Sir Edward Faulks, who is a Conservative Party peer in the House of Lords.

IPSO follows the Editor's Code (written by editors) that will only allow complaints around discriminatory coverage relating to named individuals and not coverage targeting groups of people. So discriminatory coverage about Muslims, transgender people, women, etc., is beyond the mechanisms of complaint and is effectively legitimised. Under pressure, they have recently introduced guidelines for reporting on Muslims but these are unenforceable and largely impotent. In 2017 more than 8,000 complaints were made to IPSO relating to discriminatory coverage, only one of which was upheld. The mainstream media elite avoid press regulation on the grounds of protecting press freedom. The rhetoric of press freedom that is supposed to support the public interest then comes to stand in for the power of the press to do and say whatever they like for commercial gain. Rather than expanding the distribution of information, the aim is to monopolise attention to reap profit from advertising and sales. Ingrained forms of oppression and discrimination are built-in structural features of the power dynamics of capitalist society and include class, gender and racial subordination, imperialism and political domination. In a neoliberal context where effective independent regulation has been thwarted in favour of market freedom and power, capitalism's racial formations are all too clear and are underwritten by the state that refuses to address them for fear of negative media coverage of their own political party decimating their chances of election success.

Just as we can recognise capitalism's racial formations in legacy media, these can also be identified in the ways in which technology has developed. Crawford refers to embedded forms of bias as artificial intelligence's 'white guy problem':

> Sexism, racism and other forms of discrimination are being built into the machine-learning algorithms that underlie the technology behind many "intelligent" systems that shape how we are categorized and advertised to. (2016, *New York Times*)

In the digital world of big data, Steyerl (2019) explains how the process of algorithmically enhanced pattern recognition has to deal with the vast amount of data that it must order. The criteria algorithms used to decide what to include and exclude are intrinsically political and intimately related to the racist, sexist and classist assumptions within network analytics (Noble, 2018). Chun (2019) also notes how seemingly open and boundless networks are actually a series of poorly gated communities fostered by the market-logic embedded within most data-capture systems. Networks segregate because their formulation is based on and perpetuates a reductive identity politics which posits race and gender as 'immutable' categories. Based on the concept of homophily, which assumes people like to bond with similar people, 'Facebook packages into the idea that you are like what you like, and that you will like the things that people who are like you like' (Steyerl, 2019: 13). McPherson (2018) argues that these interlinked and mutually amplifying platforms have enabled a growing right-wing public sphere to emerge, producing a new era of racial formation and a structure of feeling that she calls 'immersive racism'. The very immersive design of platforms helps the alt-right by encouraging anonymous comments on postings, trolling and the proliferation of fake news. Hate speech, she argues, is not a bug in the platform, but a generative feature of the business model – a business model that relies on mis-recognition and feeds off human frailty to sustain a neoliberal form of capital accumulation that is deregulated, unaccountable, and whose digressions are largely untraceable.

Other research points to how software analyses of large sets of historical crime data are used for predictive policing to forecast where crime is likely to occur, perpetuating a vicious cycle of excessive surveillance and scrutiny in non-white, poorer neighbourhoods (O'Neil, 2016) that is often strikingly unreliable and reinforces discriminatory policing practices (Angwin et al., 2016): 'Algorithms perpetuate the discrimination they "find". They are not simply descriptive but also prescriptive and performative in all senses of that word' (Chun, 2019: 66). Such patterns of discrimination have of course been with us since long before the internet and data analytics. Structural inequalities have always been necessary for capital accumulation. In today's digital age this not only continues but intensifies. The subprime mortgage meltdown that ignited the 2008 financial crisis in the US revealed the deepening reliance of contemporary debt and financial power structures on the extraction of wealth from racialised communities. It also showed that such racialised debt regimes are ever more intensively digitised through racially encoded algorithms that determine credit worthiness (Noble, 2018).

It is clear, then, that in order to advance an explanatory framework for political communications it is vital to reflect on the structures and consequences of capitalism – on how manifestations and mechanisms of the state are entangled with political culture, and on historical and material bases of subject production and the relations between them. Political communications are about our economic, our political and our social worlds. A regime becomes hegemonic through a range of different social, political, economic and technological factors that come together conjuncturally to create an environment in which a certain type of politics can form and take hold. But a conjunctural analysis also reveals multiple, heterogenous and contradictory forces. Not only are the institutions of the state deemed unfit for purpose, but inequality and discrimination expose capitalism's failures. At a time when established political norms, state infrastructures and economic systems are increasingly fragile there are also huge opportunities for the renewal of politics itself. This is not just an opportunity but an imperative for left politics if we are not to give that ground to the right. Yet despite the massive discontent with the current socio-economic state of affairs, working conditions, and hollowed-out democratic processes, the outrage that is expressed at the injuries of the global liberalisation of the capitalist market economy – the discontent seems to have no place to go – there is little in our field that is able to imagine a world beyond capitalism or reconceive the nature of the state because it has not made them a central part of its analysis in the first place.

CONCLUSION: WORKING TOWARDS AN EMANCIPATORY POLITICAL VISION

As critical theorists, this book is an attempt to alert us anew to the dangers of turning our gaze away from capitalism, ignoring the state or diminishing the importance of subject production, such as the history and legacies of colonialism that bring to the fore how each has impacted on the other. The fourth key factor noted at the beginning of this chapter is less written about than all the others, but without it we have no critical theory. Critical theory is transformative. As Morozov has said, 'the radical critique of technology can only be as strong as the emancipatory vision to which it is attached. No vision, no critique (2015: 1). In arguing for political communications to rediscover its own politics we are also arguing for transformative change. For this to be possible we need to disentangle the complexity of institutional formations with power so that they are de-reified and are not deemed impervious to change. We need to articulate better what transformative change might look like. This is not to engage merely in wishful thinking that will ultimately lead to disillusionment; rather it is utopian longing melded to realist thinking about the dilemmas and constraints of building viable alternatives to the world as it is (Wright, 2010). This book attempts to begin the work of finding (and producing) these resources of hope (see Chapter 7). Chapter 8 argues that we need to bring our own politics to the fore as committed political communications scholars in order to begin to think our way out of the crises we are in.

So, our objective in this book is to assess how recent social and structural developments concerning neoliberal economics, state power and political engagement have affected the political communications environment. We cannot do this without being interdisciplinary, and without being vigilant of the big picture and attempting meta-analyses that will bring some explanatory insights, however complex and multi-dimensional. But we also need to be attendant to micro-processes and the roles of individual and collective actors in locales seeking transformative change. We know that the ever-increasing entanglement of media and communications corporations with politicians and state agencies and with capitalism constrains the opportunities and possibilities for being political through limiting public knowledge and policing dissent, whether covertly or not. We know that we cannot understand contemporary mediated society and social change without reference to the capitalist economy, without appreciating the enormous and differential constraints on the possibilities of subjects being political to effect progressive social change. Conceived of in this way we have to see capitalism as political economy and as culture supported by socially generated and sustained imaginaries, expectations, dreams and promises – values of the social lifeworld that support capitalism as a *way of life* – but also expose its failings and contradictions.

To fully interrogate capitalism as a way of life requires both a conjunctural analysis that can appreciate the historical transformation of capitalism over time and a concern with situated contingent political practice (and possibilities) in our thoroughly mediated worlds. This chapter began with the political context in which this book is being written – the Brexit vote, Donald Trump as President of the US, the rise of far right nationalist parties and white supremacist movements across Europe and the US alongside Jeremy Corbyn's recasting of the Labour Party in the name of socialism and support for the likes of Bernie Sanders in the US. These are very different responses, but all share a sense that neoliberalism isn't working for the vast majority of people and needs replacing, that the political classes and established parties have been captured by private interests and need to be replaced, and that the neoliberal hegemony is close to breaking point – it may still have the capacity to dominate but it has lost its ability to persuade.

When Gramsci describes an earlier 'crisis of authority', he writes that 'the old is dying and the new cannot be born; in this interregnum, a great variety of morbid symptoms appear' (1971: 276). We are now living through these morbid symptoms. It is crucial therefore both to pose and to attempt to answer some hard questions. How can we envisage what democracy could become? How can we live together better – co-productively and co-operatively? How can social relations be imagined differently? How can communicative structures play a role in this political reimagination? How can we put politics back into political communications?

2

INFRASTRUCTURES OF POLITICAL COMMUNICATIONS

INTRODUCTION

Political communications is often too microscopic and studied in relation only to its discrete components: for example, news framing of a specific election; the impact of Facebook on a particular campaign; the use of Twitter by a populist leader; the consequences of candidate rhetoric; analysis of reader comments; the role of a single talk show in facilitating democratic citizenship; the efficacy of political fact-checking; or the risks of political astroturfing.[1] The emphasis is on the visible and the visceral, not the elusive and opaque; on process and performance as distinct from underlying conditions of power; on institutional rather than ideological factors.

At a time of enormous uncertainty, disruption and complexity in the field (Bennett and Pfetsch, 2018), we believe that it is necessary to focus not so much on the pieces but on the puzzle as a whole, and to identify the underlying dynamics, not simply the headlines, of contemporary political communications. This requires an holistic orientation as opposed to a piecemeal approach that is absorbed above all with the latest technological innovation or the noisiest political operators. It involves conceptualising political communications as a *system* that is shaped by its relationship to broader forces of social reproduction, rather than being the product of immanent technological characteristics or the media savvy of a handful of charismatic personalities. In particular, it means that we have to evaluate political communications in relation to the fundamentally unequal relations of actually existing capitalist societies as opposed to the normative visions of the healthy democracy that we do not have.

So while Bennett and Pfetsch are quite right to argue for a 'fundamental rethinking of the political communication and press/politics fields' (2018: 245), this ought not to be simply as a result of recent changes in journalistic practices, audience behaviour, technological capacity and political polarisation. Instead we need to locate political communications as an expression of the tussles that take place when resources are unequally held and distributed within societies; political communications ought not to be reduced to isolated critiques of political machinations, digital affordances and journalistic strategy, but understood in relation to the structural conflicts that emerge in profoundly asymmetrical circumstances.

This is hardly the first call to conceptualise the field in more systemic terms. Blumler and Gurevitch, for example, first identified the need for a 'systems outlook' for political communications back in 1977 (1995: 11) as a means of enriching comparative analysis and minimising the dangers of a reductionist approach in which individual factors (i.e. technology or reception) are either exaggerated or marginalised. They argue that there are four elements to a political communication system – political institutions, media organisations, audience roles and prevailing aspects of political culture (such as levels of censorship or regulatory controls) – that are 'to some extent conditioned by mutual power relationships' (1995: 12). Yet in mapping out the structural, psychological and normative sources of power that are at the heart of what they eventually describe as a 'crisis of public communication',

---

[1]All of these examples have been taken from recent editions of the journal *Political Communication*.

they pay little attention to the socio-economic conditions that shape the contours and material practices of a broader political communication system. Some forty years later, Andrew Chadwick, in his influential analysis of a 'hybrid' communications landscape (Chadwick, 2017), highlights the systemic nature of the power relations that encompass the interactions between social actors. However, for Chadwick, it is the structuring force of complex media logics, not socio-economic factors, that ultimately triumphs in any given political communications environment. For him, 'this means analyzing how the technologies, genres, norms, behaviors, and organizational forms associated with older and newer media shape politics' (2017: 22) rather than investigating the sets of social relations that underpin these interactions and condition their outcomes.

This chapter attempts to provide a framework to achieve precisely this: to examine how the economic realities and priorities of a capitalist social system constrain the practices of political communications. In so doing the chapter draws on recent literature on *infrastructure* to emphasise the material basis of the contexts in which political actors, media personnel, tech companies and ordinary citizens generate, distribute and consume communicative content about public affairs. This infrastructural approach aims to provide a political economy of political communications: one that evaluates the 'social relations, particularly the power relations, that mutually constitute the production, distribution, and consumption of resources' (Mosco, 2009: 24) and is firmly rooted in the unequal and exploitative conditions that dominate contemporary societies. In doing so, the chapter focuses less on the technological dimensions of infrastructure – such as telecoms networks, internet routers and social media platforms – but rather on four infrastructural features connected to existing social relations. It examines the barriers to access to the resources of political communications, the property regimes that dominate the landscape, the labour that underpins the production and circulation of content, and finally the policy frameworks that circumscribe this content.

THE TURN TO INFRASTRUCTURE

Communication scholarship has increasingly turned to the analysis of infrastructure in recent years (Näser-Lather and Neubert, 2015; Parks and Starosielski, 2015; Plantin and Punathambekar, 2019). This makes a welcome change from a long-standing preoccupation with texts, consumption patterns and effects studies that fail to interrogate underlying structures and social relations. At their most basic, infrastructures are 'built networks that facilitate the flow of goods, people, or ideas and allow their exchange over space ... They comprise the architecture for circulation, literally providing the undergirding of modern societies, and they generate the ambient environment of everyday life' (Larkin, 2013: 328). Energy, transport and communication infrastructures have paved the way for the development of productive societies, and as Paul Edwards has argued (2003: 185), they constitute the 'connective tissues' and 'circulatory systems of modernity'. What are some of the key features of infrastructures and some of the consequences of this shift towards 'infrastructuralism' (Peters, 2015) and in what ways are they relevant to the analysis of political communications?

First, infrastructures mark a fascination, as Graham Murdock has argued, with 'the material structures that underpin our communicative encounters' (2018: 365) and in particular the 'raw materials and resources' and 'chains of labour' that are responsible for the provision of the devices that enable the flows of political content (2018: 359). This is a step forward from earlier forms of materialism, as conceptualised by theorists like McLuhan (1964) and Innis (1964) examining the sensory and spatial characteristics of media technologies, towards an understanding of communications as rooted in the exploitation both of labour and natural resources and the manufacture and distribution of commodities. Infrastructuralism presents a direct challenge to theories that have sought to evacuate capitalism of some of the most fundamental (and undesirable) characteristics of commodity production, not least in relation to the alleged weightlessness (Coyle, 1999; Leadbeater, 1999), immateriality (Boutang, 2011; Gorz, 2010) and intangibility (Haskel and Westlake, 2018) of the digital world. Instead, it highlights physical sites, spaces and labour – often dirty, dangerous and devalued – at the heart of the communicative environment and invites us to study the material layers of media distribution: 'Beefed up broadband pipelines, cloud computing systems, digital compression techniques and protocols are now integral to the movement and storage of audiovisual signals worldwide' (Parks and Starosielski, 2015: 2).

This has the advantage of alerting us to the environmental costs of communications, whether that refers to the extraction of cobalt from Congolese mines for use in our smartphones, the data centres powered by fossil fuels and their contribution to global emissions, or the toxic landfills of communications detritus (Brevini and Murdock, 2017; Maxwell and Miller, 2012). But infrastructure also 'reminds us of the territoriality and geography of communication and transport, of questions of power, and of the challenge to devise new techniques and modes of visualizing these interrelations' (Rossiter, 2017: 7). Indeed, infrastructures such as railway networks, undersea cables and electricity grids have been essential to the construction, maintenance and extension of commodity production. They have laid the basis for domestic accumulation as well as for its consolidation via colonial relationships, so that just as 'infrastructure constitutes the territory of state and empire' in the nineteenth century (Rossiter, 2017: 163; Winseck and Pike, 2007), social media companies like Google are guilty of an 'infrastructural imperialism' based on their domination of data flows and surveillance technologies (Vaidhanathan, 2011: 111) in the digital present. For Tawil-Souri in her analysis of the highly politicised geography of telecommunications in Israel and Palestine, in which the latter's mobile networks are heavily circumscribed by occupation, infrastructures 'function as politically defined territorial spaces of control and are integral aspects of states' territoriality' (2015: 158).

Second, infrastructures have a systemic orientation: they are large-scale, generative phenomena that co-ordinate and facilitate the movement of other goods and services, including communications data and content. They are not reducible to their physical properties alone but to their ability to *make things happen*: 'What distinguishes infrastructures from technologies is that they are objects that create the grounds on which other objects operate, and when they do so they operate as systems' (Larkin, 2013: 329). Edwards concurs that they provide 'systemic, societywide control over the variability inherent in the natural environment' (2003: 188). They lend themselves to the kind of holistic analysis that we called for in the introduction to this chapter, and in particular are intimately connected to concentrations of power in any given society. After all, who apart from states and giant corporations has the resources and influence to build these networks of networks that play such a vital role in economic life?

Media infrastructure studies, claim Parks and Starosielski, 'sets out to understand the materialities of things, sites, people, and processes that locate media distribution within systems of power' (2015: 5). They analyse data centres, mobile phone masts, cybercafes and fibre-optic cables in the belief that both infrastructures themselves and information about infrastructures are constituted by highly asymmetrical relations of power: 'Public access to technical knowledge about infrastructures is not equal; rather it is guided and constrained by social hierarchies of gender, race/ethnicity, class, generation, and nation' (2015: 6). Infrastructural development is scarred by the inequalities we referred to in the opening chapter – by the investment decisions that are not accidental or whimsical, but designed to secure maximum returns according to the priorities of market-dominated economies. For example, in her analysis of undersea cables, Starosielski notes how a very uneven political geography affects the access to high-speed broadband across and within different territories such that 'as a result, communities on the periphery of current networks face a disadvantage in a cabled era and remain more vulnerable to disconnection or monitoring' (2015: 65). Infrastructures are crucial tools of economic and social development, but they reflect structural power imbalances and therefore are more to reproduce, rather than to ameliorate, existing asymmetries.

Third, the very nature of infrastructures inverts our sense of what is important by diverting our attention from what is immediately visible to hidden relations of power. Infrastructures are usually obscured from public view – buried under the sea or housed in inaccessible private compounds where there is no right to public access – and viewed as support systems rather than as productive phenomena in their own right. Infrastructures constitute 'the invisible background, the substrate or support, the technocultural/natural environment of modernity' (Edwards, 2003: 191). Even though Google now promises to make its data centres transparent and 'hypervisible', Holt and Vonderau dismiss this as a form of public relations and contend that they are likely to continue as 'information infrastructures hiding in plain sight' (2015: 80). Not surprisingly, therefore, we are more likely to be absorbed by what we can touch, hear and see. We fetishise consumer technologies, devour hours of media content every day and obsess over memes without asking questions about the platforms, raw material and labour practices on which they are based.

An emphasis on infrastructure, however, can help to shift our critical gaze. According to John Durham Peters (2015: 33), infrastructuralism is related to an interest in 'the boring, the mundane, and all the mischevious work done behind the scenes.

It is a doctrine of environments and small differences, of strait gates and needle's eye, of things that stand under our worlds'. These are precisely the material processes that are, in reality, not that boring and that reveal the underlying power dynamics, economic priorities and political preferences of prevailing social systems. Infrastructuralism adds depth to our understanding of the communicative experience by locating it in relation to a productive process in which actors, institutions and texts are embedded and shaped by specific social relations.

What's more, we tend to notice infrastructures not when they are functioning smoothly but precisely the opposite: when they seize up. The National Grid becomes frighteningly real when the power goes out and we can't make a cup of tea; switches and routers suddenly assume enormous significance when we're locked out of our Instagram accounts; submarine cables are by no means 'boring' when damage prevents millions of people from going online. 'Infrastructure', according to Ned Rossiter (2017: 5), 'provides an underlying system of elements, categories, standards, protocols, and operations that ... are only revealed in its moment of failure and breakdown'. Of course, this can be seen a 'first world' problem in that the default for many poorer countries is one where infrastructural networks function only intermittently (and in some cases may not exist). As Paul Edwards notes, the notion of infrastructure 'as an invisible, smooth-functioning background "works" only in the developed world' (2003: 188). Despite this geopolitical truth, in a neoliberal age in which communications infrastructures remain vulnerable to privatisation and are subject to permissive regulatory oversight, there is likely to be less public confidence in the seamless operation of key communicative backbones and greater expectations that digital networks, just like transport ones, are increasingly bound to fail.

Fourth, a focus on infrastructure can help to challenge the determinism that, as we discussed in Chapter 1, threatens to overwhelm public and scholarly understanding of the role of digital technologies. It is true that infrastructures are usually understood in relation to their status as (large and immovable) *objects* like roads, railways, power lines, sewers and cables; it is also true that attention to the material forms of, for example, media and communications provides a welcome contrast to accounts that dwell primarily on text and discourse without providing sufficient context for their provenance. Infrastructuralism, however, does not suggest that we can read off the impact of technologies from their physical properties or evaluate how communication shapes the political world through some sort of overarching 'media logic', no matter how 'expansive' it may be (Chadwick, 2017: 25). Instead, its more nuanced advocates follow on from Raymond Williams' argument that technology refers to a set of relationships as opposed to a fixed or stable object and that it is 'necessarily in complex and variable connection with other social relations and institutions' (Williams, 1981b: 227). Infrastructures are 'sociotechnical systems' (Edwards, 2003: 185) that are irreducible to their technological affordances; they comprise 'material forces as well as discursive constructions' and 'are the products of design schemes, regulatory politics, collective imaginaries, and repetitive use' (Parks and Starolsielski, 2015: 5).

Infrastructures, therefore, embody a sense of both materiality and sociality that highlights the fundamentally political and contingent nature of technological innovation. Subject to the balance of power at any particular time, infrastructures are neither organic nor predetermined but are the product of concrete decisions in specific circumstances, not least in terms of what we understand as 'infrastructural'. For Larkin (2013: 330), '[t]he act of defining an infrastructure is a categorizing moment … a cultural analytic that highlights the epistemological and political commitments involved in selecting what one sees as infrastructural (and thus causal) and what one leaves out'. This suggests that the design and maintenance of infrastructures – whether related to transport, banking or communications – reflect certain priorities about who should be connected and what objectives should be prioritised. Under capitalism, argues Darin Barney (2018), 'infrastructure remains irreducibly political, because it distributes and concentrates resources and advantage, enables and disables mobility (including migration), organizes spatial and temporal relations, and manifests inequality and power'. This is a crucial point: in unequal conditions, infrastructures can facilitate not connection but disconnection, not access but egress. For example, immigration infrastructures are there to keep people out, not to entice them in, while communication infrastructures are often designed around systems to exclude certain audiences through payment systems and intellectual property regimes. Infrastructure, in other words, is not simply about enabling movement and generating content, but about providing the conditions in which movement can be controlled and content barriers erected.

INFRASTRUCTURE: A WARNING

Invocations of infrastructure, however, will not magically rid us of deterministic, metaphysical or simplistic accounts of contemporary political communications. There is a danger here of grasping infrastructures either too narrowly – in other words, not as a key element of a *chain* of production and circulation but as significant in themselves – or too broadly – in which case, everything can be seen to be infrastructural. Indeed, infrastructure becomes a very vague concept if it is used simply to refer to *any* underpinning system or to *any* platform or network that facilitates movement and flow. For a start, all infrastructures have their own infrastructures. The internet, for example, is seen as a key infrastructural feature of developed economies, but the internet relies on a series of other infrastructures including electricity, commodity production, software and educational skills. Each of these will have their own infrastructures that are increasingly likely to involve digital platforms, thus generating a kind of endless cycle of infrastructural traces. As Larkin notes (2013: 329–30), any 'simple linear relation of foundation to visible object turns out to be recursive and dispersed'.

Infrastructures can also be expanded – to include norms, values and rationalities – to the extent that they risk losing an association with systemic features, underpinning logics and above all asymmetrical social relations. Infrastructures are at times endowed with a series of semiotic qualities that threaten to overwhelm their very materiality; they are seen as 'performative' (Cordella, 2010) and permanently unsettled such that the 'basic unit of research' is itself decentred (Larkin, 2013: 339). This kind of infrastructuralism, shaped by 'epistemologically relativistic theories, such as ANT [Actor-Network Theory]' (Benson, 2014), serves to flatten structural inequalities and to foreground a sense of flux and heterogeneity that renders the concept of causation virtually redundant. As Benson argues (2014), the very fact of power imbalances means 'some accounts must be privileged over others, and this is precisely what ANT not only will not but cannot do, given its epistemology'.

Despite this warning, infrastructures have provided the basis for a 'new materialism' (Coole and Frost, 2012) characterised by complexity and volatility in which material systems are shaped by a dazzling array of human and non-human interactions. This appears to be a direct challenge to what is perceived as the linearity and causality of the traditional Marxist notion of historical materialism that famously posits an economic base 'upon which a legal and political structure rises and to which particular forms of social consciousness correspond' (Marx, 1977). For example, in their collection on *Materialist Approaches to Media, Mobility and Networks*, Packer and Crofts Wiley argue that the base/superstructure model is something that their contributors specifically want to 'move beyond' (2012: 5). Similarly, John Durham Peters – a key figure in the emergence of infrastructuralism – notes that materialism has always had a 'tough guy' image and that its advocates have engaged in 'a kind of rhetorical blackmail in being more materialist than thou' (2012: 41). Infrastructuralism, apparently, can offer a path beyond both abstract idealism and crude materialism.

The problem, however, lies not with the exercise of materialist muscle, but with how one carries it out. The desire to transcend historical materialism misrepresents its underlying characteristics and exaggerates its economic determinism and thus its value as an analytical frame for approaching political communications. Historical materialism doesn't suggest that the economic dimension predetermines every outcome, or that superstructural forces, including politics, law, ideology and media, are irrelevant to the dynamics of the base. Indeed, social relations, 'which in their totality form "the economic structures of society", should be recognised first of all as human relations' (Jakubowski, 1976: 33). This understanding of historical materialism, Jakubowski argues, has little connection to the 'economic fatalism' with which the base/superstructure model is often associated. Instead, the model proposes that the economic base fundamentally shapes the possibilities of social reproduction; it both sets limits on the operations of the superstructure and is simultaneously shaped by it. There doesn't have to be a 'simple' or 'linear' relationship, as Larkin argues above, but there is no escaping from a relationship in which the power asymmetries of the base fundamentally constrain what occurs in wider society.

Darin Barney (2018) notes that some in the Marxist tradition have actually referred to 'infrastructure' as a synonym for 'base' (although Marx himself never used the term). Crucially, he argues that infrastructure – precisely as Marx referred to the concept of 'base' – is a term that denotes both material objects and 'material *relationships* – wage relations, property relations, class relations'. Indeed, for Barney, infrastructures are 'the prevailing social relationships materialized, and they contain all the contradictions characteristic of those relations, contradictions that can burst forth at any moment' (Barney, 2018). In the context of capitalist inequality, infrastructures have provided the basis of, for example, misogyny, racism and exploitation as well as the rise of a far-right populism – together with the opportunities to resist these developments. In other words, if we see the 'turn to infrastructure' as an expression of a desire to evaluate media in relation to the underpinning structures and social relations of a capitalist social system – and not simply as a marker of the messiness and scaleability of contemporary technologies – then this can provide an extremely useful conceptual tool with which to evaluate the main features of today's political communications environments. This is the basis for a critical and historical materialist analysis of twenty-first century media systems.

INFRASTRUCTURAL FEATURES OF POLITICAL COMMUNICATIONS

As we have already noted, back in 1977 Blumler and Gurevitch outlined the main structural features of political communications (Blumler and Gurevitch, 1995). Their identification of political and media institutions, together with audience orientations and the prevailing political culture, was designed above all to assess the interactions of the key elements of a communicative system that pointed to a 'crisis of civic communication'. We can see traces of this approach in more recent work by Davis (2019), where he evaluates the main conceptual frameworks, political trends, organised interests and technological developments that are at play in the communication of politics. So, for example, he highlights contextual factors such as the hollowing out of democracy, the fragmentation of political parties, the growth in populism and the impact of interest groups in an elite dominated system. McNair, in the most recent edition of his textbook (McNair, 2017), describes the main actors and trends in contemporary political communications and discusses specific elements such as the role of advertising and public relations, the impact of pressure groups, and the consequences for 'mediated politics' of globalisation and digital technologies.

Yet none of these influential texts focus specifically on the infrastructural pressure points and broader social relations that underpin political communications. In a rare exception to the rule, W. Russell Neuman, at a time when US Vice-President Al Gore was vigorously pushing the idea of a National Information Infrastructure that would allegedly revolutionise the public's access to knowledge and ideas, published an article wholly focused on a 'political communications infrastructure [that] is not predetermined by immutable laws of digital electronics but remains under our collective control' (Neuman, 1996). However, despite making some important points about the economics of and access to information, Neuman ends up identifying many of the same features as Blumler and Gurevitch in relation to political culture and freedom of speech (albeit from a far more optimistic perspective) without penetrating the 'substrate' of the social system itself.

This chapter follows on from where Neuman left off and interrogates the foundations of political communications and the infrastructural dynamics – beyond those solely related to platforms and technologies – that influence the contours of media flows in relation to public affairs. So while we might want to consider the metaphorical highways and canals of political communications and the architecture of its 'plumbing', the chapter focuses instead on some underlying factors that shape the more visible aspects of political communications, such as the articles, ads, images, tweets and posts that both enlighten and misinform together with the branded content, opinion polls and editorial judgements that shape political campaigns and public knowledge. In short, it addresses the economic and social relations that create the conditions in which, for example, trust is falling, misinformation is rising and legacy journalism is panicking. Drawing on specific examples and data, we now examine four ways in which structural forms of inequality are reproduced inside political communications environments through infrastructural failures.

1. Barriers to access and participation

We are often absorbed by the way that infrastructural platforms – for example, cheap air travel, mobile phones and the internet – connect people and ideas. In the context of the inequality outlined in the opening chapter, more attention should be paid instead to how infrastructures fail to connect people, in other words to the barriers that prevent citizens from acquiring the resources needed to play a meaningful role in political communications. This draws on Göran Therborn's argument that exclusion is one of the central ways in which existing inequalities are reproduced under capitalism. This takes place when 'a barrier is erected making it impossible, or at least more difficult, for certain categories of people to access a good life' (Therborn, 2009: 21). While he was reflecting, above all, on the dangers of economic protectionism and nativism, this form of 'resource inequality' is pertinent to the way in which access to political communications is policed through a range of socio-economic indicators and material forms of discrimination.

Attention to the structural roots of inequality has not always been a central preoccupation in political communications. 'Inequality', argues Peter Golding (2017: 4305), 'has seldom been in the foreground of communication scholarship' despite the groundbreaking study he carried out with Graham Murdock into the relationship between political inequality and information poverty some thirty years ago (Murdock and Golding, 1989). Now, however, shaken by the 2008 financial crisis, the ensuing resistance to austerity and a stubborn digital divide, inequality is making a welcome comeback (at least as a focus of research) in media analysis. Josef Trappel (2019), for example, in a collection entirely dedicated to exploring digital media inequalities, maps out the technological, institutional, textual and policy-related dimensions of inequality in relation to legacy and online media. Golding himself focuses on the material roots of information deprivation by analysing 'the mundane, everyday limits to becoming informed' (2017: 4306) and concludes that the resources required to play an active role in public life are systematically skewed in favour of the wealthy. Engagement with political communications is, after all, a costly business with restricted opportunities for some social groups and open doors for others.

We can see this clearly if we consider the relationship between income levels and access to the technologies that operate as portals to political communications.

In the US nearly 30% of the poorest households (with an income under $30,000 a year) don't own a smartphone, in contrast with the 3% of the wealthiest households (over $100,000 a year of income) who presumably choose not to own one (Pew Research Center, 2019). Similar discrepancies can be found in relation to access to desktops, laptops and tablets. While 44% of the poorest households don't have access to broadband and thus are thus shut out of a whole array of interactive and streaming services, a mere 6% of top-income households are broadband free. This means that lower income Americans are more dependent on smartphones (where they have one) for a range of functions that wealthier citizens can access on multiple devices. Pew also report that over one-quarter of adults in the poorest households rely on their smartphone for going online without access to broadband while only 5% of the wealthiest are in that position, leaving the poorest households especially vulnerable to mobile data charges (Pew Research Center, 2019).

In the UK, Ofcom notes the 'stark differences in internet use by socio-economic group' (2018a: 65) with the poorest households four times less likely to be internet users than the richest ones. While 4% of the most affluent adults are internet non-users, this figure rises to 34% of those on low income with these households also less likely to have access to internet-connected devices (2018a: 69). So just 36% of low-income households have a Smart TV and 52% have any type of computer at home in comparison to the 62% of wealthy households who have a Smart TV and nearly 90% who have at least one laptop or desktop. Of course, when it comes to owning a standard TV set, a greater number of low-income homes have one (68% v 63%) (Ofcom, 2019a: Table 7). 'Media lives', as Ofcom describes them, are therefore heavily circumscribed by socio-economic circumstances: 97% of 'high status' indviduals use a mobile phone, 73% watch on-demand or streamed content, and 74% have a social media profile; and when it comes to the least affluent individuals, 93% use a mobile, 46% watch on-demand or streamed content, and only 56% have a social media profile (Ofcom, 2019b: 4).

Despite having less access to increasingly infrastructural devices, the poorest households spend far less in absolute terms but proportionately more of their disposable income on communications services.

This leads to what Golding describes as 'citizen detriment' (2017: 4313), a form of harm caused by economic inequality and the resulting lower levels of disposable income that prevent poorer communities from securing access to a rich diet of information services. It also maps onto the differential use of platforms that are particularly relevant to the communication of public affairs. According to the communications consultancy We are Flint (2018), there are substantial disparities in engagement between high- and low-income individuals across much of the social media on which political debate takes place. In both the UK and the US, sites like Tumblr, Instagram, Reddit, YouTube and Twitter are disproportionately dominated by higher income individuals with, for example, 65% of UK ABC1 individuals active on Twitter in contrast to only 36% of C2DE individuals (We are Flint, 2018: 18). In the US, nearly twice as many high-income people engage with Reddit and Tumblr as low-income ones (2018: 44, 46).

Table 2.1   UK household expenditure on communications services 2018

	Spending (£/week)	Spending (£/week)	% of all expenditure	% of all expenditure
	Poorest 10th	Wealthiest 10th	Poorest 10th	Wealthiest 10th
Telephone	7.60	16.60	2.9	1.5
Internet	2.40	4.90	0.91	0.45
TV (inc. cable, satellite, licence fee)	4.40	9.90	1.66	0.92
Newspapers and magazines	1.20	2.70	0.45	0.25

(*Source*: Office for National Statistics, 2019: adapted from Table 3.1E)

These material differences in class and income are also a central driver of unequal news consumption habits. For example, while both rich and poor in the UK turn to television for news in equal numbers, wealthier audiences are more likely to use the internet, radio and newspapers as an additional source of news (Ofcom, 2018b: 15). And when they are online, these wealthier audiences access, on average, both a greater number of sources and ones that are likely to be traditional, 'reliable' outlets as opposed to the social media sources that are sought out by poorer audiences. This has led researchers to conclude that 'social inequality in news consumption is already high [and] that it is likely to increase as we continue to move towards a more digital media environment' (Kalogeropoulos and Nielsen, 2018: 2). Of course, it may also suggest that lower income individuals – those who are at the sharp end of austerity and insecurity – have a greater (and understandable) distrust of established news sources and are anxious to seek out new voices where they have the opportunity and the financial resources to do so. Either way, we agree with Nic Newman's analysis in the Reuters Institute's *Digital News Report* that 'people with higher levels of formal education are more likely to evaluate the news media positively along every dimension than the rest of the population, suggesting that the news agenda is more geared towards the interests and needs of the more educated' (Newman, 2019: 11).

It is not simply access to but participation in political communications that is stratified by class and opportunity. For example, research by the Sutton Trust found that the news media is one of the most elitist sectors of British society with a substantial overrepresentation of people with a privileged educational background. While just 7% of the UK population are schooled privately, 44% of newspaper columnists, 43% of the top 100 senior journalists, editors and presenters and 29% of BBC executives went to 'independent' schools, and 44% of columnists, 36% of the 'News Media 100' and 31% of BBC executives attended either Oxford or Cambridge – hardly proportionate to the less than 1% of the UK population who studied there (Sutton Trust, 2019: 37). The researchers identify a 'disconnect' (2019: 38) which leads to an agenda-setting that reflects the news media's own priorities and class situation and diminishes those experiences with which they are less familiar.

Socio-economic status, however, is certainly not the sole factor in determining access to and participation in political communications. Gender, ethnicity and disability all impact decisively on citizens' use of communication technologies, entry to associated professions and representation in political culture. There is an enduring digital divide which, as Vartanova and Gladkova argue in their study of inequality in Russia (2019: 195), should not be seen simply as 'an access problem but as a complex multidisciplinary phenomenon closely affiliated with the political, economic and cultural development of a society'. Yet we cannot afford to underestimate the huge impact of class in relation to the asymmetrical opportunities afforded to citizens that frame their ability to participate in political communications. As Peter Golding rightly notes, 'problems of ideology and democracy are impossible to interrogate without a clear understanding of the inequitable distribution of material resources and the implication of such inequalities for both acquiring and communicating information and ideas' (2017: 4318).

2. Private property rights

The second infrastructural feature concerns the character of the property regimes that underpin communications across the globe. Are they privately owned or publicly controlled? Are they subject to full democratic oversight or are they accountable simply to shareholders or individual proprietors? Given that the vast majority of the dominant platforms and outlets that facilitate, generate and disseminate content about public affairs (excluding those state bodies with a specific remit to do so) are commercial operations, this means that political communications is subject to a commodity logic in which transactions are valued above all for their ability to be exchanged in a market relationship. It is true that there are exceptions to this rule – for example, the BBC and other public service media organisations, Wikipedia and ProPublica, which perform a valuable function in offsetting the commercial instincts of their rivals and, ideally, in treating their audiences as citizens and not consumers. However, even these non-profits are forced to operate in a communications *market* and are hardly able to insulate themselves from the need to attract good ratings and plenty of traffic. Political communication flows and the structures that underpin them are therefore determined by their ability, above all, to generate profits and attention rather than to engage publics in open dialogue or to hold power to account as a precondition of democratic accountability. This marketised logic permeates every level of political communications and shapes decisions about which audience, what platform and what kind of content are most likely to secure a surplus or at least a click-through.

Commercial interests dominate traffic whether they are 'classic' infrastructure operators like Comcast, AT&T, NTT, Sprint, Cisco and Deutsche Telekom, who operate major telecoms and data networks, or 'new' infrastructure companies like Alphabet, Amazon, Facebook and Tencent, owner of WeChat, who manage the platforms and portals of the digital age. Infrastructure ownership confers monopoly or oligopoly powers on these companies, presenting them with a gatekeeping authority akin to that of the telegraph and undersea cable companies of the nineteenth century. As with these earlier operators, these highly centralised structures – at odds with the allegedly decentralised nature of the online world – exercise their power not simply by facilitating movement but by controlling the terms on which this movement takes place. As Yochai Benkler noted in *The Wealth of Networks*:

> In a pure (i.e. proprietary] property regime, infrastructure owners have a say over whether, and the conditions under which, others in their society will communicate with each other. It is precisely the power to prevent others from communicating that makes infrastructure ownership a valuable enterprise. (2006: 155)

Benkler proposes a 'commons-based' system in which power is shared equally by senders and receivers and which is 'not built around the asymmetric exclusion of property' (2006: 62). Only a non-proprietary model can challenge the commodification of human experience that is at the heart of the economic logic of the 'surveillance capitalism' (Zuboff, 2019) enforced by tech giants, resist the 'privatization of our common culture' fostered by corporate-friendly copyright rules (McChesney, 2013: 80) or prevent the kind of abuse by an infrastructure owner that we saw, for example, with Facebook's enabling of anti-Muslim disinformation in Myanmar (Vaidhyanathan, 2018: 194).

Political content, however, is also – and more traditionally – associated with the ouputs of legacy media companies such as the *New York Times*, Asahi Shimbun in Japan, Grupo Clarín in Argentina, Globo in Brazil, or Germany's Bertelsmann. Many of these powerful corporations operate in contexts in which, far from there being either healthy competition or meaningful plurality, we find patterns of ownership concentration and elite power (Freedman, 2014: 31–59) that inhibit diversity and lead to the amplification of dominant viewpoints. A Media Ownership Monitor report assessing concentration in Argentina, for example, identified the negative impact of a handful of groups with close ties to the country's economic and political elites on the public policy agenda. It concluded that concentrated market power 'connects show business (exclusive celebrities), sports (purchase of TV rights), the economy (by including financial and banking institutions) and politics (when politicians become media moguls or shareholders in media holdings) with information areas. The implications of these ties impact the autonomy of media outlets eventually' (Media Ownership Monitor, 2019).

While this phenomenon of 'media capture' (Schiffrin, 2017) is especially common across parts of Latin America and Eastern Europe, media moguls and politicians in liberal democracies are not usually as intimately intertwined at the level of ownership (Berlusconi excepted) but the corrosive impact of media concentration remains just as intense. In the UK, just three companies – Rupert Murdoch's News UK, DMG Media (publisher of the *Mail* titles) and Reach (publisher of the *Mirror* titles) – account for 83% of national newspaper readership, with five conglomerates dominating 80% of all local titles. By themselves, News UK and DMG, purveyors of anti-immigrant and pro-Conservative agendas, dominate over 60% of the market share for national newspapers and exercise a disproportionate influence over news and political agendas (Media Reform Coalition, 2019b: 5). Despite huge drops in circulation for their leading daily titles, their prominent presence in online spaces – where *The Sun* and *Daily Mail* alone account for nearly 40% of total daily offline and online UK newsbrand reach (2019: 6) – guarantees them continuing attention from politicians and, evidence suggests, from broadcasters. For example, Cushion et al. (2018) studied intermedia agenda-setting during the 2015 UK general election and found that television news, while bound by impartiality regulations, nevertheless 'pursued a similar agenda to UK newspapers during the election campaign and followed their lead on some of the major stories' (2018: 178). More than half of all BBC stories on election policy issues had previously been published in newspapers, a figure that rose to nearly two-thirds of stories on Sky News, controlled at the time by Rupert Murdoch's 21st Century Fox (2018: 171). As Justin Schlosberg has argued, we are witnessing 'not the demise of concentrated news "voice", but its reconstitution within a more integrated, complex, and less noticeable power structure' (Schlosberg, 2018: 203) underpinned by a commodity trade in political information.

3. Exploited labour

Political communications is not a rootless or intangible sphere but the result of very different forms of concrete labour. Attention is often focused on the most high-profile purveyors of public affairs content – including government ministers, news anchors, celebrity bloggers and top reporters – and the informational and promotional duties that they perform. We spend less time, however, assessing the conditions that characterise the labour of those working in what seem to be more mundane roles: programmers designing the algorithms that decide what story rises to the top of news feeds, interns working for a PR company, or journalists making their way in what remains of the local news media. We spend *even* less time reflecting on the material practices of those who produce the 'tools' necessary to perform all these roles, whether they are tin miners on Bangka Island in Indonesia, skilled staff making fibre optic cables at Tratos' huge factory in Tuscany, or assembly line workers at Foxconn in China making the latest iPhones. Not enough questions are asked, argues Graham Murdock (2018: 363), 'about the manufacture and maintenance of the machines media workers use and the infrastructures they rely on', despite the ethical and environmental implications of this labour for the circulation of communicative content.

An emphasis on labour is rather different from one preoccupied with work more generally and with the changing dynamics of particular occupations like journalism or public relations. Labour, following Marx, is a form of productive activity that, under capitalism, generates value – often in the shape of profits – through its exploitation by employers who seek to extract as much as they can from their workers. This applies both to traditional manual workers and to so-called 'knowledge workers': 'digital labor cannot be regarded as a discrete form of labor, separate hermetically from the rest of the economy … the existence of a separably visible sphere of non-manual labor is not evidence of a new "knowledge-based," "immaterial," or "weightless" realm of economic activity. It is simply an expression of the growing complexity of the division of labor' (Huws, 2014: 157).

Yet as Örnebring notes, the majority of studies on, for example, newsrooms 'are primarily ethnographic and do not contain much information about, for example, salary levels, job security, degree of management control of labour processes and conflicts in the workplace' (2010: 59). These issues are by no means incidental to the character of the content produced: it matters if there is weak union organisation and highly precarious conditions, which makes it harder then to challenge unfair or unethical practices. It matters that journalists have been under pressure in recent years to file more copy for more platforms in less time and that the pressure of these multiple deadlines has led to more desk work (Fenton, 2010; Paulussen, 2012) and to the emergence of 'churnalism', a reliance on public relations material instead of original sourcing (Davies, 2008). Under pressure from the capitalist imperative to maximise profits and reduce labour costs, the labour of political communications has been rationalised, leading, as the *Columbia Journalism Review* once labelled it, to 'fast and wrong beats' (Nyhan, 2013) and a 'public relations democracy' (Davis, 2003) that is a long way away from normative accounts of a vigorous and egalitarian public culture.

Issues of labour and exploitation are all the more salient in a digital landscape given the abundance of user-generated content in political communications. Comments, blogs, videos and social media buzz are said to be expressive of the 'free labour' that is an 'important, yet unacknowledged source of value in advanced capitalist societies' (Terranova, 2004: 73). Christian Fuchs has written extensively on digital labour and argues that this kind of 'prosumer labour is infinitely exploited by capital' (2014b: 104) and ultimately subject to the same process of value generation as that of a Congolese miner or Indian programmer. Social media users freely posting, uploading and tweeting 'become productive labourers who produce surplus value and are exploited by capital' (2014b: 103). Others are keen to point out that there is a significant difference between wage labour and voluntary work, especially in relation to experiences of exploitation and possibilities of resistance: free labour, as Ursula Huws puts it, may contribute to commodity production but is formally 'outside the knot' of capitalist exploitation and a labour theory of value (2014: 173).

This is particularly important when it comes to thinking about how to press for infrastructural reforms to political communications content. While it is very difficult to collectively organise dispersed users, it is possible to devise campaigns to unionise paid labour. Improving the working conditions and security of programmers, podcasters, journalists and promotional workers would allow them more effectively to challenge unethical and illegal practices whether that is in relation to, for example, sexual harassment, Islamophobic content or the abuse of personal data by tech companies. Similarly, it is essential to tackle the structural barriers to employment upheld by the reliance on unpaid internships in journalism, publishing and politics that favour the wealthiest entrants or the precarious contracts that disempower workers and fuel a 'crisis of agency' (Allan, 2018: 259). Graham Murdock's point about the production of hardware is relevant to political communications more generally: 'the pleasures and conveniences offered by digital objects rest on a largely concealed trail of social exploitation and environmental despoilation' (2018: 364) that then raises the obligation to press for a communications system based on social justice and equality.

4. Neoliberal policy frameworks

Political communications operates within a particular set of rules and regulations wherever it takes place. Legislation on campaign finance, electoral advertising, media ownership, data protection, taxation, discrimination, intellectual property and a whole host of other issues all constrain the autonomy of political communications actors and provide a further infrastructural basis for their actions. There are laws on net neutrality, guidelines on impartiality, subsidies for public media and fiscal incentives for infrastructure development that materially shape the communication of public affairs. There are agendas and agencies, directives and departments, committed to managing the policy underbelly of contemporary communications flows (Flew et al., 2016).

Of course these take very different forms in different countries, so that, for example, rules on transparency of media ownership are extremely opaque across Eastern Europe but stringently applied in China; in the UK, broadcasters are required to be studiously impartial during an election period – something that significantly boosted the Labour Party's fortunes in the 2017 election because of an anti-Labour bias in the unregulated written press – while American elections are dominated by money and a cavalier commercial media in what Nichols and McChesney (2013) describe as a 'dollarocracy'. In all cases, however, these rules are neither developed nor implemented on a level playing field because of the ideological affinity and mutual interests of policymakers, regulators and industry voices. Under the guise of neoliberalism, communications markets around the world have been restructured since the 1980s to better enhance corporate profitability and inscribe a commercial logic ever deeper into the media field. Tech companies, central to political controversies over 'fake news' and misinformation, were never subject to high levels of state oversight. Political communications, as with politics more generally, is increasingly in thrall to 'reckless opportunists' (Davis, 2018) – the deregulated elites who lurch from crisis to crisis with no long-term plan other than to stay in power or receive handsome rewards.

This kind of liberalisation has been facilitated not simply through stark acts of regulatory and legislative realignment with corporate interests, but often through flawed decisionmaking processes that simply remove certain issues – often those concerning concentrations of media and tech power – from the policy agenda. Trappel argues that 'the digital regime seems to be out of hand for policy altogether, due to the transnational and even global nature of the services provided by the dominant media and communication companies' (2019: 26). Thus we have both 'media policy silences' (Freedman, 2014) and the regulatory failures that take place when 'a captured agency *systematically* favors the private interests of regulated parties and *systematically* ignores the public interest' (Horwitz, 1989: 29).

Freedman (2018) has shown how right-wing populist movements have taken advantage of these policy silences to great advantage. First, a failure to rein in media concentration has led to the consolidation of giant companies with significant political influence and a commercial orientation that privileges the kind of sensationalist content that authoritarian populist leaders are only too happy to provide. Second, the reluctance of governments up to this point to scrutinise tech giants and subject them to anti-monopoly controls that remain in place in other fields has led to a situation in which unaccountable social media companies are able to abuse their dominant positions. For example, Facebook's commercial model and lack of oversight has led to its status as both a 'surveillance' and 'disinformation machine' (Vaidhyanathan, 2018). Third, this commercial impulse, together with a failure to meaningfully protect press freedom and instead subject journalists to more immediate national security priorities, has disabled reporters from asking tough and complex questions about the electoral success of right-wing populism. Finally, the failure to support independent public service media and instead to tilt the policy environment in favour of large, commercial interests (while simultaneously narrowing the remit of public media) has further undermined the ability to develop a counterweight to vested interests and a trusted platform that can challenge the false promises of authoritarian populists. Freedman concludes that while media policy failures did not cause the rise of Trump or the AfD in Germany or the People's Party in Austria, right-wing populist movements have thrived on the fact that these neoliberal policies 'have been unable to lay the basis for independent critical and representative media systems that would articulate and respond to the very diverse sets of concerns that citizens have in their respective environments' (Freedman, 2018: 615). These policy regimes constitute a further dimension of the largely unseen but nevertheless extremely powerful set of infrastructural relations that shape contemporary political communications.

CONCLUSION: THE STRUGGLE FOR POLITICAL AND ECONOMIC DEMOCRACY

This chapter has sought to *materialise* political communications: to highlight the socio-economic inequalities that distort access to and participation in the communication of public affairs, the marketised property relations that transform communicative goods and services into commodities and diminish their democratic value, the exploitative labour conditions that characterise a range of roles in the communication process from the extraction of the natural resources needed to produce mobile phones to the rank-and-file journalism that shapes our knowledge of politics, and the policy infrastructures that constrain what is permissible and that reflect neoliberal values of 'corporate libertarianism' (Pickard, 2014).

In doing so, it has drawn on a recent turn to infrastructuralism not only in order to make visible the physical support mechanisms on which communications depends and to lend communications analysis a more systemic quality, but also to draw attention to the underlying social relations that shape what is privileged and what is marginalised under capitalism. This is a complement to, and not a substitute for, the other foci of political communications – the effects studies, ethnographic analyses and text-based investigations that dominate the field – but it serves to remind us of the impact of the profoundly unequal structures that compromise the lives of billions of people that we discussed in the opening chapter. It is not enough simply to draw attention to the 'pipelines' and 'sewers' that characterise political communications. We also need consistently to contextualise their flows in the light of social relations that are in themselves 'infrastructural' and associated with the socio-economic drivers of the capitalism that remains hegemonic today. Such an approach may assist us in avoiding deterministic or impressionistic accounts of technological change and political realignment and orient us towards the fundamental features and contradictions of contemporary societies, as well as illuminating both the central challenges and paths of resistance that we discuss later in this book.

Above all, it suggests that we should focus on how best to secure a democratic political communications infrastructure that would require us to confront the monopoly control of information flows exercised by the biggest tech and media companies as well as the economic inequality in wider society. As McChesney and Nichols argue (2016: 263) in their vision of a democratic reform programme for the digital age, 'The information we need to utilize and maintain a democratic infrastructure will be ours if we make the struggle for that information part of an agenda that recognizes the necessity of political and economic democracy'. A democratic infrastructure for political communications will have to involve commitments not only to social justice, technological innovation and political representation but also, crucially, to economic equality.

3

THE STATE OF POLITICAL COMMUNICATIONS

INTRODUCTION

When top civil servants anonymously briefed *The Times* in June 2019 that then Labour leader Jeremy Corbyn was 'too frail' to become prime minister, was this simply an inappropriate intervention by two maverick mandarins or evidence of a more systematic effort on behalf of the British state to discredit him and undermine his chances of taking office? Should the fact that military and intelligence personnel provided source material for 34 different stories in the UK media representing Corbyn as a 'threat' to national security ahead of the 2019 general election (Kennard, 2019) be of concern in a liberal democracy? That these questions could even be posed reveals the lingering power of the unaccountable interests that are vested in the state. Some fifty years ago, Ralph Miliband opened his influential book on *The State in Capitalist Society* by insisting that we live increasingly 'in the shadow of the state ... It is possible not to be interested in what the state does; but it is not possible to be unaffected by it' (1969: 3). For Miliband, the state – as both institutional arrangement and instrument of power – was perhaps *the* critical actor in the political, economic and ideological battles that mould contemporary society. Fast forward to today, and despite the degree of state surveillance, penetration and oversight of our communication systems, many theorists insist that the state is not the powerful force it once was and that our lives are shaped more by private interests than by the command and control structures of a centralised state.

This is reflected in the paucity of work in recent political communications literature that focuses on the role of the state in liberal democracies. This ought not to be confused with work that highlights the activities of government or the administration of particular territorial units or content that focuses on general processes of governance or policymaking. Instead, what we lack is research that interrogates the state as a unique formation of power or, as Bob Jessop puts it (1982: 228), an 'institutional ensemble of forms of representation, internal organisation, and intervention' in capitalist society. This is not to argue that political communications has become politically complacent. Inspired by global pandemics, technological innovations, economic catastrophes, political earthquakes, military interventions and socio-cultural transformations, today's political communications researchers have discovered a rich seam of material to be mined and evaluated. At the heart of this new atmosphere are a whole host of actors including populists, presidents, prime ministers, programmers, protesters, podcasters, pollsters, bloggers, demagogues, editors, elites, journalists, slacktivists and influencers. But where in this frenzy of activity is a distinctive and complex conception of the state and a specific emphasis on state actors in relation to communicative power? Where is the updated analysis of the 'domination of official sources' that marked Herman and Chomsky's propaganda model (1988: 23), or the use of communication technologies to extend US imperial power that Herbert Schiller referred to in *Mass Communications and American Empire* (Schiller, 1969)?

Consider a recent 'state of the art' summary of 'Ferments in the Field' in a special issue of the influential *Journal of Communication*. Of the 20 essays, only one – by a Marxist academic exploring the 'interpenetration of state and capital'

(Sparks, 2018: 396) – engages even remotely with questions of state power. Most fail entirely to acknowledge the state as a meaningful actor, while others touch on related issues but use a very different terminology. Bennett and Pfetsch (2018), for example, speak of a range of processes (including gatekeeping, framing, indexing and agenda-setting) and reflect on a number of agents (including parties, leaders, journalists, protestors, audiences and publics) in their 'Rethinking Political Communication in a Time of Disrupted Public Spheres' without a single mention of the state. Entman and Usher (2018), in their fascinating account of the impact of digital technology on power and ideology, concentrate on 'elites' rather than state actors, while Turow and Couldry encourage scholars to 'give primary attention to [datafied] surveillance as a key infra-structural dimension of social and economic life' (2018: 422) in relation to 'capitalism' but not state activities per se.

Analysis of the state is not even guaranteed in work on the state itself. In an edited collection on *Global Media and National Policies: The Return of the State* (Flew et al., 2016), critical debates on the definition and scope of state power are confined to a small minority of chapters even though the editors acknowledge that 'the state remains the primary site of governance with the capacity to make decisions, assign resources and enforce laws' (2016: 7). Most contributions, however, assess policy and regulatory debates simply from the perspective of specific territorially bounded, geographical entities – a semantic confusion noted previously by Bourdieu in his extensive lectures on the state. Does the state, he asks (2014: 31), refer to 'the bureaucratic apparatus that manages collective interests' *or* to the 'territory on which the authority of this apparatus is exercised?'. All too often, the state becomes short-hand for 'nation-state' rather than a particular configuration of elite power and control that may be played out in different ways across the globe. The book ends up, therefore, mostly discussing national media policies and not the underlying conditions of power and control that make decisionmaking (and non-decisionmaking) possible.

So what has happened in the last forty years since Stuart Hall and his col-leagues wrote one of the most influential books in the field of media, communications and cultural studies, whose full title is *Policing the Crisis: Mugging, the State, and Law and Order* (Hall et al., 1978)? This account of the construction of a particular ideological discourse around crime placed the state (as well as the media) squarely at the heart of the action. The book locates the emergence of 'mugging' in relation to the 'historically developing "crisis of hegemony" of the British state' (1978: 217), and indeed argues that it can only be understood 'at the level of the state' (1978: 306). Of course there are other important socio-political variables, but Hall et al. insist on a conception of the state as an 'organiser' (1978: 205) of the economy, of political representation, of social life, of the family, and not least, of ideas through its power over education and the media.

Four decades later, globalisation, neoliberalism and technological innovation have re-shaped the debate such that, at least when it comes to political communica-tions in liberal democracies, it appears that the state has become a rather unfash-ionable and outmoded concept. This is not necessarily the case in other academic disciplines or, especially, in activist circles where there has been a re-emergence of interest in questions of the state and a rebuttal of its marginalisation in neoliberal circumstances (see, e.g. Mitchell and Fazi, 2017; Nineham, 2019; Wayne, 2018). For scholars working on the politics of race, immigration and gender – not least in relation to the impact of COVID-19 – ignoring the role of the state is not a luxury they can afford (Barrow and Chia, 2016; King, 2016; Massoumi et al., 2017). However, it appears that for many political communications scholars, the liberal democratic state is seen as an increasingly irrelevant contributor to what has been described as a 'kaleidoscopic mediascape' (Bennett and Livingston, 2018: 129; see also Chadwick, 2017; McNair, 2017).

It is a rather different matter when talking about authoritarian countries which are partially defined by the existence of an 'overbearing' state which presides over domestic communications structures. For example, a glance at the programme of the International Communications Association's 2018 conference, the largest of the academic fora in the field, reveals that while the state is virtually absent as a topic of research, it pops up almost exclusively in relation to 'illiberal' regimes, including China, Venezuela, Ethiopia and Indonesia. It seems that authoritarian countries have *real* states worthy of analysis, while liberal democratic countries, despite recent revelations about the scale of state surveillance, have official structures that are, as David Held once wrote (1983: 23), merely 'an institutional mechanism for the articulation of the general interest'. So to the extent that there are states in the West, they are likely to be cuddly, benevolent and diffuse – unlike China, which has a highly effective and coercive state, Venezuela, which has a failing state, Iran, which has a clerical state, and Hungary, which has a nasty state.

This chapter argues that the state should be a concern for political communications researchers wherever they are based, given its continuing role as a major source of and influence over media content. The chapter reflects on some of the arguments in political sociology and politics more generally that are used to justify the marginalisation of the state in relation to liberal democracies; it then proposes a critical understanding of the state that suggests it remains a key strategic actor in the contemporary world. In the second half of the chapter we discuss six ways in which the state retains a major influence over the media, before concluding that it would be extremely premature to write off or ignore the state at a time when it is accruing additional powers and capabilities that circumscribe our political communications landscapes.

THEORIES OF THE 'DISAPPEARING' STATE

The most obvious reason for the decline in interest in the state is empirical: it is claimed that state bodies no longer play the co-ordinating role that they used to in a global, interconnected world. This will no doubt change given the levels of state intervention in response to the Coronavirus pandemic. Susan Strange famously wrote in *The Retreat of the State* that thanks to the growth of private enterprise in finance, industry and trade, the 'domain of state authority in society and economy is shrinking' (1996: 82). Despite the fact that state expenditure as a proportion of GDP has not actually declined (Mitchell and Fazi, 2017: 95), she insists that global markets are now 'more powerful than the states to whom ultimate political authority over society and economy is supposed to belong' (Strange, 1996: 4). This is not just about the volume of economic activity tied to the state, but about its 'quality' and the degree to which the state has lost its sheen as a hegemonic force. In many countries, the state has out-sourced many of its responsibilities to the private sector (see Meek, 2014 for the UK), has been outstripped by the market in terms of its dynamism and its potential to gen-erate growth, and has been hollowed out to such an extent that its sphere of operation is limited to a few remaining core responsibilities such as welfare, defence, national security and immigration. It appears, therefore, that you can have *a* state if you live in the West – after all its officials issue passports and wedding licences, they stop migrants from entering the country and they directly administer (admittedly declining levels of) social security benefits – even if it is not quite *the* state which is what less fortunate people in illiberal countries appear to suffer from.

This is connected to a wider debate on the 'end of the nation state' (Ohmae, 1995) and its overshadowing by capital, corporations, commodities and consumerism. For some theorists, 'nation states everywhere are in an advanced state of political and moral decay'. These '20th-century structures are drowning in a 21st-century ocean of deregulated finance, autonomous technology, religious militancy and great-power rivalry' (Dasgupta, 2018). The notion of some sort of co-ordinating force, articulated in the very idea of the state, together with its frequent realisation in the territorial entity of the Westphalian nation-state, now appears almost quaint. So while Joseph Nye, the theorist of 'soft power', was content to talk back in 1990 of the specific 'instruments' needed to secure the legitimacy of states, for example in relation to security, trade and culture (1990: 166), his more recent work highlights the shift towards 'smart power' marked by a 'power diffusion away from all states to nonstate actors' (2011: xv).

Secondly, some scholars have virtually theorised the liberal democratic state out of existence. This is not simply because of (misleading) claims about falling levels of state spending or the growth of new transnational sites of power, but because the world is now seen as too complex for the seamless exercise of state power. In a multipolar and distributed environment, to speak of the state is to conjure up totalising structures of authority and co-ordination. It generates talk of 'deep states' and 'parastates' promulgated by conspiracy theorists and supporters of Donald Trump. It fetishises control, order and centralisation when the world appears to be out of control, savagely disorderly, hugely fragmented and utterly unpredictable (Bauman, 2000; McNair, 2006).

So instead of the machinery, personnel and instruments of the state, we have a new language that represents more contingent forms of power. We have blocs and coalitions, executives and technocrats, judiciaries and parliaments, elite networks and patrimonial regimes, authoritarian leaders and populist demagogues, and non-state forces and rhizomatic structures. We have loosely defined Establishments (Jones, 2015), multiple forms of governance (Bevir, 2012) and even a range of 'quasi-states' (Jackson, 1993), but what we don't have, apparently, are committees 'for managing the common affairs of the whole bourgeoisie' as Marx and Engels put it 170 years ago when reflecting on the emerging capitalist state. In this context, it is tempting to focus on more fluid and dynamic non-state actors in Wall Street and Silicon Valley, or in civil society and social movements, and to talk about *Indignados*, hackers and brand managers, rather than harking back to a time of bureaucrats, civil servants, spooks and 'officials'.

REINTRODUCING THE STATE

By doing this, however, we threaten to miss the continuing and very real capacity of state actors to shape contemporary political landscapes and, in particular, political communications systems. In order to avoid this mistake, it may be useful to return to some key debates on understanding the state as a specific formation of power rather than a series of discrete territories, people or institutions.

Marxist accounts argue that the capitalist state emerges as a means of cohering and representing ruling-class interests against challenges to its authority. For Engels, 'the modern state ... is essentially a capitalist machine, the state of the capitalists, the ideal personification of the total national capital' (Engels, 1947: 338). Far from articulating a 'universal' or 'public' interest, the state promotes and protects the values, protocols and property of only one section of society. The state may feign a more generalised loyalty to conflicting interests, and at times may be forced into recognising competing claims, but above all it seeks to secure hegemony and to neutralise its opponents through the use of both coercive and non-coercive means. As such, the state is able to mobilise repressive forces, for example the security services, the police and the army, together with 'administrative' institutions such as the civil service, education and communications, in order to defend or develop the necessary infrastructures for social and economic reproduction. In this way, the state is linked but not reducible to concepts like 'government', 'public sector' and 'nation', all of which lack the particular emphasis on an underlying 'apparatus' and a set of relationships around which capitalist interests can coalesce. Governments, for example, are necessarily more fragile and impermanent than the more durable structure of the state which is 'staffed by "professional" people who owe their position not to any election, popular or otherwise, but to the allegedly rational internal bureaucratic norms of the sector of the state for which they happen to work' (Sparks, 1986: 76).

Jessop (2002: 45) outlines some core 'functions' of the capitalist state: that it needs to secure the general conditions for capital accumulation, to assert the rights and capacities of capital over labour, to define the boundaries between what is seen as 'economic' and what is seen as 'political', and crucially, to address the consequences of capitalist contradictions. The state, according to this logic, presides over large infrastructure projects that private interests might not otherwise invest in, polices trade unions and opposition groups that challenge specific accumulation strategies, regulates the political and legal circumstances in which capitalism operates, and supervises the 'social equations' (Hall et al., 1978: 214) that naturalise the status quo. Despite recent developments, for example the increased use of outsourcing, the growth in transnational bodies and the shift from 'government' to 'governance', the state remains for Jessop 'the most significant site of struggle among competing global, triadic, supranational, national, regional and local forces' (2002: 211). Mitchell and Fazi, confronting the idea that globalisation somehow supplanted state power when it was 'largely the product of state-driven processes' (2017: 7), conclude that the state has not declined but is in the process of being reconfigured: 'Capital remains as dependent on the state today as it was under "Keynesianism" – to police the working classes, bail out large firms that would otherwise go bankrupt [and] open up markets abroad (including through military intervention)' (2017: 9). The prevalence of wars of occupation, inter-national rivalry and bank bailouts after the 2008 financial crash appears to bear out this conclusion.

Yet for some critics, this invocation of the continuing power of the state smacks of an instrumentalism that fails to do justice to the incoherence of and fractions within class rule. There have been decades of debate on the left about the extent to which the spheres of 'economy' and 'politics' are autonomous of the state, including Poulantzas' assertion that the state involves 'the condensation of a relationship of forces' (1978: 128) rather than maintaining the interests of a specific class, and more recently the concerns of Trottier and Fuchs (2015: 20) about whether traditional Marxist accounts involve 'monolithic concepts of the state that conceive it as a homogeneous apparatus or machine of the ruling class for dominating the ruled class'. The British political theorist Philip Abrams provides a particularly evocative critique in which he argues that the state is simply an 'ideological project' (1988: 76), not in the sense that it seeks to naturalise mystifying social relations like a *camera obscura*, but that it is a fiction dreamt up to suggest that there is some kind of 'hidden hand' behind the social order. The state, he claims, is a 'triumph of concealment. It conceals the real history and relations of subjection behind an a-historical mask of legitimating illusion' (1988: 77).

These quite different positions – characterising the state either as a clumsy yet brutal instrument of class interests *or* as a myth that exaggerates the ability of elites to act in concert in pursuit of shared aims – resonate with contemporary arguments that the state is no longer the major player in the political arena, and that even if it were, it would be an example of conspiratorial thinking to suggest that class fractions could overcome their differences in the flawless exercise of state power.

Of course there is an instrumentalist tone to, for example, Marx and Engels' conception of the state in *The Communist Manifesto* and in Lenin's description in *The State and Revolution* of the state as 'an organ of class *rule*, an organ for the *oppression* of one class by another' (Lenin, 1977: 9, emphasis in original). This reflects their origins in conditions in which state power was exercised in quite brutal ways. But this hasn't prevented Marxist theorists from acknowledging that the state is far from 'homogeneous' in its composition, that different fractions are constantly struggling for hegemony within state circles, and that there is a need for both coercive and ideological methods for reproducing class power. Instrumentalism need not mean predictability or the absence of contradiction; it simply refers to the determination, on the part of those with power, to act in ways that are designed to secure the reproduction of unequal power relations. As such, the state is engaged every day in what could be seen as 'instrumental' activities to secure the established order even if it does not operate as a 'monolithic' bloc.

Ralph Miliband (1969: 46), for example, argues that the state is not a simple object, a 'thing', but instead 'a number of particular institutions which, together, constitute its reality.' It is bound to be a 'nebulous entity' (1969: 47) until it is materialised by actual people and structures in very different and unpredictable circumstances. Miliband is particularly interested in the state's participation in what he calls 'political socialisation':

> Processes through which values, cognitions and symbols are learned and internalised, through which operative social norms regarding politics are implanted, political roles institutionalised and political consensus created, either effectively or ineffectively. (Miliband, 1969: 164)

This is far from a mechanical picture of social reproduction, but refers instead to an ongoing process of legitimation. Miliband draws very heavily here on Gramsci's description of the state as 'the entire complex of practical and theoretical activities with which the ruling class not only justifies and maintains its dominance, but manages to win the active consent of those over whom it rules' (Gramsci, 1971: 244). Here we have not a blunt instrument or a singular object, but a hegemonic *architecture* composed of government, administration, media, civil service, military, police, judicial branch, parliament and so on, that ultimately supports the reproduction of class power. It is the relationship between these institutions that 'shapes the form of the state system' (Miliband, 1969: 50), a point developed by Pierre Bourdieu when he conceptualises the state as a relational force: 'a set of specific resources that authorizes its possessors to say what is good for the social world as a whole' (2014: 33) – and, we might add, that allows them to defend this authority vigorously. For Bourdieu, the state is responsible for the 'organization of consent as adhesion to the social order' (2014: 5) *and* acts as a form of 'meta-capital' and a 'regulator of subjectivities' (2014: 197). It is, therefore, both a co-ordinating and a regulating force.

It is worth noting that the state is just as visible and interventionist in some 'classic' liberal accounts, except that here the state is not structurally wedded to reproducing class power but simply to mediating between conflicting forces. The state, according to this perspective, has a sort of 'watchdog' function – much like the classic liberal theory of the press – protecting the public interest in a neutral, disinterested fashion. It is seen as a vital response to the increasing complexity of modern societies and a necessary bulwark against the vagaries of individualised forms of exchange. So for Max Weber in his *Economy and Society*, a 'compulsory political association with continuous operations will be called a "state" insofar as its administrative staff successfully uphold the claim to the monopoly of the legitimate use of physical force in the enforcement of its order' (1978: 54). The state is an archetypal bureaucratic structure, characterised by an ultimate 'monopoly' on coercion specifically so that it can settle conflicts in an ordered and productive way. This is only possible as long as its domination is seen as 'legitimate' and its authority is validated by the creation of a formal legal system with a codified set of rules. Durkheim too conceptualises the state as a decisive social institution, describing it as both 'the very organ of social thought' (1992: 50) and 'above all, supremely, the organ of moral discipline' (1992: 72), related of course not to class interests but to a more mellifluous collective conscience.

While the Weberian and Marxist perspectives may disagree about many things, not least the purpose and beneficiaries of state power, both concur with the argument that the state refers to a set of relations, institutions and processes that are at the heart of economic and social reproduction. The state, according to the neo-Weberian theorist Theda Skocpol, 'is a set of administrative, policing, and military organizations headed, and more or less well coordinated by, an executive authority' (1979: 29). Given this conceptualisation, it is surprising that the state remains a marginal actor in some of the most popular political communications literature (e.g. Chadwick, 2017; McNair, 2017; Norris, 2000) and that its productive, disciplinary and regulatory authority is largely ignored in favour of an emphasis on the activities of governments, media corporations and tech platforms. This chapter seeks to counter this approach and now goes on to discuss the ways in which the state continues to set the parameters for what is possible, and what is not possible, inside contemporary political communications environments.

HOW DOES THE STATE SHAPE POLITICAL COMMUNICATIONS?

Back in the analogue days of 1986, Colin Sparks produced a very useful account of the different roles adopted by the state in its effort to influence media systems and cement its power. The state, he argued, could be seen as a 'patron' (in terms of its subsidies to media outlets), a censor, an 'actor' (providing source material), a 'masseur' (involved in public relations to shape coverage), an 'ideologue' and a 'conspirator' (representing shared class interests) (1986: 77–85). Sparks highlights the mutual bond between the unelected personnel of the state and the unaccountable structures of a corporate media: 'The state and the media are two of the weapons that the people who rule us use to ensure their continuation in power' (1986: 84). To what extent can this be argued to fit contemporary realities marked,on the one hand by experiences of fluidity, hybridity and heterogeneity, and on the other by residual concentrations of power and influence? In what ways have globalisation, neoliberalism and digitisation reshaped the role of the state vis-à-vis communications and how do these developments affect the relevance of Sparks' model?

The argument in this chapter is that while the language may require some updating, the core assumptions remain largely accurate, and indeed the state remains a powerful structuring force in the communications field. We identify six roles that better reflect the specific activities and typologies of the twenty-first-century state even if there are significant continuities with Spark's twentieth-century model. This list conceptualises the state as *propagandist*, *bully*, *data controller*, *rulemaker*, *entrepreneur* and *sponsor*. Of course these roles overlap – for example the state's interest in sponsoring media is often connected to a propaganda pay-off while its use of targeted surveillance is predicated on its control of the regulatory landscape – but they refer, nevertheless, to some of the key ways in which the state is able both to leverage and to naturalise its power over political communications.

Propagandist

The state is an energetic and prolific communicator. It exerts a significant amount of time and money in generating its own original content as well as source material for third parties, notably the media. Vast resources are poured into the production of public information campaigns, press releases, social media content and advertising material that seek both to inform and persuade citizens about specific initiatives whether they relate to public health promotions, electoral contests, benefit entitlements or national security. This is usually discussed in relation to 'government communication' (Sanders and Canel, 2013; Stanyer, 2007), referring to the promotional activities of, for example, the Government Communication Service in the UK, the Federal Press and Information Service in Germany and the Government Information Service in the Netherlands, and is often seen as an inevitable consequence of a 'public relations democracy' (Davis, 2002). Indeed Sanders and Canel argue that government communication takes place not on behalf of the state but of '*public* institution(s)', and that it is 'constituted on the basis of the *people's* indirect or direct consent and charged to enact their *will*' (2013: 4, italics in original). Perhaps not surprisingly, therefore, the strategic communication of liberal democracies is sometimes conceived as a relatively harmless and consensual form of information exchange in contrast to the 'propaganda' emanating from authoritarian regimes.

While some government communication may indeed be the routine output of bureaucratic political life, it is nevertheless far from an innocent form of PR that simply reflects the responsibilities of an elected government. Instead we should see it as a constituent element of a larger system of 'organized persuasive communication' (OPC) that is 'central to the exercise of power across all social spheres' (Bakir et al., 2018: 2), not least the more permanent interests that circumscribe the actions of specific governments. Indeed, if we understand propaganda not simply as lying but as 'the deliberate manipulation of representations ... with the intention of producing any effect in the audience ... that is desired by the propagandist' (Briant, 2015: 9), then we should see propaganda not as an exception or an affront to democracy but as one element of the broad terrain of OPC undertaken by all powerful interests, including states. David Miller and Rizwaan Sabir talk of propaganda in this way: not as biased or 'distorted' communication but as the 'weaponization of information' by powerful groups. Propaganda, they argue, is 'not simply a matter of discourse, not just about content, but a matter of concrete material action by particular institutional interests' (Miller and Sabir, 2012: 79) where the line between coercive and consensual forms of behaviour is increasingly blurry.

Bakir et al. (2018: 15) argue that there is a 'scholarly blind spot toward manipulative OPC' where 'citizens are routinely incentivised, deceived and coerced by powerful actors', and an overemphasis on things like public relations and branding that are seen as relatively benign forms of organised persuasion. So while it is easy to condemn the 'fake news' coming out of Putin's Russia and Xi's China, it is also important to be attentive to the multiple forms of propaganda emanating from inside democratic states that have been used, since 9/11, to market the 'war on terror' and install security regimes in which Muslims have been positioned as prime suspects. Media operations, strategic communication, public affairs, public diplomacy, perception management, information warfare, information operations and psychological operations (PSYOP) – these are just some of the ways of labelling the means by which Western states have justified military interventions like the Iraq War, legitimised domestic surveillance apparatuses and evoked threats to 'national security' (Briant, 2015).

The state continues to be a prolific and persuasive source for everyday news content, often operating behind a protective cloak of anonymity. Just as 'senior civil servants' were behind the *Times* story (28 June 2019) warning of Jeremy Corbyn's frailty that we mentioned at the start of this chapter, 'senior government sources' and a 'senior Home Office official' were also behind the unevidenced assertions in the *Sunday Times* (14 June 2015) that Edward Snowden's whistleblowing activities had endangered the lives of British spies. At times, entire units are set up to influence public perception of key events. Consider the work of the Coalition Communications Cell set up by Dan Chugg, a senior UK Foreign Office official, in 2015 specifically to challenge the increasingly widespread narratives of Daesh. Working with 15 coalition partners, Chugg sought to 'change the narrative around Daesh from one of success to one of failure' (Chugg, 2017). The CCC circulated a daily media pack to more than 1000 officials in 60 countries, ran a website and social media channels, and produced content that was reproduced in the speeches of the prime ministers of Spain and Australia. The trade magazine *PR Week* described this as 'a successful propaganda offensive waged by comms professionals in the UK and other countries' (Owen, 2018). Consider also the Research, Information and Communications Unit (Ricu), housed within the Office for Security and Counter-Terrorism within the UK Home Office, to generate content for the government's highly controversial counter-radicalisation programme, Prevent. The *Guardian* describes this as a 'covert strategic communications programme' that 'uses YouTube, Twitter and Facebook as well as more traditional propaganda methods, such as feeding stories to newspapers, including the Guardian, and leafleting' (Cobain et al., 2016). Ricu works with outsourced agencies to minimise its own role in the campaign but has employed a team of media professionals, marketing consultants, academics and counter-terrorism experts. According to former home secretary and author of the government's anti-immigration 'hostile environment' policy, Theresa May, Ricu was 'road-testing some quite innovative approaches to counter-ideological messages' (quoted in Cobain et al., 2016).

States take very seriously these 'counter-ideological' operations and have comprehensive propaganda systems that rely on intermediate agents, including for example editors, politicians and academics, to circulate and re-purpose this material. These apparatuses both pre-date and are galvanised by today's 'fake news' platforms but they are not simply the product of conspiratorial imaginations. The UK's intelligence service MI6 has an 'Information Operations' (I/OPS) division just as the CIA has its own National Clandestine Service to engage in 'non-attributable activities' (Briant, 2015: 44). In Israel, it is the responsibility of the Ministry of Strategic Affairs to 'guide, coordinate and integrate the activities of all the ministers and the government and of civil entities in Israel and abroad on the subject of the struggle against attempts to delegitmize Israel' (quoted in Blau, 2017). This involves propaganda campaigns against, for example, proponents of boycott and divestment initiatives and pro-Palestinian interests. According to *Haaretz*, the Ministry's 'leading figures appear to see themselves as the heads of a public affairs commando unit engaged in multiple fronts, gathering and disseminating information about people they define as "supporters of the delegitimization of Israel"' (Blau, 2017). In the UK, the Foreign Office poured money into the Institute for Statecraft's 'Integrity Initiative', housed in an old mill in Scotland, an outfit that was set up to counter Russian disinformation but ended up attacking the leader of the Labour Party, Jeremy Corbyn, and supporting anti-Putin politicians in the Ukraine (Ferguson, 2018).

'Strategic communication', whether covert or overt, is a core element of the contemporary state and bears witness to a propagandistic underbelly through which state interests are promoted and opposing ideas undermined, whether this is in relation to clientilist relationships in Latin America, authoritarian tendencies in China or liberal democratic norms in Western Europe.

Bully

The state's 'monopoly of the legitimate use of physical force' means that it is well placed to use coercive tactics both to control information flows and to delegitmise voices with whom it disagrees. Traditionally, this has meant formal and informal systems of censorship that range from pre-publication bans and the seizing of material that contravenes rules on what is argued to be legally publishable, to the use of official 'flak machines' (Herman and Chomsky, 1988: 28) to undermine opponents and voluntary mechanisms like the UK's 'D-Notice' that pressures editors to avoid publishing sensitive political content.

In a digital age these more blunt forms of censorship are obviously more difficult to get away with, but censorious authorities – from China and North Korea to Sudan and Eritrea – still persist in policing media outlets and clamping down on any semblance of independent journalism. The annual World Press Freedom Index, curated by Reporters without Borders, demonstrates the extent to which media censorship still remains a hallmark of authoritarian regimes. The most dramatic illustration of the coercive power of the state, of course, is the number of journalists killed while carrying out their professional duties. This includes the high-profile murder of the *Washington Post* journalist Jamal Khashoggi, allegedly by Saudi officials in their embassy in Istanbul in 2018, and the murder in 2006 of the *Novaya Gazeta* journalist Anna Politkovskaya, a firm critic of Putin's war in Chechnya. A search of the database of the Committee to Protect Journalists (CPJ) reveals that 213 reporters were killed by 'government officials' between 1992 and 2019.

In liberal democracies, First Amendment absolutism and libertarian conceptions of speech undergird arguments against the suppression of what are seen as fundamental speech rights. Pre-publication censorship is therefore relatively rare even if there still exists a barrage of legislation that can be used against journalists, including, for example, official secrecy, anti-terror, libel and bribery laws. This has allowed even the most 'liberal' states to attack investigative journalism, one of the hallmarks of a functioning 'fourth estate' and a vital defence against demagogues and tyrants. In the US, before 2008, a grand total of three cases had been brought against whistleblowers and leakers under the terms of the Espionage Act for helping journalists to report on classified government programmes. The Obama administration (2008–2016), however, used the Act to launch nine cases, leading the *New York Times* to comment that if 'Donald J. Trump decides as president to throw a whistle-blower in jail for trying to talk to a reporter, or gets the F.B.I. to spy on a journalist, he will have one man to thank for bequeathing him such expansive power: Barack Obama' (Risen, 2016). Obama's war on journalists led to the first CPJ report on the US in which former *Washington Post* executive editor Leonard Downie Jr. concluded that:

> The administration's war on leaks and other efforts to control information are the most aggressive I've seen since the Nixon administration, when I was one of the editors involved in *The Washington Post*'s investigation of Watergate. The 30 experienced Washington journalists at a variety of news organizations whom I interviewed for this report could not remember any precedent. (Downie, 2013)

The British state has been especially proactive in relation to curbing independent media coverage of the war in Northern Ireland (Miller, 1994). The 1988 Broadcasting Ban that prevented UK viewers from hearing the voices of the representatives of specific proscribed organisations (and indeed even songs that may have been seen to support the Republican movement) may have been lifted many years ago (Curtis, 1998), but restrictions on journalists still remain. For example, in August 2018, Trevor Birney and Barry McCaffrey, two British journalists behind a documentary, *No Stone Unturned*, that alleged collusion between the state and the killers of six Catholics in a massacre back in 1994, were arrested and accused of stealing official police documents. The pair were initially set to face charges under the Official Secrets Act and the Data Protection Act in a move that was widely seen as an attack on freedom of expression and an endorsement of a cover-up involving the security forces and the local police (Carroll, 2018). Under pressure from journalists and civil rights campaigners, the police finally dropped their investigation in June 2019.

That journalists continue to be enmeshed in political controversy is hardly a surprise, especially when the state is at its most tense and polarised. In 2017, the Spanish prime minister, Mariano Rajoy, reacted to the huge independence movement in Catalonia by attempting to consolidate the Spanish state and enforce punitive measures on the media. This involved warnings that it would prosecute any media outlets that advertised the independence referendum and then threatening to take control of Catalan public broadcasting including its main television station, TV3. According to Rajoy, taking over the Catalan media would guarantee 'truthful, objective and balanced' coverage (quoted in Minder, 2017), despite having more in common with the censorship of the Franco dictatorship than with an enlightened twenty-first-century state in which one might expect a free and independent media to be the cornerstone of its democracy.

Data controller

The state's monopoly of coercive power also allows it to gather extensive information about the lives and activities of its citizens. This is nothing new. For years, the Stasi in East Germany and the FBI in the US built up enormous, bureaucratic surveillance operations that generated huge amounts of data concerning personal communications and political affiliations. Digital technologies, however, have allowed the state exponentially to increase the volume of personal data that can be collected and processed and to track the movement of capital, people and communicative interactions with unprecedented detail. This is what underpins the Chinese government's plans for a Social Credit System in which, as of 2020, the behaviour of all citizens and organisations will be rated and ranked (Botsman, 2017). Of course, the state is by no means the only institution with surveillance power. Private sector tech companies like Facebook, Amazon, Google and Apple have accumulated reams of data about consumer preferences and have used this to disrupt and reshape fields from business to politics and from media to shopping. We now have what Shoshina Zuboff calls 'surveillance capitalism', a new form of data power that 'replaces legitimate contract, the rule of law, politics, and social trust with a new form of sovereignty and its privately administered regime of reinforcements' (2019: xx). Yet even under 'surveillance capitalism', the state retains a unique capability to link the collection and storage of data to issues of, for example, 'national security', and to enforce sanctions against those it deems to be acting in ways that run counter to the 'national interest'.

The events of 9/11 and the emergence of a 'homeland security agenda' accelerated and legitimised the construction of a datafied security state. This has generated what Frank Pasquale (2015: 216) describes as a 'defense/intelligence/policing complex' that is part of a wider 'Black Box Society' based on opaque algorithms and the fusion of corporate and state interests. This was, of course, most dramatically illustrated by the revelations of the American whistleblower Edward Snowden about the scale of the surveillance apparatus overseen both by the US National Security Agency (NSA) and the UK's GCHQ. Programmes like PRISM, which took data straight out of the 'back door' of the largest tech companies (who handed the NSA the keys), and BOUNDLESS INFORMANT, which processed billions of phone calls and emails in the US, demonstrate the capacity of the state to monitor the communications landscape *beyond* any single private sector organisation (or indeed all of them combined). According to Glenn Greenwald, who assisted Snowden in publishing the leaked data (2014: 94):

> ... the Snowden archive led to an ultimately simple conclusion: the US government had built a system that has as its goal the complete elimination of electronic privacy worldwide. Far from hyperbole, that is the literal, explicitly stated aim of the surveillance state: to collect, store, monitor, and analyze all electronic communication by all people around the globe.

It seems hardly necessary to argue that this kind of surveillance machinery is incompatible with a democratic political communications environment and that there is an asymmetrical link between increased surveillance and the 'diminished oversight and accountability' of those who exercise power (Andrejevic, 2007: 7). Yet given the relative absence of the state from political communications literature, it is worth repeating Pasquale's point that the most pernicious consequence of surveillance is that 'it freezes into place an inefficient (or worse) politico-economic regime by cowing its critics into silence. Mass surveillance may be doing less to deter destructive acts than it is slowly narrowing the range of tolerable thought and behaviour' (Pasquale, 2015: 52).

This would appear to be the direction of travel in Narendra Modi's India, where the home ministry in 2018 allowed government agencies to monitor all digital traffic. This followed an attempt by Modi to establish a 'real time new media command room' to snoop on all 'digital media chatter', a proposal that was only scrapped after substantial public opposition yet with other elements of the surveillance apparatus still in place (Kazmin, 2018). This form of 'chilling' also has a direct impact on journalism. The UK government, for example, passed The Data Protection and Investigatory Powers Act (DRIPA) in 2016, facilitating unprecedented surveillance of journalists by the security services. According to the general secretary of the National Union of Journalists, the legislation was a 'snoopers' charter' that will 'trample over the very principles of journalism and will be a death knell for whistleblowers of the future' (Stanistreet, 2016). The legislation was so draconian that additional protections for journalistic sources were eventually included after a vigorous campaign by media organisations and reporters. Nevertheless, even then, sections of the Act that allow for access to phone and digital records without the suspicion of criminal activity were ruled to be contrary to European law by the High Court in 2018 (Kakar, 2018).

Rulemaker

Some commentators argue that there has been a dilution of the state's power to control the communications landscape as part of a shift from *government* to *governance* in which outsourced actors assume some of the responsibilities previously performed by the state. According to Petros Iosifidis (2016: 21), 'The role of the state as government certainly appears strong as it is the sole authority that rules and controls, but in a state of governance, the state typically *manages* and *orchestrates*' (emphasis in original). This would certainly appear to be the case in relation to the internet, where a range of non-governmental organisations and private companies are instrumental to online regulation and 'manage' internet protocols (Freedman, 2016). Yet as we have seen from some of the examples in earlier sections of this chapter, the state has not yielded its legislative role and continues to provide the legal infrastructure through which rules affecting the communications environment are developed, implemented and policed. Supranational bodies like the European Union and trade agreements like the North American Free Trade Association place limits on the autarchy of the state's role, but they do not supersede its status as the central domain of decisionmaking even in a more globalised world. For example, rules on media ownership, election advertising, intellectual property, tax breaks and spectrum allocation all shape the character of political communication in relation to specific countries, and are subject to oversight and sanctions by regulatory bodies whose authority is vested in the state.

The state, therefore, has certainly not divested itself of the power to set the terms of debate and devise the rules that structure communicative interactions. Indeed, given the rise of online disinformation and misinformation as a public policy priority in recent years – that 'fake news' is disrupting democratic elections and undermining trust in established sources of authority – we are likely to see a raft of new laws being passed that will probably grant additional powers to the state. France was the first country to pass a law on the 'manipulation of information' that enables judges to demand the immediate removal of fake content online during an election period. The law hands the regulator, the Higher Audiovisual Council, a series of new administrative and executive powers to police enforcement and even to suspend media outlets that are deemed to be controlled or 'under the influence' of a foreign state. While there are some welcome initiatives concerning the transparency of algorithms and the labelling of digital content, the law was criticised both for strengthening the power of the state and for failing to address the underlying causes of the problem of misinformation. 'The concentration of property in the media sector, the low working conditions of journalists, and the conflicts of interests within the sector are the three main diseases of contemporary journalism', argued the leader of the left-wing La France Insoumise party, Jean Luc Mélenchon: 'The law appears to deal with the symptoms, not the causes, of the diseases of the media sector' (quoted in Ricci, 2018).

Of course, the state's ability to make and police rules does not mean that it will *always* intervene in such a decisive fashion. While, as we have already seen, there is little hesitation in using its more coercive powers to resist immediate and pressing challenges to its core interests, the state also has at its disposal a range of less contentious options with which to secure its hegemony, including outsourcing, co-regulating and non-decisionmaking. The reluctance, for example, by US antitrust authorities to prevent the relentless buying sprees of Google and Facebook has led to a situation in which we now have 'giant monopolistic machines for the circulation of misinformation and propaganda that liberal commentators have argued have distorted recent ballots in the US and UK' (Freedman, 2018: 611) and that are now likely to generate new policies that the state will have to implement.

Entrepreneur

Thus far we have identified only negative roles where the state uses its power to further its own interests and diminish its opponents. What about situations in which the state can mobilise its power and resources for the public good and not only for the special interests with which the capitalist state is intimately associated? This might suggest a *welfarist* role in which the state guarantees a minimal allocation of communication rights, acts as a counterweight to market failure and privileges the public interest in communications. This approach is perhaps best expressed in the public subsidies for non-mainstream content and continuing support for public service media that we consider in the next section. The state, however, also has a *developmental* aspect in which it seeks to build up capacity – in terms of infrastructure, skills and technologies – both to accrue economic advantage and to improve opportunities for its citizens. This involves large-scale public investment, partnerships with industry and a focus on the end-user as well as the bottom line.

We might want to describe this role in terms of a 'developmental state' (Chalmers Johnson, 1982), a 'promotional state' (Abramson, 2001) or an 'enabling state' (Flew, 2007), but perhaps the most persuasive analysis has come from the economist Mariana Mazzucato in her book on *The Entrepreneurial State* (Mazzucato, 2013). Here she argues against neoliberal advocates of a 'small state' that, far from being a bureaucratic restraint on innovation and creativity – where it is confident and not apologetic – is able to take risks and engage in long-term planning that market forces have little appetite for: 'An entrepreneurial State does not only "de-risk" the private sector,' she argues, 'but envisions the risk space and operates boldly within it to make things happen' (2013: 6). The book contains a detailed analysis of innovations in the technology, health and energy sectors in which the state has played a leading role, and focuses in particular on the role of public investment in generating the conditions in which digital transformations became possible. Apple, she notes, 'was able to ride the wave of massive State investments in the "revolutionary" technologies that underpinned the iPhone and iPad: the Internet, GPS, touch-screen displays and communication technologies. Without these publicly funded technologies, there would have been no wave to foolishly surf' (2013: 88). In the UK, crucial developments in colour television, microcomputing and digital broadcasting have all emerged out of the laboratories of the publicly funded BBC.

For all the democratic possibilities of a forward-thinking and risk-taking state that is committed to serving the public interest, it is, however, virtually unthinkable for the capitalist state to shrug off its underlying commitment to existing property relations. Mazzucato is quite right to challenge the myths about a 'sluggish' public sector versus a 'dynamic' private sector, yet even the most entrepreneurial states remain in hock to the logic of capital accumulation and the reproduction of the status quo. Neoliberalism has not eviscerated the entrepreneurial state but has instead changed its immediate priorities, such that we now see 'a shift in the emphasis of state action from securing the market through the provision of various kinds of social welfare (primarily but not exclusively directed at heading off internal challenges) towards the provision of various kinds of productive infrastructure (primarily but not exclusively directed at attracting investment and ensuring its profitability)' (Sparks, 2016: 68). There may yet be productive and large-scale investment by the public sector into artificial intelligence, personalised algorithms and broadband infrastructure, but as long as the state maintains its intimate connections to vested interests it is hard to see how the fruits of the investment will be both controlled and enjoyed by the majority of ordinary citizens.

Sponsor

Whereas Sparks talked of the state as a 'patron', 'a direct economic benefactor of the media' (1986: 77) through its direct funding, granting of licences, tax breaks and advertising subsidies, we prefer to use the more commercial language of 'sponsorship' to indicate the different financial relationships that the contemporary state maintains with media outlets. Broadly speaking, this refers to two types of arrangements: public funding for media that is independent of the state and funding that is seen as an extension of the state. We are concerned that, in current circumstances, the crucial distinction between these two categories is under enormous stress.

True, there is a significant difference between the systems of press subsidies in Sweden, Norway, Finland and Denmark that Syvertsen et al. (2014) describe as a crucial pillar of the Nordic 'Media Welfare State', and state-funded international news channels that are wholly answerable to their funders and that in some cases appear to fulfil the propaganda function discussed earlier. It is worth noting, however, that while the former system is under increasing strain, the latter approach is booming with a growing number of states more than happy to underwrite their own broadcast iterations of 'soft power'. Early adopters like the Voice of America and the BBC's World Service have now been joined in a very crowded marketplace by Al Jazeera, Russia Today, China Global Television Network, France 24, Press TV, Rai Italia, Globo TV International and many more. Each channel has a quite different relationship to its state sponsor, but none can be said to be wholly independent of the sphere of influence and control exerted by its paymaster. The lack of operational autonomy may be more obvious when it comes to China's recent overhaul of its overseas outlets and the creation, as part of a $6.6 billion global expansion campaign, of a consolidated 'Voice of China' to promote China's brand across the world (Yip, 2018), but this is a matter of degree. So while Al Jazeera prides itself on its BBC-inspired commitment to editorial independence, it remains a pawn in the foreign policy dynamics of its Qatari funders. Even the BBC World Service is hardly immune to this kind of strategic power play given that the introduction of new language services was funded by the UK government's 2015 Strategic Defence and Security Review. Acknowledging that the World Service does not operate according to the same logic as Chinese state media, Kate Wright nevertheless argues that 'it no longer seems adequate to conceptualise Western-state-funded international media as simply having an "arm's length" relationship to the governments which support them' (Wright, 2019). Instead, she argues, we need to evaluate the varied strategies by which journalists attempt to stay independent of what she describes as their 'funding states'.

Domestic public media services are equally embroiled in the politics of these 'funding states'. For example, both Hungarian and Polish public service broadcasters have faced legislative reform and political attacks that have curbed any semblance of independence. In Poland, the ruling Law and Justice party has introduced the state appointment of broadcast executives and presided over the sacking of 120 journalists (Goclowski, 2016), while Hungarian public media is now answerable to a regulator dominated by government appointees, resulting in a visibly pro-government tone (European Federation of Journalists, 2018). Public service media across Europe are reined in by funding crises and political interventions such that even the much-heralded independence of the BBC has been undermined: 'Far from retaining its independence from all vested interests, and delivering a critical and robust public interest journalism, the BBC is a compromised version of a potentially noble ideal: far too implicated in and attached to existing elite networks of power to be able to offer an effective challenge to them' (Freedman, 2019: 206; see also Mills, 2016). It has reached the point that even the accomplished former World Service journalist Owen Bennett-Jones (2018: 32) argues that 'there is plenty of evidence that the BBC, in both its international and domestic manifestations, deserves the epithet "state broadcaster"'.

CONCLUSION: NAMING AND EVALUATING THE ROLE OF THE STATE IN POLITICAL COMMUNICATIONS

Given the scale and scope of state intervention into contemporary political communications landscapes, we are somewhat baffled by the lack of attention that has been given to this 'nebulous' (to use Miliband's term) but nevertheless powerful institutional arrangement in recent literature in our field. When we look at the communicative element of the Covod-19 pandemic, at the 'war on terror', at the surveillance apparatuses and datafied infrastructures that circumscribe political communications, at the full range of promotional technologies and apparatuses that legitimise the status quo, at the funding regimes that support specific media outlets, and at the propaganda systems that may go by other names but nevertheless attempt to normalise state power, we are surprised that 'naming' and 'evaluating' the role of the state is not a bigger priority for political communications scholars.

It is true that globalisation, digitalisation and neoliberalism have introduced new actors and trends into popular discourse that we need to focus on. It is also true that the state may have a significant role to play in rolling back the domination of corporate power in the shape of proposals for public media subsidies or calls for the break-up and nationalisation of Facebook and Google (Srnicek, 2017). This makes a robust and expansive critique of the state all the more necessary in order to disentangle measures that enhance the unaccountable power of elites as distinct from those that involve the further mobilisation of publics in social and economic life.

Neoliberalism has not made the state disappear from our communication landscapes. Indeed, due to the outsourcing and hollowing out that has taken place in the last thirty years, the state has become *more* concentrated, *more* hierarchical, sometimes *less* visible, but just as fierce in its articulation and defence of the capitalist interests with which it is intimately connected. State power is neither a conspiracy nor a seamless instrument of class domination. It is messy, contradictory, self-denying and opaque, but it is certainly not passé. We need, therefore, a political communications network that both identifies and challenges the logics, dynamics and strategies of the state as it seeks to shape communicative exchanges wherever they take place.

4

ELITES, EXPERTS, POWER AND DEMOCRACY

INTRODUCTION

This chapter explores the power of modern-day elites. It asks two things: how is elite power currently maintained and what has media and communication got to do with it?

Its focus is the growing disparity between the visible mediatised public sphere and the more private communication networks and spaces that largely operate outside of the public eye. It argues that, as the former has become louder and more ubiquitous, the latter has quietly been extended and consolidated. Thus critical media and political communications scholars need to be less side-tracked by the loud and brash aspects of mediatised politics, and devote more of their attention to invisible forms of communicative power.

On the one hand, democracy seems more visible than ever. Between tabloidisation, click-bait news headlines and alternative news sites, 'leaders' with charismatic authority (Weber, 1948), celebrity symbolic capital (Bourdieu, 1984) and populist views gain a greater public profile. They are opposed loudly on these planes by alternative leaders, news journalists and high-profile protesting groups and movements. However, on the other hand, beneath this vibrant public sphere, increasingly powerful and well-resourced business, financial and technological elites are influencing politics, economics and wider society through more covert means. They operate through opaque think tanks, flexible networks and more private communication channels. They use their extreme wealth to employ a range of expert intermediaries in law, accountancy, lobbying and public relations, to both avoid the public spotlight and achieve insider access and influence. Their greater mobility enables them to move across jobs and sectors, private and public, nations and regions, exploiting their advantages and reducing their risks and losses.

Consequently, just as public mediatised democracy becomes more unstable and visibly chaotic, private invisible forms of polyarchy (Dahl, 1961) become more ordered and entrenched. Thus the space between symbolic politics and the actual institutions, networks and decisionmaking of elite power has got slowly larger. Inequalities, between classes, regions, races and generations, continue to rise, while national polities and economic systems move towards fragmentation and dysfunction.

The chapter is in three parts. The first asks how key elites have endured amid the social, political and economic breakdowns they have helped to engineer. The second interrogates the relationship between elite power and visibility, arguing that the two are not as connected as we might imagine. The third explores the various ways that modern elites have managed to draw on an alternative set of resources to maintain their wealth, influence and power.

THE STRANGE NON-DEATH OF ELITE POWER AND INFLUENCE

There is a glaring conundrum here. Opposition to the foundations of elite hegemony gets ever more vocal and effective. Elites appear more precarious than ever. Their institutions and prevailing ideologies are being strongly challenged and undermined.

And yet, those at the top seem to be as rich, influential and powerful as ever. How do we explain this?

Before launching into this question, it seems important to define elites and the basis of their power. Classic elite theorists (Mosca, Pareto) viewed elites as those who gravitated to the top on account of their superior abilities. Later, more critical elite scholars, from C. Wright Mills (1956) onwards (Domhoff, 1967; Sampson, 1962; Scott, 1991; Useem, 1984), departed from this. Instead they focused on the social conditions which elevated elites and then sustained them in 'higher circles' of power, via their positions atop large private and public institutions. They documented those at the top of key professions, from politics and the judiciary, to business, the military and media. As with classic (post-)Marxist thinkers, they viewed elites as constituting a class who were well-positioned to take advantage of whatever manifestation of capitalism, democratic or otherwise, prevailed at the time. Thus, such elites shared a cohesive 'class consciousness' born of shared educational and social backgrounds, and maintained through interlocking board memberships, exclusive clubs and other shared social spaces. Their influence over public discourse justified their positions and advantages to wider publics. Their dominance of both capitalism and democratic political institutions resulted in elites maintaining and perpetuating themselves, their wealth and their power, at the expense of the rest.

Taken together, the bases of elite power in capitalist democracies rested on the following: positions at the top of large private and public bodies, superior education and wealth, shared social and cultural world views, control over technical and institutional practices of decisionmaking, and influence over media and public information systems.

Looking around today, many of these same foundations of elite power appear to be in poor health. Elites appear more split than cohesive across a number of political and corporate sectors. Recent social science studies of elites have argued that leaders have become increasingly fragmented and precarious. For one, they are no longer as bound together by their social, cultural and educational ties as they once were. Those with top private school and Ivy League or Oxbridge educations are still highly over-represented in large corporate and state institutions, but their numbers have dropped considerably (Carroll, 2008; Davis, 2018; Mizruchi, 2013; Useem, 2015). Business leaders are far more split by globalisation, and conflicting forms of capitalism: 'industrial', 'financialised' and 'platform'. In many ways, they are as conflicted and divided as political elites. Thus even as multinationals get ever larger, the collective power of their CEOs to influence central governments is rather haphazard.

In addition leaders themselves have also become far more mobile, insecure in their jobs and precarious (Davis, 2018; Davis and Williams, 2017; Naim, 2013). Those at the top move position ever quicker, either being pushed out or leaving before things break down. Whether a government minister in politics or a large business chief, average tenures are often no more than two to three years (Davis, 2018; Freeland, 2012; Ho, 2009; Luyendijk, 2015), and it is even less in the cutthroat world of high finance or in Britain's Brexit governments or Trump's White House. Under such circumstances, elite rule and influence appear increasingly difficult.

More fundamentally, capitalism seems to be floundering under its own contradictions, with no sign of immanent reinvention around the corner. The government institutions, parties and political establishments of democracies are buckling and unstable. Crises – economic, financial, environmental, viral, geopolitical and social – are confounding leaders who have no answers, and it is clear that public media and information is no longer a means of keeping publics in tow. Indeed, many citizens have lost faith with elites of all kinds. Trust in, and support for, institutions, from parties to the police and legacy media, continue to plummet powerfully (see also Chapter 1). Mainstream parties, having dominated polities everywhere for decades, are being wiped out (see Chapter 5). Outside formal politics the very visible signs of discontent with capitalist democracy are everywhere, from radical new social movements challenging capitalism to mass protests directed at repressive states.

And yet despite the contradictions, instabilities and precarity, elites are still here, richer and seemingly more powerful than ever. Why?

Starting with the economy, the capitalist part of capitalist democracy no longer seems to be delivering. In its current dominant manifestations, driven by neoliberalism, globalisation, financialisation and platform capitalism, the economic system is faltering with no clear upturn in sight (Crouch, 2011; Streeck, 2016). The neoliberal turn, taken in the 1980s, has had its ups and downs for mature democracies everywhere. Yet policymakers could still claim the positives outweighed the negatives. The rise of the service sector, development of finance and new technologies appeared to offer alternative jobs and growth for countries with declining manufacturing bases. World trade flourished, bringing cheaper food and commodities from poorer economies, and in those same economies hundreds of millions were lifted out of extreme poverty. Despite some big hits, political and economic leaders seemed to have found new ways to manage their way through the down-cycles that followed. By the end of the 1990s a neoliberal consensus had developed in governments, both left and right, about the core elements of modern economic management: free markets, free trade, inflation-targeting, lower taxes and less regulation (Mirowski and Plehwe, 2009).

It took the crises of finance 2007–2008 and COVID-19 – to show that not all was as it seemed in the economy (see Cable, 2009; Elliott and Atkinson, 2009; Ferguson, 2012; Krugman, 2008). In 2008 many banks and financial institutions collapsed or were nationalised. The wealthier and once stable economies were revealed to be both more precarious and unsustainable than previously thought. Huge trade imbalances had built up between exporters (e.g. Japan, China and Germany) and importers (e.g. the US and UK). Financial deregulation had enabled vast amounts of capital to be created and circulated in the financial system rather than the real economy. Much of this activity was opaque and spread extreme levels of risk and debt through the system. Conventional economics and economic policymakers had bracketed out these issues. They were then taken completely unawares by the crash and could not explain what had happened or be sure it wouldn't happen again.

But more than this, beyond the national and global economic flows, glaring inequalities and disparities were building up within countries (Dorling, 2014; Piketty, 2014; Wilkinson and Pickett, 2010). Working-class wages had been stagnating for some years. In the wake of the crash, many middle-class occupations experienced protracted wage stagnation too. Property prices grew well above inflation or income rates and sent home ownership into decline. Disparities between wealthy cities and regions and poorer ones grew even faster. Many local economies, in the UK, US and Continental Europe, experienced a harsh decline and increases in unemployment or precarious employment. Welfare state supports were cut in the name of austerity economics. Particular sectors of society, including women, ethnic minorities and the younger generation, were all hard hit. In the last decade, rises in life expectancy began going into reverse and the global numbers in poverty have begun rising once again. Even the institutions of the international community, from the UN and IMF to the OECD and Davos, began to publicly acknowledge that the global economic system was neither stable, sustainable nor fair. At the time of going to press in 2020, the capitalist system is enduring a more profound crisis still with many of these same trends even more in evidence.

It was not just capitalism that was not delivering. Party-based democracy had lost its sheen too (see Chapter 5). For much of the latter half of the twentieth century democracy seemed to be spreading inexorably. By 2015 two-thirds of existing nations were holding competitive elections, even if many of those were only partial democracies (International Institute for Democracy and Electoral Assistance [IDEA], 2016/2017). Even as citizens became more negative about political parties and governments, they still retained a strong faith in democracy as a political system per se (Hay, 2007; Norris, 2004; World Values Surveys).

However, by the 2010s things seem to have turned. The 6th World Values Survey, taken between 2010 and 2014, found over half of respondents had little or no confidence in their governments, and two-thirds had little or no confidence in their political parties. Freedom House (2017) and the Economist Intelligence Unit (EIU, 2016), which have been evaluating the health of democracy in all nations for decades, began noting a clear downward trend in global democratisation. In some countries a substantial minority had become overtly more critical of the democracy concept itself (IDEA, 2017). In the UK in 2018, only 29% of people were satisfied with the British system (Hansard, 2018), and in the US, only 35% had a positive view of federal government. Across the UK, the US and Continental Europe, people who earned less, were younger, BAME, from lower classes, less educated, or non-home-owners all felt substantially less 'satisfied' with their system of democratic government (Armingeon and Schadel, 2015; Hansard, 2015, 2018; Pew Research Center, 2018; Stefan and Mounk, 2016). Such publics all had less faith in parties, parliaments and mainstream media, felt more alienated and disenfranchised, and were less likely to vote or participate in formal politics.

As with the post-1930s depression, nationalism has been rising starkly, bringing a new wave of anti-democratic nationalist and populist leaders. The new politicians are tearing up international trade and military treaties. Western democracy has been challenged, on the one side by an expansionist Russia, and on the other by the power of China and to a lesser extent India. A series of leaders, both democratic and authoritarian, have become overtly critical of globalisation, international institutions and liberal democratic values (Barnett, 2017; Goodhart, 2017; Inglehart and Norris,

2016). For many (Cohn, 2016; King, 2017; Luce, 2017) the hegemonic world order, developed on the ideas and practices of capitalist democracy and Western liberalism, is facing substantial challenge.

All of this looks to be bad for all those ruling elites that have done so well out of this combination of capitalism, globalisation and liberal democracy. For decades they have sat atop these ever-growing corporate, financial, media and political institutions. Their wealth and influence were predicated on being in charge of both private and public sectors, and making sure the combination worked in their favour. However, if a growing majority of publics are increasingly antagonistic to established elites and the institutions they are attached to, then their days look numbered.

Certainly, the opposition of the last decade has been regular and highly visible. In the wake of the 2007–2008 financial crash, public attacks on bankers, big finance, the super-rich and over-paid CEOs were frequent. Politicians, parliamentary committees and mass media each began questioning neoliberalism and the financial system. In 2011 there was a global explosion of protest (Bennett and Segerberg, 2013; Gerbaudo, 2012; Gitlin, 2011; Mason, 2012). The *Indignados* of Spain and the Occupy Wall Street movement in New York spurred protest movements in multiple countries. In the same year, violent mass anti-government protests began in Yemen, Syria, Libya and Tunisia. The high point of this 'Arab Spring' was the forcing out of the Mubarak government in Egypt after hundreds of thousands collected in Tahrir Square (Eltantawy and Wiest, 2011; Howard et al., 2011). Others followed their lead, including in Turkey's Gezi Park, Hong Kong's Umbrella Revolution, Brazil's Movimento de Junho, and Mexico's Yo Soy 132 (Castells, 2015; Gerbaudo, 2017).

Very visible protests have continued to gather support and media coverage on a range of issues that challenge the dominant positions of elites in other ways (see also Chapter 7). In 2013, the Black Lives Matter campaign, focusing on institutional racism and police brutality, took off. In 2017, the #MeToo movement challenged male dominance and sexual harassment across the worlds of entertainment, politics, business and news media. In 2019, millions of schoolchildren around the world followed Greta Thunberg's lead to miss school and protest about the environmental crisis.

Each of these movements became highly visible. They rapidly gathered supporters in the hundreds of thousands or millions. They spawned local protest networks and gained mass media coverage in dozens of countries, often becoming the lead news story for weeks at a time. They also made extensive use of social media, spreading their ideas and protests, and by-passing mainstream media gatekeepers and negative framing.

Although few governments collapsed in the face of such protests, this widespread dissatisfaction with many of the ranks of today's power elite had damaged them. Many mainstream parties, of the kind that had dominated their nation's politics for several decades, were either wiped out, pushed into political obscurity by new upstarts or forced into taking more extreme/populist positions (see Chapter 5). So too, many large multinationals and banking institutions, once household names on the Financial Times Stock Exchange (FTSE) 100 or Fortune 500, have been wiped out or taken over (Cable, 2009; Cox, 2012; Kay, 2013).

A common trope of this alternative politics, whether supported by regressive nationalists or progressive organised interests, is a direct attack on elites themselves. Several analyses of recent elections, in the US, the UK and Continental Europe, observed that publics were revolting against political establishments (Barnett, 2017; Conti et al., 2018; Frank, 2016; Luce, 2017; Muller, 2016; Rennie Short, 2016). This anti-elite sentiment often included those in business, civil services, the media and finance. Several leaders of right-wing populist parties tapped into this anti-elite feeling, ironically as many themselves were 'elite' (e.g. Trump, Macron, Lopez Obrador, Farage).

And yet, despite all these indicators of elite decline, there are many signs that those in the top 1%, or more accurately the top 0.001%, are as rich and powerful as ever. Their wealth has continued to increase over and above everyone else's, whatever the state of the economy. In 1979 the average US CEO's pay was 38 times that of the average worker. By 2005 it was 262 times (Palley, 2007: 14). In the UK the ratio went from 47 times in 1998 to 185 times in 2012 (High Pay Commission, 2012). This clearly continued in spite of the poor post-crash economic conditions. The number of billionaires and ultra-high-net-worth individuals (UHNWIs) continues to increase by some 10% or more per year. In 2010 Oxfam reported that the total wealth of the richest 388 people in the world was the same as the bottom 50% of the global population. By 2017 the figure was just eight people, six of whom were in information and communication technologies (e.g. Bill Gates, Jeff Bezos and Mark Zuckerberg).

The companies and institutions controlled by elites also continue to get bigger and more dominant too. The major stock exchanges of Britain (FTSE 100) and the US (NYSE) still break new records, peaking in 2000, 2007 and 2018. Banks have maintained the expansion of their asset bases over the last four decades. For example, up until the 1970s, UK total bank assets had been roughly equivalent to half of UK GDP for a century. By the time of the crash they were at five times UK GDP, a ten-fold increase (Haldane, 2010). When the crash hit, the international banking system managed $516 trillion, equivalent to ten times the GDP value of the whole world economy (Cable, 2009: 146). Today's digital giants are becoming more globally dominant than in any previous era (Birkinbine et al., 2017; Srnicek, 2016). In 2014, some 90% of smartphones used either Google or Apple operating systems, and some 87% of online searches were done on Google or Baidu (Birkinbine et al., 2017: 400). Facebook had over two and a quarter billion active monthly users. Such companies have become too big and too global to manage or regulate.

And on the other side of the balance sheet, despite the many loud and visible challenges to elite authority, real political and social change seems to be a long time in coming. Many movements and revolts, such as Occupy or those of the Arab Spring, declined as fast as they had appeared. Military authorities regained control and the forces of the status quo, whether democratic or authoritarian, continued as before. Progress in achieving gender and racial equality, and the radical steps required to halt the environmental crisis, are all far too slow.

In effect, whatever the changing circumstances, the institutions and corporations of capitalist democracy, and the elites atop them, still seem to be holding firm.

The hoped-for paradigm shift has not happened at the higher levels. The haves have even more and the have-nots even less.

Why is this so and where do media and communication come into the equation?

POWER, VISIBILITY AND THE MEDIATISED PUBLIC SPHERE

To engage with this conundrum, inquiry into media and political communication needs to acknowledge the growing gap between the visible public sphere and the private communicative spaces of elite power.

For too long critical scholars have overly focused on the visible at the expense of the invisible. Thus default critical paradigms have linked mass media to ideologies, visibility and discursive power. Media power is about voice and prominence. Those who can influence or control public mediatised spaces have communicative power.

Hence one enduring strand of work focuses on mass media as constituting the space between the elite at the top and the masses below (public sphere 101). In simple Habermasian (1989) terms, it was printed outputs such as newspapers and pamphlets which, along with public spaces in coffee houses and clubs, created the communicative spaces of European public debate in earlier centuries. Such spheres were key to evolving democracies in which top-down ruling elites (of the monarchy, church and state) were challenged. A wider range of individuals were able to use such spaces to open up subject agendas, rationally deliberate on issues, and expose rulers to 'critical publicity'. As mass and then new media developed through the centuries, so public spaces, visibility and critical publicity expanded with them (Coleman and Blumler, 2009; Curran, 2002; Dahlgren, 1995; Kellner, 2000; Polat, 2005).

Although Habermas' original historical accounts and more modern media analysis have been subjected to a range of criticisms (Calhoun, 1992; Fraser, 1997), we are still left with a set of democratic norms around modern media, public debate, visibility and accountability (see Curran, 2002 for a discussion). Much work in politics and political communication similarly revolves around this combination of public communicative space, legitimacy-seeking leaders, mediating journalists and engaged citizens (for overviews see Coleman and Blumler, 2009; Held, 2006; Keane, 1991). How political leaders appeal to voters, respond to the public will and are held to account necessitates reasoned, rational and widely visible media. How publics are informed and educated about their shared interests and their choices depends on the same.

For critical scholars in media and cultural studies the concern is also with visibility, media and power. For a variety of reasons (ownership, advertising, powerful sources, regulation, censorship), elites influence the production, content and framing of news (Curran, 2002; Golding and Murdock, 2000; Herman and Chomsky, 1988). Elites are the 'primary definers' (Hall et al., 1978) and chief 'information subsidy' suppliers (Gandy, 1982) of the mediatised public sphere. The media 'encode' dominant ideologies within their content and 'interpellate' publics through messages.

Mass consent is effectively manufactured through control of public media. Thus, the status quo is legitimated and elite activities are not properly scrutinised.

In recent decades this focus on visibility and power, almost without noticing, has been extended by various developments. The first of these is the sheer exponential growth of media itself. As Blumler and Kavanagh (1999) noted, at the end of the twenty-first century we had entered a 'third age of political communication'. A fundamental part of that was the ever-increasing 'media abundance, ubiquity, reach' of multiple new media formats. From an era of the press and limited terrestrial channels, we had leapt to a multi-channel environment of cable and satellite, and to 24-7 wall-to-wall coverage. That was prior to the huge expansion we have since witnessed of the world wide web, broadband and mobile technology. All manner of online news sites, blogs, podcasts, social media networks and so on have followed. Text and imagery now surround us, instantly accessible, whatever we are doing and wherever we are. Although much of the content is not directly linked to politics and power, we have become ever more focused on media, the visual and symbolic in the 'fourth age of political communication' (Blumler, 2013; Davis, 2019).

Second has been the rise of promotional culture and its deployment by all manner of commercial, public and political organisations and individuals (Davis, 2013; Wernick, 1991). Professional communication in politics has advanced, in terms of employment, budgets and techniques, with each decade (Lilleker and Lees-Marshment, 2005; Scammell, 2014; Swanson and Mancini, 1996). Following on in parallel have come corporations, interest groups, charities, public institutions and media organisations themselves (Cronin, 2018; Davis, 2002; Miller and Dinan, 2008). Each of these seeks to compete to gain a dominant position across the expanding media landscape, to catch the attention of publics be they voters or consumers. This fight for visibility and a dominant media position is also a feature of platform capitalism (Srnicek, 2016). The new digital giants continue to create new online spaces and services at a pace. They give these away for free to users, drawing in more paying suppliers and larger amounts of valuable big data in the process. Winning in these markets means rapid expansion, universal visibility and accessibility.

Third, and related to the first two, is the rise of populism itself: populist media and populist politics. In the increasingly desperate and cut-throat world of ubiquitous media space and declining revenues, news organisations and cultural producers have gone to more extreme lengths to capture audience (and advertiser) attention. News-makers focus on celebrities, gossip, scandal and outrage in their headlines, seeking to draw off-line casual observers and online click-bait (Braun, 2015; Elvestad and Phillips, 2018; Graves, 2016). Meanwhile, politically motivated organisations, from governments to campaigning groups, create memes, gifs and stories, trying to push them to go viral across social media networks. And politicians look to tap into this media ecology of celebrity entertainment values to grab the attention of apolitical audiences (Corner and Pels, 2003; Stanyer, 2007; West and Orman, 2003).

All of this has helped the rise of the new wave of populist politicians (see Chapter 5). For those in more authoritarian countries, the attempts to win the information war, online and in mass media, are packaged through the cult of leadership.

'Charismatic authority' (Weber, 1948) is clearly manufactured for the likes of Putin, Modi, Erdogan, Bolsonaro and others. Media and entertainment backgrounds also aid aspiring political leaders in democracies, from Berlusconi and Grillo in Italy to Schwarzenegger and Reagan in the US. Thus Donald Trump moved from 14 seasons of a reality TV show to the US Presidency in 2016. In 2019 Volodymyr Zelensky, famed for playing the president in a TV show in Ukraine, was then elected as its actual president.

In each case, media visibility has been used to step from one occupation into a position of power. The public recognition factor of a celebrity, as well as an ability to play up to tabloid news values and capture extensive media coverage across formats, leads directly to electoral success. Hence we are left with an impression, more than ever, that mass visibility begets a form of mediated symbolic capital (Bourdieu, 1984) which can be traded in for political and economic power. Ipso facto, visibility has become another resource for elites to accumulate and utilise to gain or maintain power.

However, there are several reasons to argue that elite power derives as much if not more from non-visible as visible sources. In fact the more mediatised and visible politics and business become, the more elites are able to operate and sustain themselves in the shadows. The more 'refeudalised' and corrupted public media become, the more public democratic processes become distracted and distracting from hard political practices and decisions taking place in private.

First, many of the most powerful elite individuals in society operate outside the media. They do not need mass recognition or media exposure to be effective. In politics, leading politicians thrive on their visibility, yet behind them exist expert advisors, big party funders and civil servants, many of whom are barely known to ordinary citizens. In general, government bureaucrats last far longer in their administrative careers, including in senior posts, and have more expertise in government and policy areas than the politicians they serve. Big funders have far more income and assets than the parties they donate to. In 2016, just 158 individual families and their companies donated half of the $6.5 billion spent in the US elections (Hershey, 2017: 296). In the 2017 French elections, it has been estimated that only 2% of donors contributed between 40 and 60% to Emmanuel Macron's victorious En Marche party (Cage, 2018).

In business we are used to seeing the CEOs of our largest companies regularly appear in news coverage. And clearly some of the world's richest people (Jeff Bezos, Mark Zuckerberg and Bill Gates) are frequently reported on. However, although an average CEO may earn millions, lesser known top financiers and super-rich investors earn tens or even hundreds of millions each year. In the UK, of the 20 best-remunerated FTSE 100 CEOs in 2017, only two featured on the *Sunday Times Rich List*. But even the perceived wealth of those leading the tech giants is somewhat misleading, based as it is mainly on the value of shares held in their own companies. For some years the four largest companies quoted on the New York Stock Exchange have been Alphabet (Google), Apple, Microsoft and Amazon. But quoted companies have values based on speculative expectations of future rather than current real value and assets. When these companies are ranked according to real accounting measures, such as profits and assets, the rankings are quite different. In 2016 Apple was 8th, Microsoft 23rd, Alphabet 27th and Amazon 237th (Forbes, 2016). The seven largest companies in the world, using these standard measures, are all banks. Few of these top financiers, super-rich investors or bankers are known beyond the financial world.

Second, whether publicly visible or not, powerful elites tend to influence others through private networks and communication channels. In classic studies of elites and power (Bachrach and Baratz, 1962; Wright Mills, 1956; Useem, 1984), elites have more say in politics because they have far greater representation on top decision-making committees. They not only get to decide, they also get to set agendas and the terms of debates (see Lukes, 2005). Studies of influence-seeking by powerful corporations and individuals find that they are far more prone to using private channels to access both political and business decisionmakers (Ferguson, 2012; Marsh, 1998; Miller and Dinan, 2008; Mitchell, 1997). They use either routine means, such as committee or advisory board positions, or have regular access to senior ministers and bureaucrats. In such accounts, insider connections enable powerful interests and particular demographics (older, white, wealthier males) to push decisionmaking and 'non-decisionmaking' clearly in their favour.

In effect, the most important forms of elite communication are more likely to take place outside of public spheres. Both media and the mass of ordinary citizens do not observe or monitor this. Thus, as Lukes' classic study of power argues (2005: 1), 'we need to attend to those aspects of power that are least accessible to observation: that, indeed, power is at its most effective when least observable'.

Third, what is becoming painfully clear is that the mass mediatised public sphere, in all its current guises, may be loud and visible, but it is also extremely volatile, untrusted and unstable. Rather than acting as a form of power and influence, it is becoming quite the opposite: something anarchic, fractured, untrusted and polarised. It is not so much being 'refeudalised', as Habermas feared, as dismantled.

For some decades mainstream news media have found their operations under increasing economic strain. With each new technology and increased area of news space to fill, journalists have had to produce more with less (see Davies, 2008; Freedman, 2009; Kovach et al., 2004; Pew Research Center, 2009). The steady decline had become a major crisis by 2010 as the combination of financial crisis, increased global competition and huge losses of revenue to the digital, non-news world pushed many operations towards breaking point (Anderson et al., 2015; Davis, 2017b; Pew Research Center, 2016a). This breakdown of the news business model led to all sorts of cost savings which, in effect, have thoroughly undermined the core product of media organisations: news content. Investigative reporting and well-researched and fact-checked stories have slowly been replaced by wire service outputs, user-generated content, recycled and cannibalised material, celebrity Twitter spats, 'soft' news and public relations material (McChesney and Nichols, 2010; Miller and Dinan, 2008), at which point mainstream news content, while not pure fakery, is still highly spun, distorted, unbalanced, over-sensationalised and partial.

News, whether mainstream or alternative, has become unreliable, untrusted and ignored for other reasons. The Reuters Institute's (2017) 36-nation study noted that

54% of citizens get more of their news via social media algorithms. Even established producers inadvertently disseminate actual fake news from social media (Narayanan et al., 2018; Woolley and Howard, 2017), while highly partisan alternative 'news' sites, troll factories and bots actively spread fake news as fast as they can make it up. Vargo and Guo (2017) indicated that partisan online sites now set more news agendas than legacy news operations, including the *New York Times* and *Washington Post*. Meanwhile, populist politicians, taking their lead from Donald Trump, continually accuse their established media critics of producing politically motivated 'fake news'. The combination of individual choice, partisanship and algorithmic news selection is increasingly fragmenting the news audience into polarised filter bubbles (Narayanan et al., 2018; Pew Research Center, 2017; Reuters, 2017; Sunstein, 2018). The spaces and differences of opinion, between left and right, old and young, wealthier and poorer, more educated and less, keep growing.

The end result is that trust in all public information, news and leading political figures is collapsing. Only 43% of people 'trust most media most of the time' (Reuters, 2017), 32% of US citizens said they regularly spotted fake news online, and 51% viewed 'inaccurate' news (Pew Research Center 2016b). Another nine-country survey recorded 67% saying they did not trust news, viewing much of it as a mix of poor quality, propaganda, barely disguised advertising or evidently fake. Support for individual politicians, especially those who take a more populist line, is also subject to extreme volatility. Recently Donald Trump, Emmanuel Macron and Jair Bolsonaro have all seen their poll rating dive sharply within months of gaining power.

In effect, the digital and populist turns have fundamentally destabilised the visible mediatised public sphere. Citizens struggle to see the differences between legitimate relatively 'truthful' politicians, public information sources and news outputs, and illegitimate, lying or fake ones. We now have an anarchic 'wild west' of 'post-truth politics' where individuals and organisations both rise and fall rapidly. Thus if visibility and symbolic, mediated capital are resources of elite power, they are equally responsible for elite fragmentation and decline; those who live by the sword of populist visibility also die by it.

ELITES AND ALTERNATIVE FORMS OF PRIVATE AND INVISIBLE POWER

Just as the visible public sphere world appears to be disintegrating, the invisible private world of elite power and influence is being consolidated and extended. The ways and means elites are able to operate, accumulate and manipulate institutions and decisions keep evolving in the shadows. Behind the creative destruction of the public democratic world, private structures, networks and practices of inequality and power are maintained. It is these many spaces, forums and networks that critical social scientists and media scholars should be focusing more of their attention on.

One of these forms of influence is through the infiltration of ideas and personnel from the corporate world into governments. As states and parties become more 'depoliticised' they look for sources of expertise and practices from outside, ceding definitional and operational power to invisible unaccountable others from business (Crouch, 2011; Hay, 2007; Mair, 2013). Thus Chicago School-educated economists have found their ways into the economic and finance departments of multiple countries, as well as national banks and international financial institutions such as the IMF (Babb, 2005; Davis, 2017a; Kristensen, 2015). The practices of NPM (New Public Management) and auditing came from personnel and consultants who formerly operated in the financial sector (Hood, 1995; Moran, 2003; Power, 1997). More recently, corporate-style executive boards have been set up for UK government departments, with all board chairs and a majority of non-executive directors coming from the private sector (Wilks, 2015). So too former financiers have moved into dominant government positions in the US and UK, thus promoting more financialised economies (Davis and Walsh, 2017; Krippner, 2011). Such shifts, towards what Davis (2018) calls 'econocracy', have coincided with the adoption of neoliberal approaches to economic management (Crouch, 2011; Mirowski and Plehwe, 2009).

A related feature of corporate elite influence is the intermeshing of public and private networks. Janine Wedel's (2009, 2014) work in the US documents how key figures, or 'flexians', move across such networks, leveraging their influence and knowledge as they go. Thus the same ex-army generals sit on government advisory committees and the boards of arms manufacturers while also appearing as expert analysts for news media. The same financiers or tax accountants move from Wall Street to the US Federal Reserve or government positions and then back again. Such access is further enhanced by the social, informal and cultural networks that such corporate and public elites share (Davis, 2018; Freeland, 2012; Jones, 2015; Khan, 2011).

Maclean et al. (2014, 2017) find something similar amongst top French business leaders who become 'hyper agents' moving between private and public. In Britain parallel studies (Cave and Rowell, 2014; Wilks, 2015) show how the revolving door between public and private networks has continued to spin ever faster since the 1980s. Between 2010 and 2014 some 600 former ministers and civil servants took on business roles and board positions. So too almost all recent heads of the Treasury and Civil Service, as well as multiple senior officials, have moved into positions in international finance (the IMF, World Bank, investment banks; see Davis, 2017a).

For those members of the elite (the super-rich international investors or 'rentiers' and the CEOs of multinationals) who do not want to be directly involved in such 'flex-nets' of power, there is now a growing range of technical intermediaries. Various expert professions emerged over the twentieth century to grease the wheels of capitalist democracies (Abbott, 1988). Specialists with legal, accounting, business consultancy, public relations, lobbying and other expert skills have each developed in elaborate ways (Ferguson, 2012; Miller and Dinan, 2008; Reed, 2012; Zald and Lansbury, 2010).

But in recent decades within each sector there has evolved a high-end, elite-serving top tier. This is often dominated by a handful of very expensive and influential companies, with specialist networks and knowledge. Taking some examples in the UK, just three top public relations businesses came to serve half the companies in the FTSE

100, worked closely with the Conservative Party, and were awarded numerous Conservative Government contracts for work (Davis, 2002). For most of the 2000s just four international accountancies (PwC, Deloitte, KPMG, EY) provided services to 96% of FTSE 350 companies, as well as being regularly seconded to government departments and state advisory and regulatory bodies. Just five legal firms had a similar level of dominance amongst the FTSE 100 (High Pay Centre, 2015; Public Accounts Committee [PAC], 2013). Each of these firms is ever present at the main political party conferences and makes regular donations to them too. In effect, the power of very wealthy elites now includes the power to purchase each of these sources of expertise and access.

Such influence allows elites to thrive in various ways. For one, it helps them to maintain invisibility. As Davis (2002) revealed, more high-end public relations resources are devoted to keeping elites, political or corporate, out of the media. A range of industries, from arms manufacturers and fossil fuel producers to cigarette manufacturers, banks and big pharma, have successfully covered up their illegal actions (Miller and Dinan, 2008; Stauber and Rampton, 1995). In politics, corruption, incompetence, illegal military actions and human rights abuses are regularly kept from media and public scrutiny.

Such intermediaries are also a key means of achieving ever-greater profits and political advantage. Purchasing expert accounting, technical, lobbying and legal knowledge enables elites to have an insider view of the current 'rules of the game'. Knowing early on the latest regulatory or tax regimes enables one to either gain a 'first-mover' advantage over rivals or find ways to circumvent these. Better still, having input into those evolving directives allows one to alter the rules in one's own favour, or to set the initial terms and framing of the technical discussions involved (Davis, 2017a). This works equally well in the worlds of finance, national governance and local government. If the new elites want to gain exceptions to local planning, health and safety, and other decisionmaking bodies, to over-develop sites or exploit natural resources, they can (Atkinson et al., 2017). At the international level, if they want to prevent international regulations on tax, the environment or the misuse of personal data, they will (Freeland, 2012; Tsingou, 2015). And in banking and finance, if they want to develop very lucrative but highly risky and under-regulated financial products and forms of lending, they do (Engelen et al., 2011). So the workings of pure money power are put into practice in today's capitalist technocracies.

Invisible elite power is also built on finding innovative new ways to go under the radar and extract capital from publics and states. Companies and individuals, from the liberal democratic West to an authoritarian Russia and China, have spent decades profiting from state-led changes to economic policy. The privatisation of state industries, natural resources, land and property has created a new set of giant firms, super-rich oligarchs, corrupt party officials and international investors (Freeland, 2012; Wedel, 2009). Unsuspecting publics have been sucked into supporting big finance through their pension funds and the securitisation and trading of credit card and mortgage debt. Private finance initiatives or public–private partnerships have been very profitable to companies, but have left states with long-term, high-interest debts amounting to hundreds of billions (Benjamin, 2015). A similar trick has been pulled off with the rise in the outsourcing of state services to independent providers (Bowman et al., 2015). So too have multi-billion-dollar bank bailouts, quantitative easing and costly investment incentives to foreign businesses to relocate all transferred public reserves to private shareholders. In addition, large companies and super-rich individuals have found multiple ways to avoid paying tax (Shaxson, 2011; Tax Justice Network [TJN], 2015). In 2010 some 83% of such companies had offshore accounts in tax havens, with estimates of $21 trillion held in them (Urry, 2014). In the UK 98% of FTSE 100 companies use such tax havens directly or indirectly through their subsidiaries, and 90% of top-end property was acquired or sold via these.

Lastly, a great resource and source of power for the modern power elite is its enhanced mobility (Birtchnell and Caletrio, 2014; Davis, 2019). The emerging international top tier may be less socially cohesive and more unstable in their leadership positions, but they have also managed to turn precarity to their advantage. Globalisation, neoliberalism and new transport and information technologies may have destabilised both capitalism and democracy, but they have also facilitated elite mobility (Elliott, 2014; Featherstone, 2014; Freeland, 2012). Corporate and political leaders can now move across the globe with great speed. They can communicate and move their liquid financial assets anywhere and everywhere in an instant. They have multiple properties and assets in multiple nations and jurisdictions. They can move themselves, their families and entourages from place to place. Thus they are far more mobile than the poor precariat lower classes, the real local communities, industries and governing structures, they pass to and from.

This mobility both offers strategic opportunity and acts to mitigate personal risks (Bauman, 2007, Davis and Williams, 2017; Featherstone, 2014). Opportunities are there to leap from one top job or sector to another, gliding across one's personal networks. Investments can be withdrawn from failing industries and countries and reallocated to new emerging sectors or nations. Wealth can be channelled invisibly through multiple countries. Differing tax and legal regimes can be leveraged by global elites as they move through alternative jurisdictions. And if national political and economic systems collapse, or social instability sets in, modern elites can relocate rapidly. Under these circumstances the new elites thrive on their flexibility, their disconnection from the majority (nationally, politically, socially) and their liquid mobility.

Therefore, although we live in a more mediated visible and unstable world, we also exist in one that is more technocratic, specialist, complex, precarious, liquid and hidden. These shifts have affected everyone but, within the chaos, elites have adapted and thrived. They glide across their exclusive flexible networks. They have the resources to employ a range of connected and knowledgeable experts to make sense of the Kafkaesque technical, political and legal corridors of power. And they have the mobility to leave failing regimes, industries and regions to set up anew and with minimal losses in new ones. Such skills, networks and resources are only available to a select few; the rest have to live with the consequences. For such reasons, elites can keep under the radar and continue to thrive amidst the increasingly chaotic political, economic and media systems they have helped to create.

CONCLUSION: INTERROGATING THE PRIVATE COMMUNICATIVE REALMS OF ELITE POWER

What has been argued here is that as elites and society have evolved, so have the bases of their power. Decades ago, their maintained hegemony relied on shared cultures and ideologies linked to parallel educational, social and economic backgrounds. It also rested on their positions at the top of large public and private institutional hierarchies, enabling them to set agendas and make self-interested decisions. And it rested on their influence over the mediatised public sphere of more limited media outputs and access. This combination allowed them to thrive in capitalist democracies.

Today, several of those elements endure but others do not. Social and ideological elite cohesion is fragmenting. Public institutions and capitalist democracy are far less stable than they once were. Control over the public 'means of mental production' has broken down. Elites of all kinds are loathed and distrusted, except when condemning 'elites' themselves. All of which suggests that elite rule, as we have come to experience it, is more chaotic and less in control than before.

Yet as this chapter has argued, elites have evolved and so have their sources of power and influence. They work ever more across private communication networks and spaces. They use their huge wealth disparities to employ experts with insider knowledge and contacts across all the facets of government and commerce. By such means they manage to set the rules of the game and exploit them accordingly. Furthermore, they are far more flexible, light-footed and mobile than ever before and operate out of sight and under the radar. Communicative power for elites is thus more private than it is public.

In fact, the more anarchic and fractured the mediatised visible public spheres of democracy become, the more elite communicative power has been extended inside the private realm. This growing disparity is itself an explanation for the increasing dissatisfaction and distrust of democracy more generally and particular political and business elites more specifically. The louder the protests, the more they seem to be ignored or dismissed in the opaque corridors of power.

For such reasons, critical media and communication scholars need to look more at these private communicative spaces, networks and media (digital and other). Visibility and power remain connected, but invisibility and power are more connected still.

5

DEMOCRACY WITHOUT POLITICAL PARTIES?

INTRODUCTION

Political parties are fundamental to the operation of modern representative democracies. They go together like Barbie and Ken, Shaggy and Scooby, milk and cookies – or at least they used to. What happens to democracy when parties no longer function?

Looking around the globe, prior to COVID-19, democracy seemed as precarious as it had been for many decades and the breakdown of mainstream parties seemed to be at the heart of that. The party model that came to dominate mature democracies for decades, that of the electoral-professional, rational-centrist party, has quite suddenly been struggling to hold on to power. Long-term declines in party membership, voter turnout and trust, have recently produced political tipping points. Whether left or right, citizens have deserted them in large numbers. The alternatives emerging, be they nationalist-populists or progressive, social movement-party hybrids, offer change but lack coherency, stability and longevity. They seem to offer few answers to many of the big problems facing nation-states, from climate change and resource scarcity to financial instability and job insecurity.

The question is, does this mean the party-based model of representative democracy no longer functions, or merely that it is time to look beyond the electoral-professional-centrist party model that has dominated for so long?

The chapter is in four parts. The first briefly traces the twentieth-century evolution of political parties in established democracies, from ideological and amateur entities to mass, catch-all parties and then to electoral-professional ones. As the section explains, the evolution of the modern party has also coincided with the growing crisis of faith in mainstream politics. The question is, is this because of or in spite of how party politics has evolved? The second section explains the analysis offered by more conservative political scientists and commentators. In this account, public disaffection says more about publics and the complexity of modern governance than it does about parties. They regard current levels of distrust and political instability as a temporary blip in the upward progression of democracy. Part three critiques this stance, instead directing blame at mainstream parties themselves. It argues that the mixture of centrist-rational politics and electoral-professional organisation was a direct cause of public alienation and disengagement. The fourth part looks at the alternative models emerging and explains how and why they are succeeding. However, it also suggests that, as yet, each has failed to offer a sustainable long-term substitute.

THE RISE AND FALL OF PARTY-BASED DEMOCRACY?

A competitive party system is a basic element of modern representative democracy. Parties bring together like-minded political actors to develop a common political programme. They are the institutional mechanisms for representing diverse public interests in society (Mudge and Chen, 2014). They develop policies and deploy them once in government. They are then held accountable for their actions through regular elections (see Dalton and Wattenberg, 2002; Webb, 2007) and via media scrutiny. They are *the* practical, organisational body for organising politics in any sizeable 'actually existing democracy'. As Schattschneider (1942) once said, democracy is 'unthinkable' without parties. So what happens to democracy when parties cease to operate as viable, coherent, long-term entities?

As every democracy has emerged and evolved so has its political parties. Through the course of the twentieth century parties have continually reinvented themselves, both ideologically and at a practical organisational level. At the risk of oversimplifying, mainstream parties have gone through at least three historical stages of development.

Initially, they tended to emerge organically, to represent specific groups and interests in civil society. These were based on a combination of employment conditions, religions, regions, ethnicities and so on. Such interests provided both the funding for a party and its organising officials. Parties relied on local networks and amateur volunteers. Leaders came from those groups, having worked their way up the ladder over time. Parties and their supporters developed relatively enduring bonds and remained strongly aligned over decades. Ideologically, such parties had relatively clear and simple policy ideas. The most obvious stances, reflecting their constituent groups, were located along the left–right spectrum (although often complicated by factors of nationalism and religion). Parties of left or right were identified by their fairly enduring positions on a range of issues such as economic management, various forms of equality, taxation levels, defence and welfare provision (see Ball and Dagger, 2013; Dalton, 2017; Heywood, 2017).

Throughout the twentieth century parties in established democracies evolved, adapted and reinvented themselves. First, they moved beyond their initial organisational amateurism and ideological purity as they became larger 'mass' or 'catch all parties' (Kirchheimer, 1966). To grow to a significant size and become a dominant parliamentary force required both professionalism and ideological flexibility. Policy programmes were widened beyond the initial base to draw in other sets of supporters. Senior party figures became professional politicians and parties increasingly employed experts, rather than committed volunteers, to run their organisations. This inevitably led to the next party incarnation – the 'electoral-professional party' (Panebianco, 1988). As mass media expanded, and professionalism became more embedded, so parties came to rely less on their core members and local networks. Professionals from other sectors, such as journalism, marketing, tech companies and policy think tanks, all took on paid roles, either permanently or as consultants (Blumler and Gurevitch, 1995; Swanson and Mancini, 1996). Funding and managing these more autonomous organisations became more important too.

By the latter stages of the twentieth century, strong and enduring mainstream parties with strong organisational apparatus and general centre-left or centre-right policy positions had emerged. Voters in majoritarian electoral systems tended to gravitate towards one of two main parties: Republican or Democratic in the US, Labour or Conservative in the UK, the Indian National Congress or BJP in India. In proportional representation systems it was often coalitions built around two major established parties, such as the Christian or Social Democrats in Germany, Republicans or Socialists in France.

This steady professionalisation of parties over time has coincided with growing signs of public disaffection with party politics. From the 1950s to the 1990s voting levels eased down 10% in the 19 OECD countries with long-term data available. New lows below 50% were registered in nations like Japan and the US. Membership of political parties shrank from 14% in the 1970s to below 6% in the 1990s (Putnam, 2002: 406). World Values Survey data of 19 nations in the 1990s showed that only 38% had confidence in their governments and just 22% in political parties (Dalton and Wattenberg, 2002: 264). Such long-term trends led to several authors declaring that democracy was edging towards a crisis (Blumler and Gurevitch, 1995; Dalton and Wattenberg, 2002; Putnam, 2000, 2002).

Despite the doom and gloom talk, none of this seemed to matter that much. Then, in the last decade, those longer term negative trends became more pronounced. Tipping points seem to have been reached. The 6th wave of the World Values Survey (2010–2014), covering 60 nations, found, in aggregate that only 34.7% had 'confidence' in their governments next to 51.8% who did not. Only seven of the 60 nations surveyed had more positive than negative scores for confidence in parties (all seven being non-democracies). These figures were even more negative for nine of the most established democracies, such as Japan, Germany, Australia and the US. For these nations, 59.9% had little or no confidence in their governments and 76% the same in relation to their political parties. In both the US and Australia, the negative party scores were over 85%.

Democracy evaluators everywhere had, for some decades, recorded positive upward data trends in terms of the number of democracies emerging and the positive democratic indicators of their institutions and systems. That was suddenly reversed in the 2010s as they began recording a series of negative shifts. In 2016 the Economist Intelligence Unit (EIU, 2016) noted that half of the 167 countries it evaluated annually had seen declines in their democracy ratings over the last ten years. The largest declines were recorded across Western and Eastern Europe and North America. In 2017 Freedom House (2017) also observed that civil liberties and political rights had dropped in 67 countries over the past year but only 36 nations had improved in the same period. In fact, for three years running there had been a net decline in the democratic health of roughly 30 nations. IDEA (2016) noted that average voter turnout had dropped 20% since the 1980s in Europe. The declines in turnout and confidence were even more pronounced amongst certain demographics such as young voters. A growing number, more than 25% in some nations and across certain demographics, had begun to question whether democracy was still the best political system to have (EIU, 2016; IDEA, 2017; Stefan and Mounk, 2016).

As the 2010s progressed, this rather negative but abstract opinion data began to be realised more concretely in a series of shock electoral results that left mainstream parties either split or marginalised. Parties that had dominated their multi-party parliaments for several decades began losing control. In Greece in 2015, both major parties (PASOK and New Democracy) were ousted by Syriza. The 2017 French presidential elections saw both main parties ejected. Emmanuel Macron's fledgling En Marche party then beat Marine Le Pen's Front National into second place. Elsewhere, Brazil and South Korea impeached their presidents. In 2018 South Africa forced out their president, while in Mexico both the once-dominant PRI and PAN were deposed by another new party led by Andrés López Obrador. Italy ended up with a coalition of two populist parties, the Northern League and Five Star Movement, led by Giuseppe Conte, another non-politician. Jair Bolsonaro, a once extreme, marginalised politician, won the Brazilian presidential election.

The first-past-the-post systems of the UK and US hindered the rise of new parties, but instead once-dominant parties became fundamentally fractured and unstable. In the UK, since 2010, neither Labour nor Conservatives have managed a strong ruling majority. Both parties have been embroiled in deep civil wars and the Brexit vote of 2016 has utterly divided them. In the US both Democrats and Republicans have faced similar splits between their Washington establishment centres and their more radical challengers. Through these divisions and identity crises emerged Donald Trump, a non-politician, to take the presidency in 2016. In Australia, with a different voting system but many other political similarities, in 2018, after another internal party war and coup, the country was left with its sixth prime minister in eleven years.

Across Europe, where established parties maintained their presence, they were considerably weakened by election results. By 2016 newer nationalist, populist parties had become part of ruling coalitions in eleven democracies (Inglehart and Norris, 2016). Over 2017 and 2018, results left mainstream parties in Germany, Holland and Sweden struggling to hold sway and being forced into precarious coalition arrangements. Elsewhere, fragile (semi-)democracies, such as Turkey, Hungary and Poland, changed tack, moving back towards more authoritarian practices and institutions. Strong populist leaders, in China, India, Russia and the Philippines, all consolidated their holds on power, throwing out challenges to Western democracies.

All of which suggests that mainstream parties in democracies are experiencing something more than a temporary downward blip. Many have either been wiped out or are not expected to survive in the long term. The alternatives that are appearing seem to be equally precarious if not more so. They rise and fall rapidly and have few detailed policy responses to the growing list of political problems, from global financial instability and growing inequality, to impending environmental disasters and international military tensions.

What does this mean for party-based democracy? A conservative response is that party-based democracy is going through one of its many down-cycles, but as in previous times it will recover and thrive once again. The modern, centrist electoral-professional party remains the model that is most likely to deliver that in the long term. Alternatively, a more critical analysis focuses on the failings of the electoral professional party itself. If democracy is to flourish once again, another type of party model must emerge.

THE STRUGGLE TO GOVERN: A RATIONAL-CENTRIST ACCOUNT

One position, taken over recent decades, might be termed the 'rational-centrist account' of party-based democracy. Here centrist (or conservative) social scientists have joined centrist (or conservative) politicians and commentators in support of the predominant model of parties that held sway in the 1990s and 2000s: the centrist, electoral-professional party. They have advocated this model as something more positive, rational, efficient and responsive to the wider citizenry. It is the best model for party democracy and emerged as a logical response to the changing demographics, alignments and complex political fault lines of contemporary democracies. The crisis of recent years is likely to be neither substantive nor enduring, and in the longue durée democracy will prevail once again.

For rational-centrists, modern parties have evolved in response to changes in media, society and shifting political proclivities. Their development has been both necessary and positive for democracies and is not directly related to increased levels of political disaffection (Dalton, 2004; Eatwell and Goodwin, 2018; Lees-Marshment, 2008; Norris, 1999). So, to start, communication strategies have had to adapt as media have evolved. Through the last century political communication moved from localised networks and print media to centralised, mass broadcast radio and television (Blumler and Kavanagh, 1999; Hershey, 2017; Maarek, 1995; Wring, 2005). Accordingly, parties had to reorient themselves away from local and towards national media. Then, through this century, they have been steadily forced towards online communication and social media as a majority of citizens have come to obtain their news and information that way (Reuters, 2017).

So too have parties had to change in response to an evolving citizenry, economy and society, all of which have become much more fluid and mobile. This in turn makes it difficult to maintain parties based on enduring and established constituent groups. For example, employment in heavy industry and farming, along with union memberships, have declined substantially. People work in far smaller units, in services and the fast-evolving gig economy. They are more urban and more mobile, less connected to organised religion and local communities (Putnam, 2000). They are also more post-materialist in outlook (Inglehart, 1990), and no longer classifiable into simple classes (Savage, 2015). Thus parties have had to adapt and become more flexible too.

In ideological terms, parties are no longer aligned around traditional left–right party politics. Increasingly, voters have identified themselves through race, gender, religion and sexuality, as much as by class and occupation. They have become more concerned with issues such as environmentalism, animal welfare, abortion, globalisation and multiculturalism. In fact, for rational centrists (Eatwell and Goodwin, 2018; EIU, 2017; Goodhart, 2017; Inglehart and Norris, 2016) large groups of citizens have become more focused on nationalism and cultural identity. For Inglehart and Norris (2016) the recent shifts in mainstream party-political fortunes were down to a 'cultural backlash' across the US and Europe. This pitted nationalist rural people with traditional social and family values against cosmopolitan liberals who embraced globalisation, multi-culturalism and non-traditional family values. Goodhart (2017) offered a parallel thesis in relation to UK citizens and the 2016 Brexit vote. 'Somewheres', comprising 50% of the population, were also more rural, socially conservative and tied to traditional values and a sense of community. They raged against the smaller but more wealthy and powerful 20–25% of 'Anywheres' who were successfully promoting social and economic liberalism, thereby undermining the rest.

All of this is reflected in the marked increase in electoral volatility between and during elections. In decades past, a relatively small percentage of voters would change their party support during an election period. However, by the 2010s citizens were changing their vote in ever-growing numbers. This was noted across Europe (Chiaramonte and Emanuele, 2017; Conti et al., 2018), where, according to Chiaramonte and Emanuele, the average volatility shift had jumped to 18.01%. In the US presidential election of 2016 Trump benefitted from an upward swing in support of 19%. In the 2017 UK election the Conservatives' 20% poll lead was reduced to 2.4% after just a month of campaigning.

Parties have thus been pushed to adapt to the changes around them. Professionalisation in organisational management, media and communication strategies has resulted. Such professionalisation began with the employment of experts in various fields (Blumler and Gurevitch, 1995; Lilleker and Lees-Marshment, 2005; Scammell, 2014; Swanson and Mancini, 1996). These came from the worlds of advertising, public relations, polling and marketing, journalism, and media production. Political consultants and commercial agencies came in to advise. Market research became a core function for parties as they developed their policies. Forms of voter identification and classification became more complex and nuanced. More qualitative and quantitative data was collected and collated on public policy preferences. Politicians were media trained, ideas and leaders market tested. Campaigns and advertising budgets were developed in detail and targeted efficiently.

On the one hand, such developments could be seen as transforming parties into more business-like entities, acutely focused on gaining power. However, for rational centrists, changes to parties actually enhanced party democracy in real practical ways (Newman, 1999; Norris, 2000; Scammell, 1995, 2003). Because good marketing is a consultative, two-way process, its adoption by parties forced them to become more representative and aware of citizen preferences (Lees-Marshment, 2008, 2011, 2015; Lilleker and Lees-Marshment, 2005). According to the 'Lees-Marshment model' (2008), successful parties of the twentieth century did not simply become better at winning elections, they became more responsive. They therefore began as basic 'product-oriented parties' with crude, untested ideological policies that they attempted to hard sell to voters. Professionalisation first meant using more sophisticated marketing techniques to better operate as effective 'sales-oriented parties'. But, in the next stage, they became fully fledged market-oriented parties which used marketing techniques to both develop and sell policies in conjunction with citizen stakeholders.

A similar progression took place in relation to the use of modern public relations and advertising techniques in politics (Grunig and Hunt, 1984; Nessman, 1995; Scammell, 1995). Party communication, instead of being a crude top-down one-way affair, evolved to became more 'two-way symmetrical' in nature. Thus, as with market-ing, policies and messages were developed through consultation rather than imposed in a top-down way. Better communications also meant that complex policy ideas could be presented in user-friendly formats, thereby better engaging ordinary citizens.

In effect, sensible and enduring parties have had no choice but to adapt and move beyond their parochial bases, narrow policy confines and amateur organi-sational practices. Of necessity, they became more all-embracing, more technical and rational rather than ideological. Evidence-based policy production and responsive political institutions replaced dogma and disconnect.

Until recently, rational centrists had two strong responses to the slow-growing crisis of the party democracy issue. The first was to downplay the crisis thesis and suggest that it was more noise than substance. The reasoning of Norris, Inglehart (1977, 1990, 1997) and others was that if democracy generally works well then any sense of political crisis is simply superficial. The more interesting issue for them was determining why citizens in democracy did not appreciate what they had. For Ingle-hart, wealthy, established democracies have produced a generation of postmaterial-ists. These are people who have economic and physical security and an education that makes them overly critical. Such privileges bred a sense of critical entitlement in which citizens expected the rewards of capitalist democracy without being willing to actually participate. Studies show that many say they want a say in politics but it is only a small group who are willing to be involved (Dalton, 2004, Hibbings and Theiss-Morse, 2002; Webb, 2007). In effect, people are not that unhappy because, compared to previous decades, they never had it so good.

For these observers, there have been periodic times of crisis talk, but these have been shown to be merely temporary down-cycles in the long forward pro-gression of democracy. Historically, crisis talk appears at regular intervals, most especially at times of conflict, economic crisis and social unrest. But crisis – economic, political or other – often precedes reinvention and reconfiguration that then lead to further peace and prosperity. What people experience is short-term peri-ods of disruption and renewal (Norris, 2000, 2002, 2004, 2011). Over the longue durée, democracy has spread and most people in the world are far better off than they were a century ago.

They argue that over the last century, life for most people improved on multiple measures: education, lifespan, healthcare and welfare provision, living standards and civil rights. In 2014 global life expectancy was 71.5 years, significantly higher than the 40 years at the start of the twentieth century. At the same time, the number of democracies tripled in the last part of that century. In 1975 the number of nations hav-ing competitive elections was 46 but that number had grown to 132 by 2015 (IDEA, 2017). As Hay (2007) pointed out, even though the levels of voter turnout and trust in parties have continued to decline, faith in democracy as a system has remained high. Democratic principles are strongly supported even if parties and politicians are not. In 2017, despite the recent period of political instability and the downturn in democracy trends, IDEA (2017: 8) continued to argue that long-term gains are what counted. While acknowledging the current era of political turbulence, they also concluded that

'Over the past forty years most aspects of democracy have advanced, and democracy today is healthier than many contend'. In 2018, Runciman (2018) concluded that current events do not signal a return to the 1930s era of fascism. Democracy is simply going through a 'mid-life crisis' from which it will re-emerge a little battered and older. Since the alternatives, from 'pragmatic authoritarianism' to epistocracy, do not measure up, democracy will endure for some time.

The recent shock electoral outcomes in Europe and the US spurred Inglehart and Norris (2016) to look anew at the crisis debate. However, as before, their focus was on publics rather than parties or political and economic systems. Their cultural backlash thesis focused on culture, community and values, and the attraction to the emerging set of strongman populist leaders. They recognised but said rather less about those who had been losing out socially, economically and politically for decades. For Goodhart (2017) and Eatwell and Goodwin (2018), this sense of relative economic and political neglect amongst large proportions of the population was noted, but once again issues of culture, identity and individual autonomy were emphasised. In effect the crisis is born more out of irrational cultural and ideological factors, not material, institutional, party and system factors.

PARTY DEMOCRACY AND THE FAILURE OF THE PROFESSIONAL-ELECTORAL CENTRIST MODEL

An alternative starting point for explaining the sense of crisis focuses instead on the failings of parties themselves. In particular it looks critically at the once dominant rational-centrist, professional-electoral party model. Delving deeper here reveals that, ideologically, practically and organisationally, such parties became increasingly detached from a majority of citizens. Eventually, tipping points have been reached, turning seemingly more superficial problems into a more substantive crisis for democracy.

One problem has been what we might term the 'false prophets of rationality'. Rational-centrists have proclaimed their liberation from ideological dogma and their attachment to evidence and rational policymaking. For some years, centrist politicians, whether left or right, have taken what seemed a logical way forward, which was to defer to experts on a number of complex policy matters. In so doing, politics was 'depoliticised' in established democracies everywhere (Flinders and Buller, 2006; Hay, 2007; Mair, 2013). In consequence, all centrist parties came to broad agreements on a range of policy issues: an attachment to free markets, privatisation, deregulation, low taxes, free trade, weaker unions and lower welfare spending, foreign policy and so on. Ideological differences were less important than competence. Good governance meant technocratic rather than political management, non-governmental regulatory institutions, and the outsourcing of state services and functions to the private sector (Bowman et al., 2015; Moran, 2003). It also meant government putting great faith in the expertise of business entrepreneurs and highly paid consultants from law, accountancy, economics and the ICT sector (see also Chapter 4 here).

Rational centrists took a similar approach to the great forces of social change: globalisation, neoclassical economics and new ICTs. Centrist parties of all varieties adopted a similar narrative about each of these trends – that is, that they were both rational and inevitable and all smart politicians and leaders should embrace them. They both took advice from external experts and then promoted these trends in their public speeches and policy directives. In each case they argued that the embrace of these powerful forces would benefit the large majority of citizens everywhere.

So, it was said that globalisation may have posed a direct challenge to state sovereignty but it also offered much promise for states too (Albrow and Glasius, 2008; Beck, 2006; Held, 2002). It brought greater international integration, peace and stability, and greater economic efficiency. Under such circumstances states would lose some autonomy but they would also be supported and secured in other ways. Similarly, neoclassical economics (and neoliberalism), like globalisation, was widely advocated, both by particular national leaders and international institutions such as the IMF, World Bank and OECD (Mirowski and Plehwe, 2009). For those championing it, the shift in economic policy that it brought was vital for stabilising national economies in the 1970s and 1980s amidst a period of crisis. It has been central to integrating the international economic system, spurring worldwide growth, employment and prosperity, and has lifted billions out of poverty. So too, there was an unquestioning embrace of all new information and communication technologies (the internet, wireless technology, advanced computing power and data collection, digitalisation, and so on). These ICT revolutions promised to reinvigorate democracy and media, enable new voices and dialogues, and spur a thriving new economy (Castells, 2001; Norris, 2002; Tapscott and Williams, 2007).

However, after decades of embracing and adapting to these transformations, the promises have not been fulfilled for many sectors of society. In terms of the new digital economy, digital divides are widespread, and old media monopolies have simply been replaced by bigger, more dominant digital ones such as Facebook, Amazon and Google (see Chapter 2). Corporations and governments track and monitor citizens in ways George Orwell would never have dreamed of, legacy news media have been devastated, and the online public sphere fragmented, polarised and undermined by widely disseminated misinformation and fake news (Curran et al., 2016; Fuchs, 2014a ch. 1; Srnicek, 2016; Tufekci, 2014).

Globalisation has made it increasingly difficult for states to exert control over their economies, industries, trade, international flows of finance and disease, migration and environments. Local industries, regions and communities have been devastated by the consequences (Cerny et al., 2005; Krugman, 2008; Stiglitz, 2017). Neoliberal economic policies have undermined multiple state functions, from welfare systems to tax collection. Wage income stagnated or dropped for large parts of the population and inequality has shot up (Oxfam, 2017; Piketty, 2014). So too has economic instability and financial precarity as many states and individuals have found themselves with huge debts as they continue to cope with the aftermath of the financial crash of 2007–2008 and now COVID-19 (Streeck, 2017; Tooze, 2018; Varoufakis, 2016).

The difficulties of large swathes of the population in many mature capitalist democracies appear to have been ignored or glossed over by these same centrist parties and their unaccountable experts and institutions. Right-wing parties appeared to favour the rich and large corporations, and so did left and right centrists. Many ordinary people felt entirely left behind (Barnett, 2017; Frank, 2016; Rennie Short, 2016). The grand stories of progress often appeared to be a fantasy for them and their communities. As Dennis Muller (2016: 17) put it:

> ... millions of ordinary people, particularly in the Anglophone democracies, have been left behind by globalisation, and sacrificed on the altar of neoclassical economics ... voters in those circumstances know only one big truth: their living standards, share of the cake, and place in society are imperilled or reduced.

What rational centrist politicians failed to understand was that such experts and professionals were not neutral fact producers and truth-seekers. They were often employed by organised interests with agendas (see Chapter 4). Expertise was spun and over-hyped by government technocrats when it was politically expedient. Experts themselves had a personal stake in promoting their expertise and certain big ideas. As highly paid professionals they directly benefitted too. Lastly, they were far from fallible, failing to predict or explain the ups and downs of the economy or great financial crises. They over-emphasised the positives while national figures ignored the negatives and huge regional and demographic variations. Hence when populist politicians, from Donald Trump to Michael Gove, denigrated experts and mainstream media accounts, many nodded in agreement.

At an organisational level, professionalisation has also been responsible for the distancing of parties from their members and publics. This has been recorded in multiple ways. For example, as campaign expenditures have grown, to pay for consultants and advertising and promotional costs, so parties have focused more attention on enticing big funders. Between 2001 and 2017 in the UK, the Conservative and Labour Parties spent £112 million in parliamentary election campaigns (Electoral Commission, 2018). Such expenditures are tiny when compared to those in the US. In 2016 alone, $6.5 billion was spent in total during the election (OpenSecrets, 2017), half of which was raised by a small number of wealthy families and companies. Accordingly, party leaders have moved closer to big donors, be they wealthy individuals or corporate special interests (Crouch, 2004; Hay, 2007; Magleby, 2011).

The use of communication professionals to direct campaigning has similarly worked to distance parties from their wider citizenry. Such professionals are more oriented towards dominating public discourse and winning elections than they are towards 'two-way communication' or 'deliberative public spheres' (Franklin, 2004; Hall-Jamieson, 1996; Sussman, 2011). That often means utilising 'spin', negative attacks on opponents and a focus on leader personality traits rather than policy matters and core citizen concerns. In a global survey of political campaign professionals (see Scammell, 2014) asking about the 'very important' factors for winning campaigns, the top answer for US practitioners was 'budget/money' (86%). In Europe and Latin America, it was 'the candidate' (79–84%). 'Issues' was only mentioned by 47% in the US and 36–41% elsewhere. So too have campaigns increasingly focused on the small sets of swing voters and states deemed necessary to win an election, most particularly in majoritarian electoral systems. In the US in 2008, 98% of all campaign events and advertising took place in just 15 states (Fairvote, 2008). No candidate visited 35 of the states at all. In 2012, 99.6% of all campaign advertising was in just 10 swing states (Fairvote, 2013).

One obvious consequence of this targeted focus of policy and campaign messages on specific groups was that those repeatedly ignored began to lose faith in politicians of all sides. So, for example, Fairvote (2013) found that the long-term drop in US electoral turnout was more pronounced in those seemingly safe states ignored by candidates. The Pew Research Center (2018) recorded clear correlations between age, education, race and wealth on the one hand, and levels of engagement, knowledge and satisfaction with the US political system on the other. Being older, richer, more educated, and white meant a far greater likelihood of positive political engagement. The Hansard Society (2015, 2018) documented very similar correlations in relation to UK citizens, where 58% of those from higher classes were 'certain to vote' versus 40% of those from lower ones, 63% of homeowners were as opposed to 37% of renters, and 52% of whites were versus 33% of BME citizens.

One conclusion is that professional-electoral parties are prone to generating both virtuous and vicious circles of participation. In other words, some groups with a bigger stake are continually incentivised to engage. Others, such as the young, women, ethnic minorities, the poor and less educated, are less likely to feel they have a stake or participate. Such trends are only likely to have increased as a result of the targeted practices of electoral professionals. After all, why allocate funds and attention to those less likely to either fund parties or vote for them?

For each of these reasons, electoral-professional parties are a direct cause of wider public disaffection with party politics. Rather than being responsive to the larger citizenry they are meant to represent, they have become far too elite-focused. They have become what Katz and Mair (1995) have labelled 'cartel parties' or Crouch (2004) has termed 'cadre parties'.

What many recent elections have also shown is that the electoral-professional playbook is no longer working as it did. Neither Donald Trump, Jeremy Corbyn nor Beppe Grillo's Five Star Movement attempted to seize the 'centre ground', and none of them relied on experienced campaign professionals. Trump was particularly gaffe-prone and offended multiple voter groups. Hillary Clinton's political advertising budget was three times as much as Trump's (Motta, 2016). The pollsters employed by mainstream parties and news media repeatedly failed to predict voter shifts or the ultimate outcomes of several elections (see accounts in Jackson et al., 2016; Lilleker et al., 2016; Thorsen et al., 2017). The reliance on close ties with mainstream media was also shown to be problematic as Trump, Corbyn, Sanders, Podemos and others by-passed them, often looking to generate support through social media. In the US (Carlson, 2016; Lewis and Carlson, 2016) and UK (Berry, 2019; Davis, 2018), political reporting had become far too associated with the elite establishments of Washington and Westminster.

Thus, for many critics, the electoral outcomes from 2015 onwards were a conscious protest against political and connected elites of all kinds (Barnett, 2017; Conti et al., 2018; Frank, 2016; Luce, 2017). The ballot-box revolts kicked out against the larger networks of business, media, professional-expert and political elites that had continued to thrive while ordinary citizens struggled. For the public, it was electoral-professional-centrist parties that lay at the centre of this elite nexus.

ALTERNATIVE PARTIES AND THE ROOTS OF THEIR SUCCESS

If mainstream parties are struggling to survive, what are the alternatives taking their place and how are they succeeding? The model that has made most gains in the last decade is far-right nationalist-populist parties. Silvio Berlusconi's Forza Italia provided the early template here (Crouch, 2004): large corporate wealth, widespread media influence and populist appeal combined. It is a model that has served the likes of Donald Trump (US), Jair Bolsonaro (Brazil) and Viktor Orban (Hungary) amongst others (Eatwell and Goodwin, 2018; Judis, 2016; Mudde and Rovira Kaltwasser, 2017). By 2016 such parties had either gained political control or entered into ruling coalitions in eleven European nations. They had a growing presence in even the most politically and economically stable states, such as Sweden, Holland and Germany.

The other alternative can be seen in the more left social movement-party hybrid organisations that have developed since 2010. For some key sociologists (see the review in Mudge and Chen, 2014), parties, social movements and states can be more dynamically interconnected in their practices and personnel (see also Chapter 7). In recent years, a number of such entities have emerged with more democratic models and communication practices and connectivity. These have much in common with the large social movements that developed, such as Occupy Wall Street, Movimento de Junho in Brazil and the Arab Spring uprisings. Podemos, La France Insoumise, the Pirate Parties, Bernie Sanders' more radical wing of the Democrats and Corbyn's Labour Party are all examples here (Chadwick and Stromer-Galley, 2016; Gerbaudo, 2018; Mason, 2012).

Why are such parties mounting successful campaigns? How are they different ideologically, practically and organisationally, and do they offer sustainable, viable alternatives? Of course, their ideologies vary considerably, as do the conditions of their emergence and their forms of organisation. However, they do share certain elements that distinguish them from professional-electoral centrists.

One thing that unites them is their attack on elites, cosy centrism and the status quo. They openly criticise mainstream politicians, mainstream news media, corrupt business leaders and members of the establishment. It is a tactic that works despite they themselves often being wealthy elites (e.g. Nigel Farage, Donald Trump, Silvio Berlusconi) and continuing to co-operate with other elite factions in media, politics and business. Whether left or right, they appeal to large sections of society who feel disenfranchised and left behind.

However, the success of alternatives is based on more than their elite critique or appeal to nationalist feeling. In many ways they are also better attuned, both ideologically and organisationally, to the mediatised political environment of the times. This is fragmented and fluid, driven by personalities and popular culture, emotional and fashionable, fast-moving and flexible.

For one, both news media and politics have become increasingly oriented towards entertainment values and personalities, something conducive to mediagenic leaders. For several decades news providers have had to cope with the steady shrinking of their viewer and reader bases. Much of this was not to news rivals but to the entertainment sector. In an effort to compete, journalism has gravitated more to tabloid coverage, scandals, gossip, human-interest and scare stories (Dahlgren and Sparks, 1992; Delli Carpini and Williams, 2001; Franklin, 1997; Thussu, 2008). With greater losses incurred to the online world, news organisations moved to covering bizarre stories, negative attacks and personality clashes in an effort to claw back online click-bait traffic (Braun, 2015; Elvestad and Phillips, 2018; Graves, 2016; Reuters, 2017). Journalism has also devoted more space to celebrity coverage (McLachlin and Golding, 2000; Turner et al., 2000), which has included presenting politicians as celebrities or reporting celebrities who campaign for political causes (West and Orman, 2003; Wheeler, 2014).

At the same time, political parties began putting an emphasis on personal image management in their campaigns (Corner and Pels, 2003; Stanyer, 2007). They focused on leadership personalities, attacking oppositions on the same basis. They ventured into the entertainment world, with leading politicians appearing on popular entertainment shows such as *Have I Got News for You* or *Saturday Night Live* (Holtz Bacha et al., 2014; Lawrence and Boydstun 2017; McGregor et al., 2016; Stanyer, 2013). Likewise, the door has been opened the other way, as public figures from outside politics have used their entertainment profiles to run for office. Thus, after many years of appearing in *The Apprentice*, Donald Trump was more recognised than any of his Republican Party opponents when he campaigned to be the Party's nominee (Lawrence and Boydstun, 2017). Such conditions are of course conducive to parties headed by strong, charismatic leaders. Nigel Farage, Geert Wilders, Emmanuel Macron, Jair Bolsonaro and Narendra Modi are each happy to play up to a cult of personality. They are all prone to voice extreme opinions, offend opponents, make erratic policy proposals, all of which is to appeal to their core supporters and those antagonistic to centrist technocrats and the status quo. Such opinions also generate lots of news coverage.

In addition, for similar reasons, both news media and political parties have come to avoid detailed policy discussions, being more driven by short-term fashions and extreme stories. News reporting, for decades, has drifted away from in-depth coverage of political speeches and public debates. Instead, pieces prefer to present ideas in decreasingly small clips, and vice versa, politicians pepper their speeches/interviews with vague, snappy soundbites. In every recent study of electoral coverage in the US or UK, particular policy areas are rarely discussed in more than a few percent of stories. Meanwhile, by far the most common news items are 'horse-race' ones focusing on polls, followed by controversies and scandals (see most recently, Loughborough, 2015; Patterson, 2016). The shape of this political-news ecology favours populist alternatives. It allows ideology to be 'thin', flexible and fluid, according to political expediency and media fashions. It is conducive to leaders making emotional appeals and offering eye-catching policy statements. These require neither detailed research nor wider party discussion and debate.

Populist alternatives have also been well placed to take advantage of the breakdown of mainstream media and the switch to social media for news and political information. The shift to digital has not only left legacy media struggling to retain income and consumers, it has also left them less trusted (Anderson et al., 2015; Reuters, 2017; Worlds of Journalism, 2016) and less able to dictate news agendas. Alternative news sites, often more extreme and less weighed down by professional and legal restrictions, have flourished. So have numerous alternative political websites. The new political news and information environment is now increasingly fragmented and polarised, with politically interested individuals moving between the sites they chose to and avoiding all else. A majority of people in many countries now prefer to get their news via social media algorithms and shared links from chosen networks rather than from legacy news sites (Reuters, 2017). Fake news generators and armies of social media bots now also disseminate all manner of propaganda through networks (Woolley and Howard, 2017).

This new environment, which is fast-moving and by-passes mainstream media, suits alternative parties in various ways. For those on the right or centre, such as the Tea Party or En Marche, they have been useful in generating alternative political narratives and galvanising and organising new supporters. Well-resourced right alternatives do not even need many activist supporters. Instead, they can fund alt-right radio and online news sites and generate their own (mis)information to be disseminated widely through online networks and targeted social media adverts (Woolley and Howard, 2018). They are not weighed down by the machinery of ordinary parties, with their need to consult or develop detailed policy analysis. In a sense, they can go further than electoral-professional parties in acting like corporate entities and dispensing with democratic processes and organisational practices. That leaves them flexible and fluid, and able to respond quickly to what is trending or immediate in the digital information world.

For those more bottom-up hybrid movement-parties on the left, social media platforms have been extremely useful for bringing together and organising new organisations fairly rapidly (Bode and Dalrymple, 2016; Fenton, 2016; Gerbaudo, 2018; Loader et al., 2016; Weeks et al., 2017). As Gerbaudo (2018) explains in detail, these new 'platform parties' develop their own participatory platforms. The Five Star Movement has its Rousseau Platform, Podemos their Consul Participation, and the Pirate Parties their Liquid Feedback Democracy App. These enable a higher level of ordinary member participation and interaction in terms of discussion groups, online training events, consultations, ratings and votes on policy proposals. Such organisational mechanisms are particularly useful for engaging younger voters and others who feel left out by the media-party establishment. Several more radical left-wing challengers within traditional parties, such as Bernie Sanders or Jeremy Corbyn, have made extensive use of them in their campaigns (Chadwick and Stromer-Galley, 2016; Stromer-Galley, 2014; Wells et al., 2016). It is such practices that have rapidly made these hybrid entities amongst the largest parties by membership in Europe. By 2017, France Insoumise, the UK's Momentum and Spain's Podemos all had over half a million registered members.

Under such circumstances one can see that the current mediated political environment offers many opportunities for alternative parties to flourish. Those on the left are taking up the organisational and communication methods so successfully used by new social movements. Those on the right have located alternative communication platforms and can do away with the checks and balances of ordinary parties, detailed policy programmes and rational deliberations. Both a struggling legacy media desperate for consumers and the anarchic social media network alternatives suit their appeals, based as they are on charismatic leaders, emotions and knee-jerk responses. Whether left, right or centre, the new alternatives can by-pass both legacy media scrutiny and the political establishment to quickly build their projects and supporter bases.

Although such parties are currently in the ascendency there remain difficult questions in relation to their long-term sustainability and their contribution to democracies more generally. In Bolleyer's (2013) study of the emergence of 140 parties in 17 mature democracies over a four-decade period, the majority failed to make an electoral breakthrough. Amongst those that did, a third then vanished soon after their breakthrough, and many others disappeared altogether just a few years later. As she explained, the very electoral volatility that opens up opportunities for new parties is also a reason for their demise in the long run. For one, their success depends on their appeal to detached, floating voters who, over time, are equally likely to switch their allegiance once again to another party. Secondly, organisational persistence and repeated electoral success require long-term resources and organisational investment in an enduring infrastructure.

Both sets of findings are very pertinent to the new emergent parties of the last half decade. For the nationalist-populist parties of the right, there are resources but often little attempt to build member and activist-oriented infrastructures. In fact, those 'charismatic parties' (Bolleyer, 2013) rarely endure beyond the political lifespans of their high-profile leaders. Such leaders often resist the institutionalisation of their parties, seeing it as a personal threat to their positions. In general, in ideology and practice, such parties are less democratic and accountable than centrists. They present 'an illiberal democratic response to undemocratic liberalism' (Mudde and Rovira Kaltwasser, 2017: 116). They offer few detailed policy options or long-term visions. In fact, their short-term fixes are only likely to exacerbate the longer term problems of climate change, environmental degradation, declining resource issues, growing inequality and financial instability. They offer 'creative destruction' and blunt ideological zeal but no answers. More often than not, their muddled responses to the COVID-19 crisis have led to much higher per capita death rates in their nations.

For alternative left social movement-party hybrid organisations, of the kind that have developed since 2010, they offer greater democratic depth but present similar doubts about sustainability. Without high funding or allies across the political and media establishment, they struggle to compete and influence. Most of their new social movement cousins, such as Occupy Wall Street or those involved in the Arab Spring, died out as rapidly as they had come into being. Very few have emulated the success of nationalist-populist parties. As Gerbaudo (2017, 2018) explains, the very platform structures which were vital for generating large number of new members have not been that conducive to producing enduring democratic party structures and practices. They have taken the place of middle party management cadres without reproducing all their functions. They have facilitated greater participation but left a large gap between 'hyperleaders' at the top and ordinary members below. This leaves more engagement but has limited actual member influence on parties.

CONCLUSION: WHAT NOW FOR PARTY-BASED DEMOCRACIES?

Traditional party-based politics, whether more centrist or ideological, in two-party or multi-party systems, no longer seems to be functioning well. Part of the problem, as centrists explain, is that social, economic and technical changes are making democratic governance increasingly complex. Genuine democratic representation and practice are too slow to keep up with the pace of change brought by digital turbo capitalism. Parties cannot compete with undemocratic global corporations, financial networks, the mobile super-rich, and the instant emotions and fashions of social media.

However, part of the problem comes down to the parties themselves. As argued here, the rational-centrist, electoral-professional party that has dominated politics in many democracies has deep-seated issues which it is failing to address. In organisation and focus such parties have become too 'cadre'- or 'cartel'-like, tied more to funders and professionals than to members and publics. Their ideologies and techno-rational approaches, whether left or right, in the long term have benefitted certain groups and organisations, in particular the wealthy and international corporations, over others.

A paradigm shift is needed as these failings need to be recognised and addressed. That includes a more critical questioning of the positive narratives around globalisation, neoliberalism and the digital economy. The 'rational' embrace of these socio-economic shifts has caused great inequalities and undermined democratic states. Centrist technocracies may be rational, but they have also become rigged, short-termist and detached. The political system they have co-created has disembedded them from the lives of the many far away from the political centres of Paris, Berlin, London and Washington.

Currently, however, each of the other party model choices on offer is also problematic. Nationalist-populist parties are rather less democratic and accountable than traditional parties. They may be temporarily effective in electoral terms, but they offer little in the way of enduring political structures, democratic practices, or solutions to the current large-scale and long-term problems confronting twenty-first-century states. Alternative, more democratic and left hybrid movement-parties appear fragile and precarious. They lack resources and, so far, more sustained influence over political and media institutions. In effect, none of the options on offer present models that are both positive and practical. The choice appears to be rational rigged centrism, radical right, elitist short-termism, or radical left instability.

As commentators have pointed out, if political parties no longer function, then democracy is imperilled too (see Chiaramonte and Emanuele, 2017; Hershey, 2017; van Biezen and Poguntke, 2014) – in which case, either party-based systems need to be radically restructured and regulated, or alternative kinds of representative and organisational structures need to be developed, or related structures of governance and public communication need to be rethought. Perhaps all three? In effect, either a radical overhaul of party structures and representation needs to take place, or we need to think about how democracies might function without parties altogether.

6

THE VIOLENCE OF AN ILLIBERAL LIBERALISM

INTRODUCTION

No social system is neutral about its own basic values. One of the most central values of liberal democracy, and one important distinguishing feature of liberal societies, is said to be the independence of media. Indeed, democracy would not exist without the freedom to express and communicate opinions, to assemble, associate, publish, etc. Yet the idea of media as private property which is also so central to liberalism imposes a decisive limitation on the democratic value that is accorded to media. The picture is further complicated particularly by contemporary digital media, which is less regulated, more secretive, increasingly powerful and being utilised by state actors in ways antithetical to the democratic claims central to the legitimation of liberal democracies (Bennett and Pfetsch, 2018).

The clash between two conceptions of democracy, on the one hand as a form of government and on the other as a form of social and political life (Rancière, 2010), has led to what Fraser describes as a 'rejection of politics as usual' and a serious 'crisis of hegemony' (2019: 9). This 'democratic paradox' and the failure of liberalism become acutely evident before the appearance of significant dents in the authority of established political parties. Lest we forget, the financial meltdown of 2008 arrived not long after the invasion of Iraq, which is now agreed to have been one of the worst foreign policy disasters in US and British history. The appalling criminal acts committed on September 11, 2001, were used to legitimise further assaults on democracy at national and international levels and other questionable actions (including direct military interventions, occupations, torture, economic and political sanctions) under the banner of 'exporting democracy' and defending democracy.

This chapter argues that an understanding of both liberalism and war should be central in mapping the social conditions that enable a particular interplay between politics and media, for war, as we have seen, curbs the very democracy it claims to be protecting through the rapid expansion of the repressive apparatuses of the state, the upgrading of colonial security policies with digital and biometric technology, assaults on individual and collective liberties through pigeonholing citizens into the binary of 'patriots' and 'terrorist sympathisers', the limitations on civil and democratic rights, and the subordination of everything and everyone to the perceived ideals of the 'free world'. It questions how free and independent media in the UK and US have 'freely' submitted to the state's authoritarian agenda, as we saw during the invasion of both Afghanistan and Iraq, and argues that political communication has not sufficiently highlighted these questions about the impact of war on media and democracy.

Therefore, a particular focus of the chapter is on the absence of war and military interventions as an important factor and category in scholarly discussion of political communications. This is not to suggest that war itself is absent in communications journals and books. Far from it. There are scores of books and articles that examine the relationship between media and war, and even a cursory search will yield an extensive reading list on this very subject. In a rapidly segmented field of media studies there are even journals that are dedicated to this very issue under the broader title of 'conflict'. Our interest here is much broader. In recent years, political communications scholars have produced important work that has tried to 'rethink', 'revisit' and 'reconsider' the interactions between media and democracy (Bennett and Pfetsch, 2018; Blumler and Coleman, 2015; Blumler and Kavanagh, 1999; Scheufele, 2000). This chapter, however, suggests that war should be considered as central in any reassessment or reconsideration of democracy itself. This is crucial, since militarism and war are 'no longer a mere consequence but also a motor of historical development' (Balibar, 2010: 13).

Blumler and Coleman (2015), in their fascinating analysis of the relationship between democracy and media, argue that the old model of analysis of political communication systems is desperately out of date, and propose revising some of the foundational concepts of political communication scholarship. The article was published in 2015, and while they highlight some of the most important changes and transformations, including technological development, the interplay between secular and sacred and so on, there is little discussion of the relationship between war and democracy at both a national and an international level. Blumler's earlier article co-authored with Kavanagh (1999) evaluates what they describe as 'the third age of political communication' and examines a system that is full of tensions, 'sets new research priorities, and re-opens long-standing issues of democratic theory' (1999: 209). The article looks at various stages of political communications in the post-war period, which is a somewhat misleading label in an era of permanent war. But it fails to mention war as a subject of political communication. Other leading figures in this field have invariably examined the 'destabilising' impact of the internet (Dahlgren, 2005) and yet have said nothing about the destabilising impact of wars for democratic life in democracies or for the democratic aspirations of people in the global south. Bennett and Pfetsch's most recent contribution to rethinking political communication highlights the crisis of legitimacy in many democracies, and points out that the previous assumptions about a 'broadly inclusive and well-functioning public sphere' only 'made sense for most democracies in Europe and North America in the last half of the twentieth century' (2018: 243). However, that war is a significant disruptive factor is curiously missing from their rethinking. There is therefore an urgent need to offer some correctives in our thinking about media and democracy. If 'war is the continuation of politics by other means', should it not be central in any discussion of political communication?

The absence of war as a central concern for political communications can perhaps partly be explained with reference to the existing narrow focus on what Rancière has described as a 'pure' form of politics, in which politics is stripped to its abstract form and handed over to 'government oligarchies enlightened by their experts'. Politics is then freed from domestic and social necessity and 'is tantamount to the pure and simple reduction of the political to the state (*l'etatique*)' (2015: 36). However, we know all too well that, despite increased challenges to the state's monopoly of war by non-governmental forces, it is mostly states that wage wars and it is their 'enlightened experts' (including inside the media) who are tasked with justifying the most 'unjust' wars. War remains the 'purest' form of politics in which citizenship is weakened (and where even citizens are stripped of their rights), and the very idea and practice of democracy is overshadowed in the climate of 'emergency' and the need for 'national unity'. There is a dialectical relationship between the unexportability of democracy to the less 'enlightened' and the attack on the very idea of democracy in Europe and North America. In order to understand what Bennett and Pfetsch (2018) have called the 'disrupted public sphere', we have to question the very assumptions about an inclusive and well-functioning public sphere in the light of a much broader political and geographical context.

Another possible explanation for the absence of war in many assessments of political communication has something to do with taking for granted the very 'universal' promise of liberal democracy, of which war is one of the clearest manifestations of its limit or perhaps even its promise. This chapter first highlights the continuity and longevity of illiberal practices by liberal states and pays attention to the paradoxes of liberalism itself. It then examines the Chilcot Report as a case study to highlight that even when the invasion of Iraq was officially acknowledged as a disaster, the limits of liberalism, the anti-democratic and irresponsible behaviour of a large section of the British press, and the consequences of war for the most afflicted, were brushed aside.

THE FALSE UNIVERSALISM OF LIBERALISM AND LIBERAL DEMOCRACY

Raymond Williams (2014: 179) once suggested that the term 'liberal has, at first sight, so clear a political meaning that some of its further associations are puzzling'. This, as Williams demonstrated, is partly because the word itself has a long and fascinating history that dates back to the fourteenth century. The original uses of 'liberal' were mostly positive. *Liberal* was a mark of distinction, a free man in contradistinction with those who were not; *liberal arts* was a reference to skills appropriate for men [sic] who had means and status; *liberal* also came to be defined as generous, open-minded and unorthodox. The distinction, from its very first usage, was all about class, privilege and status. This positive framing of liberalism remains dominant. However, 'liberal' also had, and still retains, negative meanings. For example, cultural and social conservatives still associate 'liberal' with unrestrained and undisciplined attitudes and behaviour. *Taking liberties* is pejorative, as is a 'liberal' reading/attitude to facts and figures.

In the realm of politics, the term is just as complex and puzzling. On the one hand being 'liberal' has long been regarded as being open-minded, progressive or even radical, while on the other hand liberals are attacked for either being insufficiently radical (from the left) or being too progressive (such as in the US). The prevailing definition of liberalism (as an ideology, political philosophy and tradition) has historically revolved around tolerance, progress, humanitarianism, objectivity, respect for and promotion of reason, democracy and human rights. To be considered a 'liberal' (in this sense) can still be seen as a positive thing. Yet despite receiving a very good press throughout its history, liberalism has also been subject to passionate and sustained critiques by the left and the illiberal. For the latter, liberalism has gone too far; for the former, it has never gone far enough. Raymond Williams, for example, argues that liberalism, while referring to a 'mixture of liberating and limiting ideas', is 'essentially, a doctrine of possessive individualism' and that it is therefore 'in fundamental conflict not only with socialist but with most strictly social theories' (2014: 179–80).

The basic premise of liberal thought is the equality of individuals before the law – a conception that stresses the negative immunity of citizens from political intervention and coercion. Yet as Davies (2017) notes, private property 'has long been recognised as a fundamental individual right within liberal frameworks, which partly accounts for the connection between political and economic liberalism'. Historically, however, economic participation and entitlement have been limited to a small minority of people with resources and capital. It was precisely this liberation of men to 'own property' that Marx criticised so trenchantly: 'None of the so-called rights of man', he argued, 'therefore, go beyond egoistic man, beyond man as a member of civil society – that is, an individual withdrawn into himself, into the confines of his private interests and private caprice, and separated from the community' (1978: 43).

The variety of uses and connotations certainly makes a sweeping generalisation about liberals and liberalism impossible. Yet the seed of contradiction was visible from the very first moment of liberalism: the strength of liberalism – its commitment to emancipation – is also its main weakness in that there were at least three major exclusionary clauses in this project. It was not only love for liberty but also contempt for people of the colonies, the working class and women more generally, that were factors that united liberal thinkers. In his book on liberalism, Domenico Losurdo reminds us that liberal thinkers – including Locke, Smith and Franklin – shared an enthusiasm for 'a process of systematic expropriation and practical genocide first of the Irish and then of the Indians', as well as for 'black enslavement and the black slave trade' (2011: 20). The contradictions at the heart of liberalism are sharply expressed in its approach to 'liberty'. Losurdo stresses that slavery was not something that preceded liberalism, but rather something that fostered its maximum development after the success of liberal revolutions. The total slave population in the Americas increased from 330,000 in 1700 to three million in 1800 and then to over six million in the 1850s. The tangle of emancipation and enslavement also shows itself in the slogan of the rebel colonists during the America war of independence: 'We won't be their Negroes' (2011: 20).

Even for the most radical of liberal thinkers, John Stuart Mill, democracy was fit only for a 'civilised' community. 'Despotism', Mill asserted, 'is a legitimate mode of government in dealing with barbarians, provided the end be their improvement, and the means justified by actually effecting that end' (2005: 14). In fact he argued in favour of the colonisation of India on the basis that 'vigorous despotism' of civilised British imperialism would make Indians 'capable of a higher civilisation' (Mehta, 1999: 106). It is no accident that the celebrated 1789 *Declaration of the Rights of Man* says nothing about the rights of slaves or the people of the colonies, or women. The power of capital in the land of 'barbarians' came not through 'peaceful competition' but via the barrel of a gun. The scars are still deep and still fresh. Slavery continued by other means in both the colonies and the metropolis. The ideology of superiority and difference that underpins this barbarism is liberal in its origin and in its make-up. Contemporary versions of this thinking about freedom and democracy – as evidenced through recent 'humanitarian interventions' – continue to evince a sense of superiority in which liberals enforce 'democracy' upon the 'less enlightened'. The love of freedom and liberty that is central to the idea of liberalism is indeed one that, in its realisation, has all too often been easily sacrificed on the altar of the interests of capital and (imperial) states.

Liberty, for Mill as well as other liberals, was exclusive to those with 'developed' faculties. As such, it was not just the 'barbarians' but also the native working class and the illiterates who were considered ineligible for the right to vote. Nothing was considered worse than giving representation (and the right to vote) to the working class for it would give them the chance to negotiate for better wages and working conditions. The lack of freedom in the colonies, therefore, was extended to the metropolis and issues of race and class were intertwined from the start. The 'disruption' to the public sphere, noted by Bennett and Pfetsch (2018) in relation to the current era, began much earlier than is usually assumed and acknowledged.

In short, while liberty has provided an ideological bulwark against authoritarianism, it has also always been connected to the configurations of the liberal democratic capitalist state. Linked to this, therefore, is a further contradiction: the equation of liberalism with democracy. The Italian philosopher and political scientist Norberto Bobbio, who was on a (peaceful) mission to bring liberalism and the left closer together, argued that a 'liberal state is not necessarily democratic'. Indeed, while liberalism is about 'a particular conception of the state', democracy 'denotes one of the many possible modes of government' (1990: 7). Bobbio further suggests that the relationship between liberalism and democracy raises a more problematic relation between liberty and equality. The question, contrary to rigid liberal thought, has not been simply about liberty or freedom, but about the precise nature and definition of liberty itself: freedom from what and to do what?

Much of the history of liberalism has been about separating these two historic demands for liberty and equality. Throughout the history of modern times, and even in the most 'liberal' of societies, what has been lacking is precisely the more expansive, anti-authoritarian sense of 'liberal'. The US is an obvious example. The decision to invade Iraq in the aftermath of the terrorist attacks in September 2001, revelations about extraordinary renditions and the surveillance of key members of the UN and major US allies (Svendsen, 2009), images from Abu Ghraib and the 'anomaly' (to use Tony Blair's description) of Guantanamo, have shown the rule of law to be selective, if not a myth. At times in which even the liberalism of liberal America has been tested to its limits after the terrorist attacks of 9/11, and in the period in which the much celebrated First Amendment has been hijacked variously by corporate America, the gun lobby and the Ku Klux Klan (Swenson, 2004), and with visible and increased state tyranny and violence against African-Americans, rarely has the United States been so desperately in need of a touch of liberalism.

In the contemporary context, the relationship between economic and legal liberalism and the market fundamentalism advocated by neo-liberals is another contradictory and contested arena today. If neo-liberalism is a political project at least as much as it is an economic theory, ideologically it is associated with a classically minimal liberal state, with the efficiency of 'free markets' as against what is seen as the ponderous and wasteful outcome of state planned economies and nationalised industries that characterised Keynesian welfare states. Wendy Brown (2005) has argued, in contrast to classic market liberalism, that neoliberalism starts from the state itself. Why? Because in the process, the state, as Bauman and Bordoni suggest, 'rather than being provider and guarantor of public welfare, becomes "a parasite" on the population, concerned only for its own survival, demanding more and more and giving less and less in exchange' (2014: 17–18).

In addition, neo-liberalism has been linked with increasingly authoritarian uses of state power – at home and abroad – and with the re-regulation of the economy to protect financial capital rather than the de-regulation championed by advocates of neo-liberalism. 'Authoritarianism in market enforcement', as Harvey points out, 'sits uneasily with ideals of individual freedom. The more neoliberalism veers towards the former, the harder it becomes to maintain its legitimacy with respect to the latter and the more it has to reveal its anti-democratic colour' (2005: 79). What we have witnessed is not the withdrawal of the state as such, but further interventions by the state and the redistribution of wealth in favour of capital. We have only to consider here the 'bail out' of banks that were 'too big to fail' following the financial crisis of 2008, and the violent repression of protests against austerity measures that were demanded by 'global markets' (more or less personified in the European Union and the International Monetary Fund). As Swenson (2015) has argued, the production of states of emergency was essential in managing and regulating the economic crisis.

Since 9/11, the issue of war and national security has been tied up with immigration in liberal Europe to justify racial profiling and discrimination (Fekete, 2016). As Fraser has suggested, the link between the disaster of the invasion of Iraq and the financial crisis of 2008 is undeniable. It is therefore no accident that since 2008 in particular we have witnessed the emergence of a renewed state of emergency not just through the threat of terror (although that is still present) but through the threat of scarcity. It is in this period in particular that the future of the welfare state has been linked explicitly to the issue of immigration. Under the banner of 'living within our means', policies that for a long time were simply associated with 'structural adjustment' programmes in the global south, are now being implemented in some of the richest countries in the global north. Scarcity constitutes the reality and the lived conditions of the most deprived people, while, as Oxfam (2017) has pointed out, only a tiny minority have benefited from and thrived in the post-2008 economic crisis. In attaching the issue of welfare to that of immigration, we are presented with false choices given that there is evidently enormous wealth concentrated in the richest societies. As Alperovitz and Dubb (2013) have pointed out, in 2011 the US economy produced almost $200,000 per family of four. The figure in Britain was around $150,000, in Germany $160,000, and in devastated Greece over $100,000. The issue is political, and the causes of hardship are the systemic design of capitalism.

Here lies a further contradiction. What has been considered as a beautiful dimension of liberalism, both in its longevity and its attachment to a basic welfare provision, is the social democratic experiment in Europe after World War Two and the use of large-scale public spending to enact progressive social and economic measures. Yet this has been the exception rather than the norm in the history of capitalism, and even here it has taken place because of the pressure of mass movements and social struggles. Similarly, the campaigns for democracy in the colonies and the metropolis came from outside liberalism. India became free not because of Western liberalism advocated by Mills and other liberals, but in fierce opposition to it. The struggle for liberation in the global south also came as part of the broader struggle for independence from the 'vigorous despotism' that liberals such as Mills had so passionately supported. The right to vote, welfare reforms and public services were gained through organised working-class movements in the metropolis. It was not liberals but emerging radical movements that made those gains after forcing the liberals to retreat from their positions that saw the law of the market as the 'divine' law: 'The laws in force today in virtually every country in the world', argues Losurdo, 'would seem to attest to the "modernity" not of colonialist aggressor, but of its victims!' (2015: 232).

POLITICS IS THE CONTINUATION OF WAR BY OTHER MEANS

Immediately after the criminal attack in Paris on journalists at Charlie Hebdo in January 2015, François Hollande, the then president of France, responded as follows:

> Today it is the Republic as a whole that has been attacked. The Republic equals freedom of expression; the Republic equals culture, creation, it equals pluralism and democracy. That is what the assassins were targeting. It equals the ideal of justice and peace that France promotes everywhere on the international stage, and the message of peace and tolerance that we defend – as do our soldiers – in the fight against terrorism and fundamentalism.

Reanimating the language of war of course has become all too common in recent years, as is making explicit the link between pluralism and democracy with what 'our' soldiers do on the international stage. Framing colonialism in a progressive cloak is not new, but if it is widely accepted that the terrorist attack on September 2001 has changed everything we need to ask for whom and how?

We have already suggested that what is generally referred to as the 'post-war period' can be misleading. As Hannah Arendt has suggested, the 'Second World War was not followed by peace but by a cold war and the establishment of the military-industrial complex" (1970: 9). She goes on to argue that 'instead of war being "an extension of diplomacy (or of politics, or of pursuit of economic objectives)," peace is the continuation of war by other means – is the actual development in the techniques of warfare' (1970: 9). The evidence is undeniable. Since the end of WW2 there have been around 250 wars, in which at least 50 million have been killed and millions more injured and made homeless. Geographically, the impact of military operations has been highly unequal. Nearly all these conflicts have happened in the Eastern hemisphere and enemy military operations have barely touched the West: hence the shock of 9/11. As Stephen Eric Bronner has pointed out, 'War has not been an exception but rather the rule. During the 20ᵗʰ century, in fact, there has hardly been a year in which the United States was not intervening somewhere' (quoted in Werbell, 2005: 521). Any assumptions about the existence of a 'broadly inclusive and relatively well-functioning public sphere' have to take this brutal reality into consideration. It is not just overt warfare that underscores global inequalities. The so-called 'long peace' after WW2 has only been relatively true for a small corner of our planet. Violence also takes many forms: 'In the past six years more children have died globally as a result of starvation and preventable diseases than humans perished in the six years of the Second World War. Every three seconds a human life that just began ceases to exist in a cruel way. At the same time in these same three seconds $120,000 are being spent on military armaments worldwide' (Brie, 2008: 240). The violence of war has mostly been directed against a perceived 'other'. This is what the history of colonialism and imperialism is about, no matter how much Hollande and others would like to frame it differently.

In pursuing their interests worldwide, imperial powers have shown little respect for international law. The legality of the invasion of Iraq, thanks to anti-war movements across the world, was indeed questioned. But what was precisely the legal basis for the horrendous war against Vietnam, the US invasion of Grenada, or the overt support given to the Contras in Nicaragua? This inconsistent adherence to international law is, as we have argued, hardly new and has its roots in an earlier 'liberal' tradition. In calling for the invading army to teach the Chinese a lesson, John Stuart Mill saw no reason to quibble about formalities: 'appeals to humanity and Christianity in favour of ruffians, & to international law in favour of peoples who recognise no laws of war at all', were 'ridiculous' (cited in Losurdo, 2015: 248).

Capitalism is based on values that privilege an irrational system based on accumulation, corruption, wreaking havoc in the market and then rewarding the culprits. This irrationalism takes an even more violent turn at the international level. The history of capitalist accumulation, according to Rosa Luxemburg, always has two aspects. The one that is usually highlighted concerns a narrative of accumulation that is defined purely in economic terms, where the exchange between capitalist and wage-labourer is seen as one of equivalence and assessed within the limits of commodity exchange. This, as we are told, is conducted within a system of fair competition, peace and equality (hiding the reality of exploitation).

The other aspect is accumulation at the international level. Luxemburg argues that it is precisely on this stage that accumulation becomes more violent, and that aggression against colonies and rivals, not to mention war, genocide and looting, are committed without any attempt at concealment: 'Bourgeois liberal theory takes into account only the former aspect: the realm of "peaceful competition", the marvels of technology and pure commodity exchange; it separates it strictly from the other aspect: the realm of capital's blustering violence which is regarded as more or less incidental to foreign policy and quite independent of the economic sphere of capital' (1951: 452–53).

Nevertheless, aggressive foreign interventions and lootings, and all major wars, were always followed by policies favourable to the poor at a domestic level. As Bronner has pointed out with particular reference to the United States, the Spanish-American war of 1898 was followed by a range of 'progressive legislations'; the vote for women came after World War One; World War Two produced GI bills and was followed by welfare reforms in Europe; and various programmes associated with the 'Great Society' were extracted during the Vietnam War. As Losurdo has argued with reference to colonisation, 'the expropriation, deportation, and decimation of the natives – made it possible for poor whites to access property, so that the reigning political power in the USA, already sheltered from attacks from without, did not have to fear the threat harboured by a bitter internal social conflicts. In other words, the liberal state (for the white community) was only one side of the coin' (2015: 252). The flipside to social stability and the rule of law for the white community was the complete lack of rights for slaves and African-Americans.

This is no longer the case. The war in Afghanistan, the invasion of Iraq, various military interventions in the Middle East and North Africa and the escalation of drone warfare have not been followed by policies favourable to native working classes. Instead they have been accompanied by the most regressive and brutal attacks on democracy, increasing the range of state surveillance, an intolerance of dissent, and even the imposition of colonial-style emergency laws (Fekete, 2016). Donald Trump, Bret Kavanagh, Boris Johnson, and an assortment of reactionary politicians in Western democracies are not produced out of thin air. It is impossible to understand their emergence without placing the contradictions of liberalism and the phenomenon of war at the centre of our discussion of democracy.

There is another way of putting this. The US share of global trade in technologies of violence in the period 2013–2017 grew by 25% compared with 2008–2012. The Stockholm International Peace Research Institute (2018) estimates that the US now accounts for 34% of all global arms sales, up from 30% five years ago. US arms exports are 58% higher than those of Russia, the world's second-largest exporter. The five largest importers in 2013–2017 were India, Saudi Arabia, Egypt, the United Arab Emirates and China, accounting for 35% of all arms imports. War as a 'metaphor' (on drugs, crime, cancer, AIDS, etc.) is hardly irrelevant in liberal democracies themselves. Between 1990 and 2000, the number of prisons in the USA increased by 80%. According to Angela Davis in 2003, there were more women in prison in California than there were women in prison in the whole country in 1970. In 2003 there were some two million people in US prisons and approximately 1.5 million in the military (2003: 88–92). In such a climate of militarised democracy, 52% of the US federal budget is spent on the military while the share allocated to health is only six per cent (2003: 88–92).

How should we reconsider and reassess the relationship between politics and democracy in the light of such evidence? The assumptions about a broadly inclusive and well-functioning public sphere in democracies were, and are, indulging in wishful thinking about the humanitarian and pacifist tendencies of liberal democracies.

Wars, as we have argued, are not something external to the 'free world', nor are they acts that are restricted to repressive non-liberal states. Of course there is no singular cause that explain all wars, but the rapid industrialisation of war, and in particular the relationship between external military power and internal surveillance and control, is an essential category for thinking about democracy at home and abroad.

Liberal democracies are not immune from this reality. If liberalism's mechanisms of self-reflection and scrutiny are part of its claims to democracy even on the question of war, then it appears that the public inquiry into the invasion in 2003 and subsequent occupation of Iraq that was announced by Gordon Brown in 2009 (referred to as the Chilcot Inquiry after its chair Sir John Chilcot) seems to provide as much a ringing endorsement of this tendency as it is a thorough going critique of the Iraq War. However, the Chilcot report also visibly illustrates the limitations, the exclusion clauses and the contradictions of liberalism.

THE CHILCOT REPORT AND THE 'DEMOCRATIC PARADOX'

The Chilcot report was published on 6 July 2016. On many levels it is an impressive piece of work. The report is the product of the examination of some 150,000 documents and over 180 interviews with a variety of witnesses, and comprises 2.6 million words in 12 volumes with a 150-page executive summary. It took more than seven years to complete and cost over £10 million. Chilcot's devastating critique of the 2003 invasion of Iraq (which, let us remember, was supported by the majority of the British press at the time) offered a timely caution against pessimistic predictions of democracy's demise. Indeed, many commentators were quick to point out that the Chilcot report was not a whitewash and its verdict was far more damning and fiercer than was anticipated. The report opens by saying that '[w]e have concluded that the UK chose to join the invasion of Iraq before the peaceful options for disarmament had been exhausted. Military action at that time was not a last resort'.

The volume of immediate media coverage of the report was equally impressive. Unsurprisingly all the national newspapers in Britain printed a picture of Tony Blair on their cover page. *The Times* called the Iraq war 'Blair's private war'; another Rupert Murdoch title, *The Sun*, called Blair a 'Weapon of Mass Deception'. The *Daily Mail*'s headline was 'A Monster of Delusion', while the *Daily Express* referenced Tony Blair's half-hearted apology with a headline of 'SHAMED BLAIR: I'M SORRY BUT I'D DO IT AGAIN'. The irony of such responses to the Chilcot report should not be lost on anyone. These papers were the cheerleaders of war in 2003, yet in the summer of 2016 they became cheerleaders for Chilcot. The consensus among these papers about the legality and desirability of war in 2003 was replaced by yet another consensus in 2016. How are we to understand and read this shift?

The report was significant for a number of reasons. While Chilcot expressed some criticism of the invasion of Iraq, the report failed to put an end to the ongoing dispute – and continuing anger – over a very bitter and devastating episode in recent

British history. Indeed, the Chilcot report spectacularly failed to address or solve what we might refer to as a 'democratic paradox' (Rancière, 2007). As we have already discussed, both the conception and the exercise of democracy have existed alongside genocide, slavery, colonialism, and the exclusion of large sections of the population, in particular women and ethnic minorities. Here we would like to focus on some elements of this 'democratic paradox' with reference to not only what the report says, but also for what it fails to say.

One of the most significant blind spots of the report is, as David Whyte and Greg Muttitt (2016) have argued, oil. The executive summary refers to oil a mere five times and never as a motive for war. In the rest of the report, oil is buried under ground despite references to government documents that clearly demonstrate the centrality of oil in the invasion of Iraq. Whyte and Muttitt rightly suggest that 'Chilcot takes at face value the Blair government's claim that the motive was to address Iraq's weapons of mass destruction'.

This brings us to the second major absence: the Iraqi people themselves. Millions of words and millions of pounds were committed to the report, yet there is absolutely nothing about the Arabs of Iraq (and Syria) who have paid a high price for the 'mistakes' of George Bush, Tony Blair and the other architects of the war. As Robert Fisk put it (2016), 'We weep for our British military martyrs, for such is how the Arabs refer to their wartime dead, yet scarcely a single suffering Arab was to be heard in the aftermath of Chilcot. The Iraqis were not allowed to give evidence; the dead Muslims and Christians of Iraq had no-one to plead for the integrity of their lives'. It wasn't just that they were not heard. The 'coalition of the willing' from the very start refused to track civilian casualties in Iraq and did not hesitate to undermine critical media voices. The report failed to provide the Iraqi people with any resources to confront the colonial aggression against them and to address the horrific consequences of the war. It says almost nothing about the civilian casualties or the massive displacement and forced migration of millions of people in Iraq. On this issue too the report sticks with Bush and Blair's claims and conduct over Iraqi casualties. Needless to say that, apart from some minor exceptions, this paradox went unnoticed.

What does this lack of rights and lack of recognition tell us about the nature of liberal democracy, considering that such aggressions were justified in the name of democracy? If the invasion of Iraq, and before that of Afghanistan, were justified in the name of the rights of victims of those tyrannical regimes, then what happens when they become the victims of liberal states such as the US and Britain? There was no shortage of Iraqi exiles and refugees who were prepared to give testimony and provide eyewitness accounts for the British media in the build-up to the invasion. Why were they not allowed to do the same later? Why is it that yesterday's victims were then denied voices and rights later on? What Hannah Arendt argued over sixty years ago, initially in a short piece about refugees written in 1943 but expanded in *The Origins of Totalitarianism*, still appears relevant. In her discussion of the dilemmas of the 'Rights of Man', she argues bitterly about the 'rightless' that their 'plight is not that they are not equal before the law, but that no law exists for them; not that they are oppressed, but that no one wants to oppress them' (1951: 295). If the Iraqi people were equal before the invasion, then why not after? If transparency, the rule of law, accountability and open debate are good for the British public, then why not for the main victims of its war?

The main point here is not simply to repeat the accusation of hypocrisy, but to stress that in the civilised, calm, measured and critical 2.6 million words of the Chilcot report, the people of Iraq fall outside of this celebration of facts and law. The people of Iraq (and the Middle East in general) are viewed as democracy's Other. But we know from history that democracy has become democratic precisely by opening itself to the Other: to women and to religious and ethnic minorities. The 'democratic paradox' has always set democracy against itself, and if democracy is to be democratised the rights of others have to be recognised and democratic rights expanded to broader constituencies.

Democracy, however, is the third and rather astonishing blind spot in the Chilcot report. Terrorism, one of the consequences and products of the invasion of Iraq, is mentioned 28 times in the executive summary, but democracy, the 'promise' of invasion and 'regime change', not even once. The invasion of Iraq is a telling contemporary example of a sense of superiority in which imperial powers enforce 'democracy' upon the 'less enlightened'. The US political scientist Ann Norton reflects on this in relation to the experience of Muslims:

> Muslims have indeed been shown to be democracy's others. They lack democracy, and it must be supplied to them, albeit by undemocratic means. The advancement of liberal democratic institutions in the political realm inhabited by Muslims, like neo-liberal institutions in their economic realms, is sought within a regime of conditionality. Democracy, like economic development, can be aided only under certain conditions. The objects of efforts to "democratize" the Middle East are required not merely to win the consent and satisfy the demands of their own electoral constituencies; they must conform to the will of the European Union and the United States. The elected government of Palestine must recognize Israel, whatever its constituents may say; the elected government of Iraq must forgo its choice of prime minister. (2013: 11)

The absence of any reference to 'democracy' in post-2003 Iraq in the Chilcot report stands in sharp contrast to how that report has been perceived; namely the promise, or indeed the possibility of 'inquiry', the visibility of debate, the importance of the 'rule of law', and the existence of accountability in a Western democracy. Chilcot, as is the case with previous, and most likely future inquiries, into foreign policy 'mishaps' and 'mistakes', was a racialised ritual in which the superior race/nation can absolve itself, learn the lessons in a civilised and calm manner and move forward, undoubtedly to the next 'mistake'. The 'feel-good factor' around this ritual was such that one of the first opinion pieces to be published by the *Guardian* suggested that the United States needs to have its own Chilcot inquiry (Timm, 2016).

This act of 'detoxing' our national conscious over yet another imperial aggression is particularly visible in relation to the British media, the fourth blind spot of the Chilcot report. One of the major cheerleaders of the invasion of Iraq, *The Sun* newspaper, went even as far as cleansing some of their stories in 2003 from its website (Dore, 2016). While fingers were pointed at Tony Blair, many MPs supported him and the majority of the mainstream British media lied to the British people. It wasn't just Blair who was a 'weapon of Mass Deception' as *The Sun* cried after Chilcot, and neither was this 'Blair's private war' as was suggested by the headline in *The Times*. In fact, all of Murdoch's titles, in Britain and elsewhere, without any exception, were cheerleaders for the invasion of Iraq. Rupert Murdoch left no doubt as to why he was supporting the invasion: 'The greatest thing to come out of this for the world economy... would be $20 a barrel for oil. That's bigger than any tax cut in any country' (Day, 2003).

Other newspapers didn't fare much better and much of the coverage of the build-up to the invasion and its aftermath by broadcasters was also dismal. The BBC ended up paying a huge price for daring to question some of the lies of the British government and after that began to toe the line. In one infamous moment from 9 April 2003, the day of 'victory' in Iraq, Andrew Marr, the BBC's political editor at the time, standing outside No. 10 Downing Street, glowingly reported that Tony Blair had shown he was not somebody 'who is drifted by public opinion, or focus groups or opinion polls'. He continued that 'it would be entirely ungracious even for his critics not to acknowledge that tonight he stands as a larger man and a stronger prime minster as a result' (Edwards and Cromwell, 2003). It is perhaps legitimate to ask how Andrew Marr feels now about his own dismissal of public opinion, opinion polls and the outcome of the war.

Millions of people knew at the time that Tony Blair, the majority of British MPs and sections of the media were lying to the public and indifferent to the overwhelming opposition to the war. Even after publication of the Chilcot report, the majority of those who supported the war or had a key role to play refused to back down. Blair himself remains unrepentant, David Cameron failed to condemn the invasion or to apologise to the British people, while Paul Bremer is still defending his record as the first governor of a 'liberated' Iraq. What about those editors, reporters and columnists who not only failed to investigate the lies about weapons of mass destruction but spread them? Nothing suggests, so far, that any lesson has been learned, least of all by British media. This is why any discussion about the crisis of legitimacy and democracy cannot ignore the devastating consequences of imperial aggression for democracy.

The main issue, as far as the invasion of Iraq is concerned, has to be about a very blatant attempt at the manipulation of facts and opinions and the complicity of a large sections of the British media in the build-up to the Iraq war. How did that happen? In an early critical reflection on media bias, Peter Golding and Philip Elliot (1979) assessed some of the suggested reforms for news broadcasts. These included lengthening broadcast news bulletins in order to overcome the stringent selection procedures and offer more coherent and comprehensive stories, introducing more background information and in-depth analysis, and training more specialist journalists who are more academically informed and oriented. In 2003, technically speaking, none of these limitations existed. Dedicated 24-hour news channels were in place with hours and hours of available slots for background information, detailed analysis, expert opinions and round-the-clock updates. The internet also had an additional and important platform for broadcasters to publish lengthy articles and opinions, providing links to similar stories or backgrounds and so on. The same technology has also taken away many of the earlier limits on the press. They could compete with broadcasters to provide up-to-date and live coverage, and offer much more than what the physically and technically limited print newspaper could offer (Sparks, 2000).

The press in particular has also at its service large numbers of commentators and analysts who can supposedly go beyond the mere act of reporting and offer more contextual and informed pieces to readers. So let us repeat the question again. How did such big lies – for example, the non-existence of weapons of mass destruction and the alleged ability of Iraq to strike Western nations in 45 minutes – get repeated by a large section of the British media? How was it possible to circulate what was effectively pro-war propaganda in a democracy? Of course we should not ignore the honourable sections of the media that challenged those lies. We also know that there was a significant challenge to Bush and Blair's false narrative by the anti-war movement. But that is precisely part of what we have referred to as a 'democratic paradox': what we witnessed in 2003 was the clash of forms of free expression with forms of propaganda that we usually associate with undemocratic states.

A different element of this 'democratic paradox' is directly related to the media. It is certainly true that in the clash between free expression and propaganda, a significant section of the British media sided against democracy. Newspaper columns, broadcast news, current affairs programmes and online comment were filled with reports by embedded journalists and pure propaganda by embedded intellectuals that simply repeated lies and distortions (Miller, 2003). The target of these lies was the British public, while the anti-war movement was either ignored, ridiculed or demonised. The fact is that liberal societies spawn liberal media that are supposed to investigate and hold power to account. However, as the case of war underlines more sharply than other cases, there are competing priorities, values and allegiances that constrain and prevent any scrutiny outside of the frame set by politicians, despite their putative independence. Most of the 'liberal media', as distinct from media in authoritarian states, are indeed formally independent from government and fiercely resistant to government control. However, what the invasion of Iraq proved beyond doubt is that media do not need to be owned and controlled by the state in order to submit to and repeat the lies of government. This paradox is not novel either.

Chilcot remained committed to the imperial sense of entitlement to wage war on 'inferior' races and nations as long as backing is received from the United Nations Security Council or committed without major national or international opposition. Perhaps it would have been naïve to expect anything else from an inquiry set up by Gordon Brown, a prime minister who, when he was chancellor, actually budgeted for the aggression, and who was the very same person who in 2005 stressed that 'the days of Britain having to apologise for our history are over'. Isolating the case of Iraq from previous colonial aggressions as well as post Iraq (Libya and Syria in particular) only serves to erase much longer colonial histories. Chilcot was an exercise and an opportunity for that history to be protected by offering a 'possibility' of a small sacrifice – the reputation of Tony Blair. In celebrating Chilcot, the British media tried to redeem itself without admitting to the shameful part they played and without apologising to the British people, to the families of fallen British soldiers, or to the people of Iraq. In 2003 the overwhelming majority of a liberal media system remained close to political power and demonised, undermined, ridiculed and attacked critical voices. They continue to do so.

CONCLUSION: FOCUSING ON WARS WAGED IN THE NAME OF DEMOCRACY

Assessment of different stages of political communication in democracies after WW2 would be incomplete without a more coherent and historical focus on the wars that have been waged by democracies and in the name of democracy. How can we defend a noble concept if the reality undermines it? To what extent does mimicking the repressive policies of authoritarian regimes in banning protests, in monitoring citizens (suspects or otherwise) and taking away their most basic rights under the banner of security stand equal to what Hollande refers to as 'culture, creation, pluralism and democracy'? Equally there can be no reconsidering, rethinking, revisiting or reconceptualising the relationship between media and democracy if we neglect to highlight the imperial dimensions of modern liberal democracies and to minimise the suffering of their domestic and international victims. In his thesis on historical materialism, Walter Benjamin offered a vision of history as a permanent struggle between the oppressed and the oppressors. But he was quick to point out the weight of history on the present generation, for there will be no redemption if we do not take seriously the claims and sufferings of the victims of history: 'There is a secret agreement between past generations and the present one. Our coming was expected on earth. Like every generation that preceded us, we have been endowed with a weak Messianic power, a power to which the past has a claim. That claim cannot be settled cheaply' (1987: 254). We will discuss the importance of committing to this in Chapter 8.

7

POLITICAL COMMUNICATIONS, CIVIL SOCIETY AND THE COMMONS

INTRODUCTION

So far, this book has been at pains to stress the multiple ways that material factors of politics and economics structure our lives as part of the political communications nexus – a nexus that is intricately woven into existing power structures in ways that are often hidden from plain sight and reach into and extend beyond communicative systems. Our contention is that starting (and ending) with media and communications systems as our objects of analysis limits our critical analytical capacities. And if we really want to understand how these systems function and therefore what is required to change them, then we need to look much more broadly at structural inequalities and political (re)alignments that are embroiled in the hegemonic perpetuation of institutionalised capitalism.

Chapter 4 discussed how elite power works behind our backs and out of view, and is largely unaffected by major forms of protest such as the Occupy, Black Lives Matter or #MeToo movements. At best these movements have brought to the fore a politics of recognition that has forced the enduring inequalities and oppressions of class, race and gender into view. At worst these movements offer up an illusion of democracy – look at how liberal our societies are to allow and engage with such large-scale political remonstrations. As political protests grow around the world, from pro-democracy protests in Hong Kong to climate change strikes in many nations, so global inequalities between the rich and the poor, the powerful and the powerless increase and environmental degradation continues apace. But Chapter 1 also situated our approach within a framework of critical theory that is emancipatory. As depressing as much of this book may be, we also want to argue that just as political struggles over the reproduction of everyday social relations interact with and are shaped by technologies and systems of communication (as part of institutionalised capitalism), they are not subsumed by them. Political imaginaries are relational. They are bound up in the matrices of lived existence that are social as well as structural, that determine what is, what fails, and what might be. This chapter is concerned with what might be.

Here we turn to the relationship between the social and the political economic as experienced in civil society and ask: how does civil society react when a specific historical conjuncture experienced as economic, political, social and ecological crisis, as outlined in the preceding chapters, looms ominously over us? How can critical political communications help people to respond? Political communications is far more than the formal structures of government, politicians, media producers and journalists – it is also about the public; yet publics are frequently overlooked. And just as we have argued in previous chapters that understanding how a neoliberal hegemony is sustained requires an analytical gaze that goes beyond media and communications technologies and systems, so this chapter argues that discovering a counter-hegemony also requires looking beyond forms of digital activism or focusing on mediated modes of opposition. Anti-neoliberal projects often have little or no trust in elite politics, and existing forms of (neo)liberal democracy reject mainstream mediations as part of the elite (see Chapter 4) or are severely marginalised and excluded from the public sphere and so have chosen to operate outside of it. In searching out alternatives we must then acknowledge that if as media theorists we wish to think seriously about the global problems of inequality, poverty and ecological crisis, then we need to break free of our disciplinary silos. To understand the role of media and communications in maintaining hegemonic rationalities and enabling counter hegemonies to emerge, we need to take account of the ways in which wider social, political and economic contexts impact on people's ability to participate and on their power to influence the wider determinants of poverty and disadvantage that affect their lives. Then we can begin the difficult job of conceiving a politics of hope.

POLITICAL COMMUNICATIONS AS POLITICS, POLICIES AND POLITY

Political science makes a well-known distinction between politics, policies and polity. Throughout this book we have argued that in order to understand contemporary political society and its relationship to the media we also need to distinguish between all three. For example, take the issue of austerity – at once a political response to the financial crash that put into play particular *policies* to deliver a form of polity. Policymakers accepting of a certain market economics reduce demand and cut public spending. Once they deem that the economy is under control, then stimulus measures are introduced. But this is also a form of neoliberal *politics* oriented towards reorganising the balance of forces in favour of capital. So in the UK, citizens were told that national debt was such that we could no longer afford key aspects of the welfare state. Welfare spending on social benefits, the health service and education was cut, while at the same time corporation tax was reduced in the name of boosting the economy. The consequences of austerity are then blamed on the poor: salaries are diminishing because migrants are taking our jobs; poverty is increasing because the poor are feckless scroungers, etc. These are all forms of discourse that are heavily racialised, heteropatriarchal and hinged on class: austerity has a disproportionate impact on black and minority ethnic households, women and those on low incomes because these groups tend to rely more on public services and benefits to survive. This has a cumulative effect – consolidating the politics and the policies that are inconsistent with the ideal of liberal democracy – that leads to a neoliberal *polity*.

Seen as a combination of politics, policies and polity, the whole notion of political communications is construed as a socially and historically constructed complex of institutional constraints and opportunities, expectations, rights, resources and capacities – unequally distributed in terms of power, status, life chances, action dispositions, identities and ways of life. So austerity is both a policy that increases inequality, politics that justifies that inequality through an economic programme of fiscal management and a polity – a site of ideological and discursive struggle. Capitalism itself is also a site of both political economy and culture supported by socially generated and politically sustained values that provide the architectural design and scaffolding for capitalism as a *way of life* – which together form a hegemonic bloc. This brings to the fore the cultural-symbolic dimension of the persistent structural inequalities of economic life that is crucial to take account of in any calculation of the possibilities for social and political transformation. From this approach, hegemony is expressed as 'the political, moral, cultural and intellectual authority of a given worldview – and with the capacity of that worldview to embody itself in a durable and powerful alliance of social forces and social classes' (Fraser, 2019: 30). So we can take a political economic perspective that is also a social constructivist perspective – something approximating a critical cultural political economy.

As Fraser (2019: 37) argues:

> ... the present form of capitalism [is] globalizing, neoliberal, financialized. Like every form of capitalism, this one is no mere economic system but something larger: an institutionalized social order. As such, it encompasses a set of noneconomic background conditions that are indispensable to a capitalist economy: for example, unwaged activities of social reproduction, which assure the supply of wage labor for economic production; an organized apparatus of public power (law, police, regulatory agencies, and steering capacities) that supplies the order, predictability, and infrastructure necessary for sustained accumulation; and finally, a relatively sustainable organization of our metabolic interaction with the rest of nature, one that ensures essential supplies of energy and raw materials for commodity production, not to mention a habitable planet that can support life.

In austerity and its entanglement with neoliberalism we see the rolling back of welfare, new forms of surveillance, the further deregulation of corporate enterprise, further liberalisation of international trade sustained by mediated narratives that are at once individualising and disconnected from global capital. Each of these elements of politics, policies and polity must be taken into account when considering how counter hegemonies may or may not emerge. Streeck (2016: 212) in *How will Capitalism End?* notes that:

> A rising share of goods that make today's capitalist economies grow would not sell if people dreamed other dreams than they do – which makes understanding, developing and controlling their dreams a fundamental concern of political economy in advanced capitalist society.

So when we seek out what these other dreams might be, we cannot simply point them out enthusiastically and cheer from the sidelines, relieved that they exist at all. Rather, we need a critique that begins with the identification of specific discourses (such as the demonisation of the poor, working class, black people, Muslim people, trans people, etc.) and discursive practices (that may exclude, marginalise and frame those with less power) that support particular policies and politics (of a neo-liberal order). This must then include an analysis of ideology and domination that accounts for the polity our counter-imaginaries exist within. We need to interrogate the factors and actors that through diverse mechanisms of variation, selection and retention (such as a continued focus on an individualised agency or technological solutionism) can also serve to reproduce these ideological effects and patterns of domination, even while they are proposing and acting upon emancipatory projects (see Chapter 4). In other words, acknowledging fully that structuring forces impinge on both the practice and realisation of our emancipatory political imaginations. And they do so differentially as capitalism feeds off the precarious and exploitable lives of the marginalised and the poor.

Counter-hegemonies must also identify a left politics adequate to counter the material inequalities and structural grievances of global financial capitalism that requires access to and a redistribution of wealth. It necessitates the protection of democracy from the footloose logic of the market or, at the very least, democratically harnessing the dynamics of the international capitalist market to the needs and interests of the majority of citizens in any given political community. It requires an understanding of who is included and excluded in what spaces and who needs to be defended – this is part of what the preceding chapters of this book have attempted to do.

This is not disconnected from political communications, but rather, it is at its very heart. As Fraser (2019: 25–26) argues, political transformation requires a break away from neoliberal economics:

> Resolving the objective crisis requires a major structural transformation of financialized capitalism: a new way of relating economy to polity, production to reproduction, human society to nonhuman nature. Neoliberalism in any guise is not the solution but the problem … we must break definitively both with neoliberal economics and with the various politics of recognition that have lately supported it—casting off not just exclusionary ethnonationalism but also liberal-meritocratic individualism. Only by joining a robustly egalitarian politics of distribution to a substantively inclusive, class-sensitive politics of recognition can we build a counterhegemonic bloc capable of leading us beyond the current crisis to a better world.

We need another politics.

REDISCOVERING ANOTHER POLITICS: THE HOPE OF THE COMMONS

Rediscovering another politics speaks to the need to identify a political vision that is consistent with and responds to the political economic critique forwarded in this book. It would be too easy to give in to the notion that utopian thought has shuddered to a halt. With the fall of the Berlin Wall and the end of the Cold War, the socialist project was left unhinged. In the field of media and communications (as in many others) we often found ourselves flailing around in postmodernism with the sense of history endlessly repeating itself. Or else media theorists seemed to be so overcome by the sheer excitement unleashed through the possibilities of new technology that they forgot to address the complexity of the contemporary conditions of global capitalism that increasingly began to appear impervious to change as 'the individualizing logic of contemporary consumer culture … and the mechanics of neo-liberalism [that] work[ed] to inhibit the emergence of any political collectivity whatsoever' (Gilbert, 2014: 22, 28).

But as noted in Chapter 1, we must also never forget that, at a time when established political norms are increasingly fragile, there are huge opportunities for a renewal of politics itself. As the relationship between capitalism and liberal democracy continues to unravel, it exposes some of the problems further still. Just as we argued above for the necessity of thinking through policy, politics and the polity together to understand the present, so we also need to combine social, political and economic analysis to reimagine the future. As discussed in this book, corporate and financial elites have substantially captured the machinery of the state and effectively neutralised the notionally centre-left party as a source of systemic reform. Where democratic government, trade unions and other citizen organisations were once thought of as countervailing forces against private corporate power, this falls short when corporate power also dominates the state (Kuttner, 2018).

Political parties have become captured by elites and are seen by the public as increasingly irrelevant (Chapter 5). The primary purpose of electoral democracies has become to gain and hold on to power rather than meet the social needs of the electorate. The conceitedness of unitary party competitiveness is then seen as entirely self-serving and disconnected from the social and political desires of voters. As inequality increases, so this exposes (endlessly) the gaps between election promises and what happens in office. It also illuminates the gaping divide between the minority of those who hold political office or circulate around the corridors of power and the majority of the population.

Rediscovering another politics means doing politics (and political communications) differently. The political fixation with economic growth at all costs was summed up in the phrase 'It's the economy, stupid', coined by campaign strategist James Carville during Bill Clinton's 1992 presidential campaign. The focus on economic growth has been the measure for success and the focus for countless election campaigns instilling short-term economic measures for superficial short-won gains. Recently, Blanchflower (2019) has argued that governments have lost sight of their obligation to act on behalf of citizens and have allowed them to become subservient to economic forces. The reach and power of a neoliberal economic paradigm is extensive but is finally being unhinged. In the UK, the glaring contradiction between the extensive cuts to public services enacted in the name of austerity to bring down national debt and get the economy under control, and the billions now being spent on leaving the European Union with apparently no adverse economic consequences at all, is startling. And everywhere, the stark contradiction of growing inequalities between rich and poor while striving for economic growth against all odds, with dire consequences for the planet and its inhabitants, is finally being understood.

Oxfam have been at the forefront of raising awareness around levels of poverty and inequality both within and between nations (Oxfam, 2019). In 2012 they also launched a report by Kate Raworth on 'Doughnut Economics': a model based on Earth-system science that consists of two concentric rings – the social foundation (the inner circle) and the ecological ceiling (the outer circle) that together encompass human wellbeing. If the boundaries of the inner circle (the social foundation) are not met then we find hunger, ill-health, illiteracy, etc; if the boundaries of the outer circle (the ecological ceiling) are exceeded then we get climate change, ocean acidification and loss of biodiversity – both of which reflect deep inequalities of income and wealth, of gender and race, of exposure to risk and of political power. The area between the outer and inner rings represents a safe and just space within which to exist. The Doughnut model (Raworth, 2017) highlights the dependence of human wellbeing on planetary health, and adeptly puts the case for economic theory and policymaking to shift away from an obsession with economic growth and capital accumulation to human nurturing and regeneration by design, but it does not in itself take us beyond capitalism.

We have also seen the concept of the commons experiencing a revival as a perspective set in stark contrast to and in criticism of the privatisation, deregulation and expropriation of neoliberalism (Broumas, 2017; Hardt and Negri, 2011; Hess and Ostrom, 2003, 2007; Ostrom, 1990) with a focus on a more equitable, just and eco-logically sustainable society. Eleanor Ostrom's (1990) seminal work on the commons outlined how commons resources (the air we breath, the water we drink, the public services we share) can be inclusively managed through decentralised and participa-tory democratic institutions to prevent or limit corporate or state exploitation. How-ever, as De Peuter and Dyer-Witheford point out,

> … [the] term commons has come to cover a proliferation of proposals, some highly radical, but also some reformist, and others even poten-tially reactionary. As George Caffentzis points out, neoliberal capital, confronting the debacle of free-market policies, is turning to 'Plan B': limited versions of commons – be it carbon trading models, community development schemes, biotechnology research, and open source prac-tices – are introduced as subordinate aspects of a capitalist economy. Here voluntary cooperation does not so much subvert capital as subsi-dize it. (2010: 31)

Clearly, not all versions of the commons or alternative economic models would fit with the critical political economic critique put forward in the pages of this book. Indeed some versions would be very happy in a reformed liberal democratic framework working with capital and the state to limit exploitation by capital and democratically harness resources for the public good – in other words, welfare/social democratic cap-italism (where both state and capital still exert considerable power). Broumas (2017) makes a distinction between liberal democratic and critical theories of the commons, with the former focusing on individual freedom in tandem with market growth and the latter positioning the commons as sites of social struggle in conflict with capitalist logics. Any alternative economics or concept of the commons must then come with a clearly defined political project. As argued in Chapter 1, clarity over the politics of any form of critical analysis is vital if we are to fully interrogate how we got ourselves into this mess, what is required to get us out of it, and what we think a better future might look like. A *politics of the commons* responsive to the critique put forward here requires public forms of ownership and social control of finance – the commons as an alternative to capitalism rather than the commons as a substitute for the welfare state (Broumas, 2017). A politics of the commons requires the displacing of a fixation on economic growth to a focus on meeting social need and creating the conditions where we can all live together better – more equitably, more democratically, more inclusively, more sustainably. This is part of what Birkinbine (2018: 291) refers to as 'subversive commoning' which insists on the necessity of a structural critique of capitalism as its premise.

RESOCIALISING THE POLITICAL

A critical politics of the commons is also part of what Fenton (2016) has called 'resocialising the political'. As politics has become so disconnected from and distrusted by the majority of people, it needs desperately to reconnect with the social – to rediscover forms of *substantive relationality*. A process of resocialising the political involves focusing on mutual recognition, dialogue and shared radical praxis. Relationality brings to the fore the ordinary everyday experience of politics and culture – it is part of what creates meaning through conversation and collaboration. It is by definition participatory and constitutive of our knowledge and understanding of places, situations and circumstances. Relationality matters politically – for understanding each other's social needs, for building solidarity, and for seeking the means to non-domination. But this is not a politics with a thin sociality lived out in fleeting and embittered exchanges online. Rather, it is politics built on an embodied and democratic social practice consciously designed to be inclusive, collective and co-operative.

Across the Western world a rise in loneliness is pervasive, occurring across all ages and socio-economic groups with Britain being named the loneliness capital of Europe (Jo Cox Commission on Loneliness, 2017; Office for National Statistics, 2018). Loneliness is defined as perceived social isolation and the lack of supportive social relationships. It has been found to contribute to multiple psychological and physiological health problems. Amongst older people it is associated with cardiovascular disease and stroke, increases in blood pressure, cognitive impairments and physical decline. Amongst young people it is associated with mental health problems, employment prospects and bullying. Meaningful social connection is vital to human development, health and survival. In recognition of the problem, in 2018 the UK government increased the remit of the Minister for Sport and Civil Society to include loneliness and launched a loneliness strategy. The minister has acknowledged that cuts to local authorities under austerity policies have impacted upon the very social institutions and community spaces where people used to come together – libraries, youth clubs and community centres – contributing further to experiences of loneliness. Extensive social media use has also been linked to feelings of social isolation, with relentless online connection (endlessly feeding data required for better targeted advertising) leading to new forms of solitude (Turkle, 2011). In other words, our social lives and selves are configured in multiple ways that are both political and economic.

And while digital activism has grown and it is easier than ever before to protest, so it is also ever easier to ignore. Online protest may spread awareness of social and political issues, enable the mobilisation of huge numbers of people in a matter of seconds and offer quick click responses for those who want to be politically involved, but on its own it is unlikely to fix society's structural problems. Social media has undoubtedly changed contemporary forms of sociality and political activism. But increasing doubts are being raised as to whether it can fulfil the democratic and social potential once accredited to it (e.g. Andrejevic, 2014; Curran et al., 2016). Growing anxiety is being expressed in relation to echo chambers, online influencers, covert advertising, bots and the role algorithms play in our daily decisionmaking as well as in our electoral and democratic processes (Hintz et al., 2019).

Although offline activism is often a desired feature of digital mobilisation, frequently it remains the domain of a lone individual connected to like-minded others but isolated from human contact. In one study in the UK on the future of civil society (CSF, 2018), participants spoke of a real need for qualitative social interactions, the importance of meeting people in person, discussing issues at length and seeking understanding over differences, so they could develop meaningful relationships. Spaces for political engagement may have expanded in a digital mediascape, but our orientation towards them is changing too. People are recognising the need for a shift away from atomised expressions of social activism, and are trying to search out new political projects that offer hope and inspiration for a different way of living and better ways of doing democracy involving deeper forms of sociality.

Across the globe different relationships of mutuality and democracy are emerging, such as co-operative forms of ownership, collaborative partnerships and alliances of workers and communities seeking to meet social need, and create new more democratic forms of existing: from the rebel cities of Barcelona, Madrid, Naples and Valencia to the community wealth-building approach adopted by Preston in the UK and Cleveland, Ohio in the USA (En Comu, 2019; Kelly and Howard, 2019). People are beginning to think through notions of co-production, co-ownership and co-operative working in an attempt to shift power and ownership from the few to the many. These constitute alternative bids for political meaning and value and swimming against the rip-tide of global capitalism often seek to discover a politics in common – the ability and will of 'the people' to come together, organise and construct a collective politics against an individualist, discriminatory and corporate agenda.

To understand how a politics in common can emerge we also need to better understand differential social and political histories and fault lines. We too often miss noticing how differently situated agents understand themselves and what spurs them to act politically. Stoetzler and Yuval-Davis (2002) argue that our ability to creatively reimagine our worlds is always situated by experiences of oppression, exploitation, embodied privilege or abjection, and how this shapes notions of what it is possible to change and what injustice is. This points to the need to creatively reimagine ways in which we can detach production from domination and enhance collective autonomy. Haiven and Khasnabish (2014: 242) argue that 'movements that fail to engage oppression critically and systematically (and its connections to exploitation and economic power) not only fail to challenge the dominant order effectively, they reproduce it'. As Lipman (2020) states, we must recognise the 'history of colonialism and imperialism and the imbrication of white supremacy and heteropatriarchy in the logics of neo-liberal capitalism' in order to challenge it. A combined social, political and economic analysis forces us to recognise that race and class need to be tackled together as neither can be overcome while the other flourishes (Fraser, 2019).

NORMATIVE CRITERIA FOR HOPE

Once we appreciate this, then how can we begin to mark out what this may look like? Fraser (Fraser and Jaeggi, 2018: 178) offers a good starting point with three normative criteria for evaluating emancipatory possibilities:

1. Non-domination – alternatives must not institutionalise the subordination of a group or groups of social actors.
2. Functional sustainability – any proposal must be sustainable over time.
3. Democracy – any proposal must be able to be institutionalised in such a way that participants are able to reflect on it, question it, decide whether it is working for them and change it if necessary.

Fraser notes that to be acceptable, a proposed structural transformation must satisfy all three criteria. Structural change must also cSonfront power with counter-power and include both large-scale forms of governance and localised forms of production and collective management. While it is hard to argue against these criteria, an insistence on non-domination and democratic practices does not necessarily seek to actively address the histories of oppression, racism and violation referred to in Chapter 1. It may be better therefore to think through these criteria expressed in slightly different terms:

1. Strong egalitarianism is vital. This speaks to Fraser's intervention on the importance of 'non-domination' but takes it further, suggesting the necessity for a redress of power imbalances in full recognition of the structural conditions of class, racial and heteropatriarchal domination in order for democratic practices to become possible. This is a form of Left politics that recognises structural differentiation but also appreciates that class and status differentials share injustices based on financialised capitalism.

A strong egalitarianism is a response to the argument put forward in this book that democracy and inequality are diametrically opposed. You cannot have one while you have the other; the more inequality you have, the more power differentials are at play and the less democracy is able to function. According to Castoriadis (1980), the essential political issue to be debated by society is the balance between liberty and equality, which he sees as the defining difference between socialism and capitalism. Put simply, capitalism values liberty through the free market, and socialism values equality through the redistribution of resources. Castoriadis argues that society makes the two concepts exclusionary when in fact they are complementary, and crucially so for a just and democratic society to exist. The first question of liberty is the equality of all in the participation of power. This is part of what Brown (2015) infers when she explains how capitalism presents the inherent contradiction of the two concepts because it assumes that total equality and liberty are impossible together. And so the exploitation of the poor by the rich, of the colonised by the colonisers, is legitimised as the only possible system. If however we take the view that democracy is impossible unless everyone has the ability to change the social and political system of which they are a part, then democracy is impossible without equality.

McChesney points out that capitalism and democracy vie for opposite conclusions – one creates massive inequality and the other is premised upon political equality: 'in conditions of extreme economic inequality [democracy] is effectively impossible' (2012: 1). The rising inequality that we are now experiencing in many parts of the world is not inevitable – government policies can reduce it. Inequality fell in most countries from the 1940s through to the 1970s. The inequality we see today is largely due to policy changes since the 1980s with President Reagan and Prime Minister Thatcher leading the way. In both the US and the UK, from 1980 to 2016, the share of total income going to the top 1% has more than doubled. After allowing for inflation, the earnings of the bottom 90% in the US and UK have barely risen at all over the past twenty-five years. And as we point out in Chapter 4, forty years ago a US CEO earned on average about 38 times as much as the average worker; by 2012 the average CEO earned about 354 times as much (Sabbadish and Mishel, 2013). Furthermore, although most wealthy countries have been subject to broadly similar economic forces, the experiences of inequality have differed within them, with the US and the UK experiencing a large increase in inequality and Canada, France and Japan much smaller increases. Patterns of economic inequality also impact on certain types of people more. The Institute for Public Policy Research (IPPR, 2018) commission on economic justice reveals how the financial health of the UK is divided along lines of income, geography, gender, ethnicity and age.

Of course, more economic equality in a country does not necessarily make it more democratic or less oppressive. Egalitarianism is about far more than economics. As Fenton (2016) argues, in order to extend the possibilities for progressive social change we must interrogate the relationship between politics and power and test power against equality. We also need to understand what powerlessness feels like, and this crucially means understanding the relationship between capitalism and *all* forms of oppression. Fraser (2019) talks about this as being the crucial relationship between a politics of recognition and a politics of (re)distribution that is vital in the rediscovery of a left politics:

> If the left hopes to revive the idea of the working class as the leading force within a new counterhegemonic bloc, we will have to envision that class in a new way—intersectionally, if you will—as not restricted to the white, straight, male, majority-ethnicity, manufacturing and mining workers, but as encompassing all of these other occupations—paid and unpaid—and as massively encompassing immigrants, women and people of color. (2019: 39)

This will necessarily involve an acknowledgement of the residual power of white, heteronormative and male entitlement. While non-domination offers an extension of social power, strong egalitarianism also requires the elimination of the entrenched political and economic power of the capitalist class.

What might this mean for our media and communications systems? Strong egalitarianism is as relevant for the media industries as it is for all other institutions and organisations. Egalitarianism refers to both external structural factors relating to the broader environment that media organisations function within and to internal structural factors relating to the workforce and working practices of the organisations themselves. The principle of egalitarianism clearly runs counter to the concentration of media ownership endemic across the globe, with the tech giants now the largest oligopolies the world has ever seen. Mergers, takeovers and consolidations of media industries accumulate great wealth and great power in ever fewer hands. Limiting concentration of media ownership is vital but only takes us so far. It may relax the stranglehold of power that certain media corporations exert, but it does not necessarily alter the neo-liberal nature of the system they operate within. So it is also crucial to enable, support and sustain forms of media ownership that are not for profit and fully independent of commercial pressures and government preferences, are organised co-operatively and democratically, and are responsive to the needs of the communities that they serve rather than at the behest of the market. Co-operative ownership has been argued to increase employment stability and increase productivity levels by discouraging an approach based on short-termism for shareholder return and the use of low-wage labour (Davies et al., 2014).

Co-operative ownership also makes firms more democratic and so responds to the internal requirements for more egalitarian employment and working practices. Of course, external and internal structural factors are linked and must be addressed in tandem. As noted in Chapter 2, mainstream media industries are largely bastions of privilege for the political and economic elite and operate with fierce hierarchies resistant to change. Public service media such as the BBC are often seen as the best redress for a contemporary journalism marked by hyperpartisanship and hypercommercialism, with the ability to offer journalism independent of the state or market, inclusive of diverse voices and with space for more critical coverage (Freedman, 2018). But Freedman (2018: 206) also argues that 'the BBC is a compromised version of a potentially noble ideal: far too implicated in and attached to existing elite networks of power to be able to offer an effective challenge to them'. Mills (2016) argues that despites its claims to be impartial and independent, the BBC has always sided with the elite and been in thrall to those in power. Over the last three decades, its independence has been steadily eroded and its programme-making increasingly commercialised. Broadcasting in the UK was originally regulated according to public service principles. That model has been increasingly marginalised as the BBC has become more and more subject to a market-based regulation. Currently, BBC activities have to be balanced with consideration for competition through 'public value' tests. They are also subjected to 'market impact assessments' by Ofcom, an independent communications regulator that has been criticised for privileging consumer interests over those of citizens. Severe funding cuts, particularly in recent years, have also caused the BBC's editorial culture to become more conservative and risk-averse. Mills and the Media Reform Coalition (2019) argue that adequate, secure public funding that is independent of governmental control is the pathway to real political independence and insulation from the market-based approach that has eroded the BBC's public service ethos. Rather than returning to the top-down, statist model on which it was founded, to fulfil its public service promise the BBC must become a modern, democratised public platform and network, fully representative of its audiences and completely independent. It is also alarmingly lacking in the diversity of its programming and its workforce. And an increasingly casualised workforce also impacts disproportionately on those from lower income families, women, minority groups, and those with disabilities.

Egalitarianism also relates to the public and to the balance of power that different publics may have in relation to various media industries. This can be summed up in approaches that stress either consumer rights (that focus on the individual and things such as privacy and complaints systems) or the rights of citizens (that stress the democratic requirements of meeting the information and communication needs of communities). This is evident in a discussion of what should be done about the phenomenal power over our data now exerted by the big tech companies. Prainsack (2019) argues that the response to big data society largely falls into two camps: those who want individual citizens to have more control over their own data, including the granting of individual property rights to personal data or implementing means of informing and consenting data subjects (Kaye et al., 2015) such as the European Union General Data Protection Regulation (GDPR); and those who advocate a collective control approach through the creation of digital data and information commons with an emphasis on collective ownership and control (Birkinbine, 2018; De Peuter and Dyer-Witherford, 2010; Hess, 2008). The hope in the latter is that the power dynamics between data givers and data profiteers will be equalised. However, as Priansack (2019: 3) points out, such approaches rarely tackle the 'categories, practices and effects of exclusion' – whether this refers to exclusion from data and information entering a digital commons, using data in the digital commons, benefitting from the digital commons or participating in the governance of the digital commons. Exclusivity and exclusions, as we saw in Chapter 2, run counter to egalitarianism and equality.

If the current configuration of neoliberalism is exacerbated by wealth inequality, is more corporate, more capitalist, built on and enhancing colonising and patriarchal interests, then a new politics is not simply about the types of political parties we elect to power and an extension of social democratic norms. A new politics must disrupt the day-to-day oppressions and injustices on which the current neo-liberal order depends; to build economic power that is owned and governed by those whose live its effects; to re-appropriate the spaces we inhabit for the social good of all and in particular for those who are currently exploited and excluded (Kelly and Howard, 2019). What we learn from experiments with different ways of doing politics are early insights into the possibilities for a different, more equal, more just and more sustainable society. Hence, insisting on the criteria of egalitarianism in relation to our media systems needs to occur alongside the same principles applied to the wider social order of institutionalised capitalism, and concurrently with the next criteria of radical substantive democracy to develop different relationships of mutuality and different ways of doing democracy.

2. Radical substantive democracy is imperative – people should be able to meaningfully participate in decisions over their lives through co-ownership and contribute to its sustenance through co-production and co-determination: democracy as a way of life not a ballot box.

In practice this will also involve a strong localism and community-managed resources like water and land run sustainably and equitably with mechanisms to progress equality and prevent anyone taking unfair advantage. This fits most comfortably with the notion of 'subversive commoning' (Birkinbine, 2018) outlined above. Within a critical theoretical approach, the commons are viewed as shared resources that are co-owned and/or co-governed by the users and communities according to their own rules and norms. This relates to physical spaces that are shared or pooled, the co-production of the resource, the means of maintaining that resource, as well as the mode of governance – how decisions are made collaboratively through collective problem solving to distribute and use the resource. The commons are intended as social systems that do not systematically separate people from their means of livelihood. They are aimed at strengthening the collective solidarity of workers and offering mutual life support to all inhabitants. They are by definition sustainable. Where capitalism revolves around competitiveness and extractive relations and practices to nature and people, a critical approach to the commons requires a generative economy to ensure the sustainability of people and planet, working towards the accumulation of the commons rather than the accumulation of capital (Ostrom, 1990). As such, this version of the commons aims to shift the form of private ownership of the means of production from a global capitalist class to the inhabitants of a given space and to change the form of power that controls economic activity.

A critical approach to the commons fits with the notion of radical substantive democracy emergent in citizen/public assemblies that inform local council decisions from Porto Alegre's participatory budgeting in the 1990s to Saillans in France and

Barcelona in Spain in more recent times. An approach that embraces these ideals is found in the concept of 'municipalism'. Barcelona city council, now governed by the citizen platform En Comu, is one of the most prominent examples of the new municipalist movement and emerged out of the recent history of the local 15M protest movement in 2011 and the anti-eviction movements across Spain. In 2015, housing rights activist Ada Colau was elected mayor of Barcelona, winning re-election in 2019 on a manifesto pledging to tackle corruption and radicalise democracy (Scharenberg, 2020). En Comu refers to 'the commons' and seeks to work with civil society actors and existing political parties to create new platforms that foster greater participation in governance and greater control over one's own forms of production (including the data we produce). In 2019, Barcelona En Comu published the book *Fearless Cities: A Guide to the Global Municipalist Movement*, which outlines 50 examples of cities in 19 countries across all continents involved in transformative local practices as part of an internationalist municipalist movement. From fighting municipal debt and poverty in Valparaiso, Chile, to tackling poor air quality and waste management in Beirut, Lebanon; from developing new institutional processes for public partnerships and experimental forms of governance to allow citizens and others to co-design processes for the city of Bologna, to the city of Naples enabling citizen-based claims on public spaces – there are multiple attempts to reinvent democratic practices from the ground up bringing activists, citizens and politicians together for a transformative politics that enables co-ownership, co-production and co-determination. Democracy is conceptualised and practised in these cases as the sharing of rule and the constant re-creation of new publics.

The question then arises, how can diverse publics with divergent views achieve sufficient consensus so that citizen participation can be translated into institutional and social transformation? How is it possible to achieve the real participation of all publics as equals? Broad participation requires the defence of the economic interests of the weakest, a renewed administrative effectiveness grounded in a new social pact and in new constitutions that give rise to new structures within a transformed state. For a renewed radical substantive democracy to work, its institutional translation must not end in institutional power for itself, rather it must create the means whereby the potential for everyone to share in power is realised. Democracy cannot work for some and not for others. Drawing on De Angelis (2017), Birkinbine (2018) argues that emergent alternative value systems, like the commons that offer a critique of and a response to the exploitations of capitalism, can bring about a change in social relations over time through a focus on and reproduction of mutuality, care, trust and conviviality. The focus on radically democratic social relations can then help realise a socialist project with institutional translations. But this will only be possible if our critique of capitalism also includes a social analysis such that the harms suffered by people of colour, immigrants, women and LGBTQ+ people are linked to those experienced by the working class.

The municipalist movement has put a feminist politics at its centre, seeking gender parity in all spaces, acts and roles and actively fighting against a patriarchal system. But we also need to ensure that fighting systemic racism, sexism and other forms of discrimination is given the same prominence in order to ensure that any new politics is about expanding the political capacities of ordinary people to realise social agency and diminish marginality. In the municipalist movement, we see the seeds of a kind of radical substantive democracy rather than state-led social democracy that stresses the need for practices of care, listening and the active seeking of understanding and solidarity to enhance collective autonomy; but they have some way to go to realise the radical substantive democracy of the sort suggested above.

As we know from the civil rights and feminist movements that have come before, re-inventing democratic practices from the ground up requires a constant process of unlearning and relearning that experiences of injustice are differential and emerge from varied histories. The felt *experience of injustice* is differently inflected but is also a crucial dynamic of democratisation – it speaks to the *senses of democratisation*. It is what inspires people to seek social transformation. The extension of this suggests that victims of injustice should be foregrounded in the development of new democratic methods that enable these injustices to be better understood and properly addressed. This means taking special measures to compensate for the social and economic inequalities of unjust social structures. It involves processes of discovery around deeply felt forms of contradiction that the world as we know it is not all that it may seem to ourselves and to others. This requires creative and sensitive approaches alive to the injuries marginalised people have suffered; approaches that build trust and relationships over time as a means of engendering solidarity and opening up possibilities for change. It is not always evident how processes of commoning and approaches to municipalism achieve this; but as Fraser (2019) notes, only an inclusive politics of recognition will be able to tackle the shared roots of class and status injustices in financialised capitalism.

A recent report on democratic policymaking observed both a 'need for change' and that 'the need to seek the voice of marginalized and disadvantaged people in decision-making processes is of undeniable and acute local, national and global relevance' (RSA, 2017). If democracy means anything today, then it must be inclusive of all those whose lives are impacted through decisions made; it must bring publics into being in the places where they live. What we are witnessing – in myriad forms, from micro-experiments to pilots and prototypes, new strategic approaches and ways of working with things like co-operative councils, participatory budgeting and community businesses – is the re-establishment of the value of the public, of the public good, and of public goods outside of the public/private dichotomy; an attempt to reframe collectivism and put more power into the hands of more people. As De Angelis (2017) enthuses, this could lay the foundations of an alternative value system to capitalism.

In terms of media and communications systems we need to apply these same criteria to reimagine how data and digital infrastructure are governed, owned and used:

> If we want to reshape the behaviour of platform companies and ensure
> that the collective intelligence explosion enabled by the mass analysis
> of data helps solve our most pressing challenges from climate change
> to the fair allocation of goods and resources, we will have to reshape the

governance and ownership of digitally generated data and the underlying infrastructure. In short, we must overthrow the data oligarchs and build a digital commons. (Lawrence and Laybourn-Langton, 2019)

A radical substantive democracy is also a means of further interrogating what a media co-operative might look like. A co-operative is an autonomous association of people who have come together voluntarily to meet their common economic, social and cultural needs and aspirations through a jointly owned and democratically controlled enterprise. They are based on values of self-responsibility, democracy, equality, equity and solidarity. Media co-ops are on the rise. The Global Newsletter for Cooperatives active in Industry Services (CICOPA) reported that in 2017 there had been a 27% increase in co-ops in the field of information and communications around the world, with many emerging in response to the need to preserve pluralism, escape commercial and state pressures and ensure independent journalism. Most of these are worker co-operatives with democratic governance at their core and the majority operate in Europe. Many face issues of a lack of finance, regulatory complexity, tax and administrative burdens, but nonetheless are increasing in number. Part of their growth is due to the emergence of platform co-operatives where users and/or workers ultimately own and control the platforms (Scholz and Schneider, 2016). Platform co-ops are a response to the exploitative, monopolistic and extractivist nature of big tech companies that exacerbate systemic inequalities and feed surveillance capitalism (see Chapter 1). The Platform Cooperativism Consortium (2019) website states:

> In the face of widespread dissatisfaction with capitalism, it is time to ask, "What kind of new economy do we want to create?" Instead of optimising the online economy for growth and short-term profits for the few, we need to optimise the digital economy for all people. Platform co-ops offer a near-future, alternative to platform capitalism based on cooperative principles such as democratic ownership and governance … Platform co-ops introduce economic fairness, training and democratic participation in the running of online businesses.

Platform co-ops are also a response to the gig economy and the uber-isation of everything. Characterised by insecure, temporary and freelance contracts, the gig economy has increased the number of jobs and kept unemployment low, but has also further eroded basic workers' rights (Armstrong, 2018) as well as contributing to consumer concerns over safety and accountability. Zero-hours and short-hours contracts, the norm of the gig economy, have disrupted dominant markets and both exploited and contributed to a low-wage workforce, with Uber growing dominant in personal transportation services and take-away food services like Deliveroo gaining in popularity. Often such workers are forced into 'self-employment' by employers keen to reduce their tax liability, avoid paying the minimum wage and deny worker rights. In the UK, the Trades Union Congress (TUC, 2018) notes that of four million adults over 25 classified as self-employed, 49% (1.96 million) are earning less than the minimum wage.

Platform co-ops offer a potential route to a fairer, more inclusive digital economy with tangible benefits for workers and users, but also struggle to raise the money needed to start and scale up (Borkin, 2019).

Worker co-ops are owned and run by the people who work in them who have an equal say in what the organisation does and how it develops, and an equitable share of the wealth created. In Cairo the online news site *Mada* was born out of the crisis in 2013 and formed by a group of journalists who had lost their jobs and were worried about the future for independent journalism in Egypt. They describe their journalism as the kind that constantly challenges, raises questions and proposes different possibilities. They operate an open and ongoing editorial conversation on the ethics of their journalism, especially with regard to protecting the rights of the oppressed and the vulnerable and preserving the privacy of sources. The workers run the business themselves, cooperatively. In Uruguay, the daily newspaper *La Diaria* was formed in 2010 as a worker co-operative focusing on independent journalism that is critical of the establishment. It has become the country's second most read daily news publication (CICOPA, 2019).

Co-ops often emerge in response to a need identified by the community, and are variously characterised in different places according to social, political and economic contexts. In the US the Banyan project is attempting to respond to the demise of local newspapers by helping to seed independent community news co-operatives that would be professional and trustworthy. The objective is to nurture sustainability and empower civic engagement and community involvement. It has adopted a consumer co-operative model, with reader-members electing the boards of local news co-ops and paying an annual membership fee. Other funding comes from crowd-funding grants and local advertising. The Banyan project provides the tools and digital publishing platform needed with the intention of increasing community events and strengthening civic infrastructure. The Banyan's pilot project, Haverhill Matters, in Haverhill, Massachusetts, is due to go live in 2019.

In the UK, *The Bristol Cable* is changing the face of local journalism as a grassroots community-led media co-operative. It prints a free quarterly magazine with a circulation of 30,000 copies and publishes investigative and community-led journalism regularly online. It also delivers free media training, equipping local people with the skills to report on issues that are important to them. It is funded by over 2,000 members, each paying a small monthly fee (who all have a say and own an equal share in the co-op), by foundation support and crowd funding. Income is also generated from advertising in the print edition, regulated by an ethical advertising charter determined by members. Each year its members vote on the annual budget, the overall focus for content and who sits on the board of directors. They rely on a strong online presence alongside face-to-face engagement and monthly community meetings. The team is paid a real living wage and freelancers get competitive rates, but they are aware that they need to do more to diversify the range of people involved. They insist on democratic decisionmaking throughout the organisation. The Bristol Cable most closely fits the description of a multi-stakeholder co-operative (MSC) whose membership includes both the workers and readers. The first multi-stakeholder co-operatives emerged in Italy in the 1990s and are often referred to as social co-ops set up to provide a range of social services such as care, prison services, mental health provision, etc. Their memberships can include workers, service users, volunteers, local authorities, and so forth, and they provide the most inclusive form of democratic governance involving the communities they are embedded within. Because of this MSCs are closely aligned with the values and approaches of municipalism.

MSCs also offer a means of financial sustainability through membership payments. *The New Internationalist*, a magazine on human rights, politics and social justice, describes itself as one of the largest media co-operatives in the world. Founded in 1973 it became a workers' co-op in 1992 and then an MSC in 2017; by 2019 it had over 3,600 investor members who have a say in how the magazine develops and enabling them to do more investigative and long-form journalism.

Media co-ops like those referred to above are trying to figure out what workplace democracy could be in the media industry – from who gets to do what jobs, to who makes decisions on content and resource distribution. A substantive commitment to democracy inside media organisations would enable the broadening of a range of voices involved in decisionmaking that in turn would help ensure that our media systems meet a wider range of needs and serve a more diverse set of interests. To guard against this evaporating into the 'diversity washing' of liberal pluralism (whereby a few more women or a few more black people are seen to do the job), it must be based on ownership models premised on genuine agency and collectivism. This links the traditions of labour struggle and unions traditionally associated with issues of work and wealth, class and poverty, to a broader politics of status and (mis)recognition associated with race and patriarchal heteronormativity. Media co-ops are collectively owned and controlled. There is no employer and employee but a membership of worker-owners. The media worker is no longer solely answerable to capital; rather, capital serves the co-operative that is democratically organised and governed. Linking this to theories of the commons, de Peuter and Dyer-Witherford (2010: 45) talk of the worker co-ops where the 'workplace is an *organizational commons*, the labour performed is a *commoning practice*, and the surplus generated, a *commonwealth*', to build what Gibson-Graham (2006) calls a 'generative commons'. Workers co-ops are not without criticism and have been variously described as being too small scale to make any difference (Marx, 1992), too weak to counteract capital (Hahnel, 2005), and even as a means of revitalising capitalism by improving employee morale (Reeves, 2007).

To avoid these dubious fates of co-option by capitalism, co-ops must also be part of a broader movement for transformational change. The fullest possible realisation of the sort of democratic egalitarian values expressed above can only be achieved by transcending the current system of institutionalised global capitalism. Systemic change means addressing the structural causes of poverty and economic inequality through redistributive mechanisms of wealth. It means foregrounding class, gender and racial subordination and political domination by sharing and redistributing power through processes of radically substantive democracy. It introduces a new spatial logic of de-commodification of the social commons where our institutions are reclaimed as part of the commons for the public good. It means refusing ever-increasing levels of extraction, production and consumption. It means reckoning with and repairing the damage done by slavery and colonialism. It means rejecting and displacing capitalism. If this seems fanciful then we would do well to learn from Wright (2010), who wrote that we are best off conceptualising alternatives to the status quo on the basis of the anti-capitalist potential of things that actually exist. He called these 'real utopias' because they exist and they reveal actual emancipatory possibilities. They are far from perfect – in particular, it is often hard to see how they can shift issues at the macro-level such as global finance, global warming, global inequalities and global justice – but in them we can find resources for hope, spaces for action and prospects for non-capitalist emancipatory futures.

CONCLUSION: NURTURING RESOURCES OF HOPE AND RESISTANCE

The assault on democratic institutions, values and imaginaries, on public good and public goods, on social justice and on citizenry, has generated a political and democratic crisis. But ideas about the enactment of a different kind of politics and different ways of doing democracy can be identified as ethnographically emergent in groups and organisations around the world. These emergent attempts at rediscovering another politics are not concerned with just trying to become an elected government (although some go in this direction). They seek instead to disrupt the day-to-day oppressions and injustices on which the current neo-liberal order depends to develop different relationships of mutuality and democracy – co-operative forms of ownership, collaborative partnerships, alliances of workers and communities seeking to meet social need where it occurs – to build economic power of their own.

Writing in *The Long Revolution* in 1961, Raymond Williams described the 'rising determination, almost everywhere, that people should govern themselves'. His idea of a revolution draws on the material, everyday nature of culture existing, often unrecognised, alongside more official forms of culture. It was Williams who pointed out that a key contribution of the Labour movement was in its creation of social institutions (unions, co-operatives, the Workers Education Association, mutual support arrangements, like the forerunners of the NHS in Welsh mining communities) that prefigured a different and more just society. It is from within certain elements of civil society with a desire for an inclusive, equal and just society that we find ideas with the seeds of hope in them based on more equality and better democracy, where political opportunities for co-determination are beginning to emerge – where it seems possible that democracy might become something that is done by us rather than something that is done to us.

Nurturing the seeds of these prospects for hope to germinate and take root puts ordinary people, as opposed to elites, back in the picture; it allows the re-imagining of the sorts of institutional and regulatory frameworks (including those that apply to our systems of media and communications) that may be required to support such a radical repositioning; it suggests social and economic forms that can be integrated into contributory forms of democracy. A political commons that is concerned to develop an alternative politics that can advance freedom, equality, collectivism and ecological sustainability while avoiding corporate, financial and market domination.

Operationally, this creates the need to formulate mechanisms of inclusive citizen participation and democratic control of the spaces we inhabit, and public spheres we produce that can interface with institutional politics – you cannot have mutuality and the pursuit of equality without entitlements and regulation. This will require new forms of state relations that prioritise the value of the public over profit, patience over productivity, and collaboration over competitiveness: economies that go beyond capital. Rethinking the media in these terms and as part of a complex of social and political relations may well help lead us to a reinvention of our democratic futures.

8

INTELLECTUALS AND THE RE-IMAGINING OF POLITICAL COMMUNICATIONS

INTRODUCTION

In much of the scholarship of political communications, it is agreed that the field is going through a paradigmatic shift. Yet the crisis of political and civic communication is almost exclusively discussed with reference to technological developments, the fragility of top-down political communication systems, and an end to the imaginary uniformity of politics and political communications itself (Blumler and Coleman, 2015). As such, remedies to the crisis – invariably framed as 'rethinking', 'revisiting', 'reconceptualising' and so on – treat the crisis as if researchers themselves are immune from, or at least not part of, the problem. Politics of course was never about the 'hall of fame' (to use E.P. Thompson's memorable description [Thompson, 1959]) and always about more than politicians, TV personalities, insiders, and charming (or otherwise) journalists. The assumption of a once prevailing homogeneous, settled, uncomplicated and coherent politics is only possible if we ignore the reality of a capitalist 'pre-history'.

In the light of the intensified marketisation of and managerialism within higher education, this final chapter asks how communication scholars should respond to a situation in which the media are seen as intimately connected to both the emergence of, and solution to, the current capitalist (and political communication) crisis. To what extent should academics remain aloof from grassroots movements or should their research and teaching inform campaigns for social justice? The chapter argues that the narrative of the 'public sphere' was, is, and will continue to be the narrative of intellectuals, and discusses how academics are simultaneously urged to 'engage' in the social world in order to achieve 'impact' and retain a scholarly detachment that protects their 'neutrality'. The chapter will also critique the way that 'neutrality' has been used by some intellectuals as a shibboleth for supporting the status quo. It argues that political communications (and media studies more generally), however, should not (and probably cannot) be insulated from fundamental questions of power and injustice, and suggests that academics should refuse the false binary between 'scholarly' and 'political' activity to pursue a 'committed' approach to their work.

THE POLITICAL PERILS OF INTELLECTUAL LABOUR

According to Gramsci '[a]ll men [sic] are intellectuals … but not all men have in society the function of intellectuals' (1971: 9). At a time in which genuine critical voices are increasingly marginalised, the role of those who indeed have the function of intellectuals needs urgent evaluation. If the task of critical analysis and critical theory is to examine the relationship between objective social realities and knowledge structures and to actively search for economic and political alternatives to existing economic and political power structures, the contribution of intellectuals to this process is not a mere 'idealist' endeavour. As such it is vitally important to address Bourdieu's (2003: 17) question: 'Must intellectuals – more precisely, research scholars, or to be more accurate still, social scientists – intervene in the political world, and if so, under what conditions can they interject themselves efficiently?'

The debate over political commitment is not novel. Neither are debates over the politics of communication. For example, the emergence of cultural studies was marked by its commitment to working-class aspiration. The work of key figures such as Raymond Williams, E.P. Thompson and those who gathered in and around the Centre for Contemporary Cultural Studies was striking for how they concerned themselves with the plights and the struggles of the wretched of Britain. This tradition of critical engagement and involvement of intellectuals in Britain of course had a lot to do with a more powerful tradition of working-class politics. Despite the pressure from Stalinism on one side and labourism on the other, radical British intellectuals could argue, as E.P. Thompson did, that:

> ... the facts of class power in our time will not allow us the luxury of self-isolation. We are committed, with a total commitment, to meet each contingency as it arises, knowing that it is our fate and our responsibility in capitalist society to see many of our hopes and energies ploughed into "the wither'd field," but knowing also that there is no force which can change this society except within ourselves. (1959: 55)

That the title of a leading radical publication was *Universities and Left Review* meant that there was at least some hope universities would play a leading role in influencing social and political choices.

In France too, the tradition of commitment was equally strong and, until the defeat of 1968, there was an intimate relationship between intellectuals and mass working-class politics. The left, having played a decisive role in resistance to fascism, remained committed to the idea of emancipation, not least in relation to the breaking down of patriarchal chains. The publication of Simone de Beauvoir's *Second Sex* in 1949 was a landmark, as was Sartre's *What is Literature?* (1950), which passionately defended the idea of committed literature. Similar trends could be observed in other countries, north and south, when the full force of liberation movements after World War 2 both in imperial and colonial states were on display.

Remembering this history of a critical intellectual tradition (and its influence on early media and cultural studies research) is crucial when the idea of reasserting literature's capacity to challenge all forms of domination is re-emerging (Rancière, 2010). But it is also worth remembering that the binary that sets the 'art for art's sake' tradition against that of political commitment not only has a much longer history, but is also part of movements and moments of history that are much bigger than the intellectuals themselves. Sartre's view on committed literature wasn't universally approved and came under attack not only by those on the right but also by figures such as Adorno (1980). The commitment to commitment was seen as rather 'vulgar', and the role of the 'public intellectual' emerged as a much weaker substitute for those who might have been encouraged to bring their 'academic pose' (Wright Mills, 1970) to what Habermas famously called the 'public sphere'.

The shift was theorised explicitly by another widely quoted guru of our time, Manuel Castells. Having produced some of the most devastating critiques of capitalism in his early works, Castells began to distance himself from the very public that he was supposed to talk to as a leading public intellectual. In the third volume of *The Information Age*, he complained that each time an intellectual has tried to answer 'what is to be done?' and to implement the answer, catastrophe has ensued. If this is the case, then there is every reason for intellectuals to avoid challenging the actually existing social order and seeking any alternatives. Emancipating himself from what he calls his obsession with the inscription on Marx's tomb and thesis eleven on Feuerbach, he wrote that 'In the twentieth century, philosophers have been trying to change the world. In the twenty-first century, it is time for them to interpret it differently' (Castells, 1998: 395).

Interpreting the world differently, in the case of Anthony Giddens, another prominent sociologist, gave us the 'third way' and a renewed effort to reach an accommodation with capitalism. Bev Skeggs has rightly argued that we 'should never forget that Giddens was an architect of New Labour's "third way", an apologist for the institutional structures that enabled neoliberal policies to be implemented. Through his publishing enterprises Giddens has saturated sociology with this apologist perspective ... Giddens and Beck both proposed the denigration of class as a key unit of analysis for sociologists; yet, analysis of class can only be wilfully ignored by those with enough privilege to do so' (2019: 28). What vanished from Giddens' social theory was the idea of the 'social' itself, for it was assumed that resources to pursue individualisation were available equally to all individuals. Giddens offered no new interpretation, but according to Skeggs merely reproduced 'the original myth of liberalism' (2014: 10). Having been recruited by Tony Blair, he became a leading example of what Peter Dahlgren has called 'house intellectuals' (2012: 98).

Giddens' attempt to shift the function of sociology from critique to legitimation of power went beyond the borders of already 'modern' capitalist countries. He visited Libya twice in 2006 and 2007 as part of a public relations effort by US lobbying firm Monitor Group designed to secure media coverage, which they described as 'broadly positive and increasingly sensitive to the Libyan point of view' (Corn and Mahanta, 2011). He wrote about his first trip in an article published in the *New Statesman* in August 2006, entitled 'The colonel and his third way'. Giddens reported that the stories of the colonel's ill health were exaggerated and informed readers that 'Gaddafi is interested in the debates and policies involved in social democracy in Europe, which is the reason he has invited me. He likes the term "third way," because his own political philosophy, developed in the late 1960s, was a version of this idea' (Giddens, 2006).

Six months later, in a comment piece for the *Guardian*, he wrote about a further trip and insisted that Gaddafi 'was not negative about globalisation, as so many politicians in developing countries are, and recognised that Libya must change to prosper'. He noted that Gaddafi was in favour of diversifying the economy, banking reform, and dismantling inefficient state-owned enterprises. Furthermore, Giddens claimed that 'as one-party states go, Libya is not especially repressive' and finished his article by offering this prophecy:

Will real progress be possible only when Gadaffi leaves the scene? I tend to think the opposite. If he is sincere in wanting change, as I think he is, he could play a role in muting conflict that might otherwise arise as modernisation takes hold. My ideal future for Libya in two or three decades' time would be a Norway of North Africa: prosperous, egalitarian and forward-looking. Not easy to achieve, but not impossible. (2007)

One has to remember that such positive commentary on the Libyan state and its 'sincere' leader Gaddafi was not extracted through the torture of an imprisoned sociologist, but volunteered willingly by an 'objective' social scientist. Unfortunately, the citizens of Libya did not have similar levels of access to the necessary resources to pursue 'individualisation', and unlike our 'objective' sociologist they did not have the luxury of remaining 'detached' from the brutal material realities of their country. Giddens has yet to practice the 'reflexivity' he has long advocated in the aftermath of the Arab revolutions of 2011.

Giddens was not alone in this PR exercise. Other luminaries that were invited by the Monitor Group included Joseph Nye, best known for developing the concept of 'soft power', Richard Perle (who reported his trip to Libya to the then Vice-President Dick Cheney), the conservative writer Bernard Lewis (who briefed the US Embassy in Israel on his trip), Francis Fukuyama and another conservative writer Benjamin Barber, author of *Jihad vs. McWorld*. According to Corn and Mahanta (2011), Barber served on the international advisory board of the Gaddafi International Charity and Development Foundation, which was overseen by Saif el-Islam Gaddafi. The willingness of conservative thinkers like Barber, Lewis, Perle and Fukuyama, to receive payment for participating in cleansing the image of the Libyan dictator should not surprise anyone. The involvement of Giddens, however, prompted Todd Gitlin (2011) to write about the perils of public intellectualising: 'Big-thinking theoretical brains can be the most treacherous. One reason why brains have gotten a bad rap is that smart people can be so fatuous, idiotic, and clueless.'

By contrast, Habermas, whose expansive writing covered not only philosophical traditions but also history and sociology, never refused to intervene in political debates and concerns in Germany and Europe and did so mainly as a left-leaning public intellectual. Yet his political interventions on two significant and controversial military conflicts, or 'humanitarian interventions', during the Gulf War of 1991 and the Kosovo War in the latter part of the same decade, tested his own commitment to cosmopolitanism, justice and human rights. Was the immediate liberation of Kuwait sufficient to justify what Habermas and many others labelled as 'just war'? In the case of Kosovo, he suggested that what changed his view was the 1995 massacre of Bosnians in Srebrenica: 'Confronted with crimes against humanity, the international community must be able to act even with military force, if all other options are exhausted' (Habermas, 2002). But was this not a 'safe area' under UN protection, and did this crime happen precisely as a result of the failure of that 'international community'?

In the case of the military intervention in Iraq in 1991, which paved the way for the total devastation of the country over a decade later, his logic was simple enough: 'the Iraqi invasion of Kuwait was a violation of international law, and Saddam Hussein moreover threatened Israel with gas warfare' (Habermas, 2002). Such a position skates over some uncomfortable facts. What has now been popularised as the 'international community' has never been international and rarely equal. Habermas had admitted that the case of Kosovo carried a greater burden of justification because of stalemate in the UN Security Council. But we can assume that on this occasion there was no reason to prefer 'communicative action' over the use of violence, even without full consensus of the 'international community'. The case of Iraq was also interesting, for it was on 11 September that George Bush Senior made his 'New World Order' speech to a joint session of Congress and announced the war against Iraq in 1990. The hypocrisy of the UN Security Council on violations of international law and its infinite patience with Israel obviously did not register or matter. As Anderson points out, Habermas' position was inconsistent to say the least:

> ... since violations of international law had never hitherto troubled Habermas overmuch – when Turkey invaded Cyprus, Indonesia annexed East Timor, let alone Israel seized East Jerusalem and occupied the West Bank, there is no record of his being moved to comment on them – it seems clear that political feelings rather than legal arguments were the principal pressure behind Habermas's endorsement of Desert Storm. On the one hand, there was his self-declared, long-standing posture of loyalty to the West. (2005: 24)

In his essay on commitment, Adorno had argued that it is futile to separate the beauty of Brecht's works from his politics and political intentions. He reminded us that in Sartre's writing on literature there is an undeniable statement: ' "Nobody can suppose for a moment that it is possible to write a good novel in praise of anti-semitism." Nor could one be written in praise of the Moscow Trials, even if such praise were bestowed before Stalin actually had Zinoviev, and Bukharin murdered' (1980: 186). This moral position was somehow lost on Habermas, who is, of course, regarded as the major philosophical descendant of the Frankfurt School.

The point is not to suggest that researchers should become politicians and abandon altogether what Wright Mills has called 'intellectual craftsmanship' (1970). Neither do we suggest that we should throw the baby out with the bathwater and brush aside or dismiss any research based on serious lapses of judgement by writers. One can easily add to such a list by considering, for example, Hannah Arendt who, despite her intellectual contributions being recognised as key texts in postcolonial studies and despite her own personal experience of racism, oppression and exile, could still write about African-Americans as those 'living amongst us' and describe imperialism as 'one great crime in which America was never involved' (quoted in Owens, 2017). The examples we have provided above, however, demonstrate that intellectuals who are central figures in media theory see no opposition between scholarship and commitment. They appear committed but lend their *symbolic force*, to use Bourdieu's term, to the dominant powers. All academic writings are political, whether acknowledged or not, and ours is no exception. All writers need to recognise, as was suggested by Williams (1981a), the 'ism' in their own criticism.

Closer to our chosen field of political communications, the 'ism' in Brian McNair's 'criticism' illustrates our point more directly. In one of his contributions to media scholarship, he once infamously wrote that some media 'are dumber than others. But so are some people' (McNair, 2003). Immediately after the terrorist attack on London Bridge on 3 June 2017, he tweeted the following: 'Enough! Islam is a cancer on the planet. It must be destroyed, or reformed. Soon. Zero tolerance!' His university, Queensland University of Technology, immediately distanced itself from his comment (Tutty, 2017). What was astonishing about this intervention by a professor of journalism, media and communication was the expression of hatred, inciting violence ('zero tolerance') and making a sweeping generalisation against a religion with 1.6 billion followers. McNair was not taking a secular position against religion in general – otherwise the tweet should have read 'religion is a cancer on the planet'. Furthermore, this was not an emotional and immediate outburst to a particular tragedy. Previously, in an article published in *The Conversation*, he favourably quoted a passage in a book by the editorial director of *Charlie Hebdo*, Stephane Charbonnier, which 'denounces the western media, politicians and those commentators who mute their criticism of Islam for fear of being accused of "Islamophobia"' (McNair, 2015). To be fair, he does acknowledge that those who brutally attacked the office of *Charlie Hebdo* had a particular interpretation of the Quran and admits that there are extreme 'Christians too, and Hindus and even Buddhists'. But effectively these are disclaimers before he gets to his main point: that 'critiquing Islam in the media and elsewhere is not "islamophobia"'. Neither is it racist, because, apparently, being Muslim has nothing to do with ethnicity, and indeed many Muslims are critical of the 'extremists in their rank'. The title of this particular intervention is 'Islam and the media – let's not fear open debate'. One could ask whether this open debate about Islam and the media would also include an open discussion about the causes of war, global economic inequalities, colonialism, international trade and development, and imperialism. In advocating the violation of certain human rights (in his call for 'zero tolerance'), McNair was firmly siding with illiberal liberal intellectuals who are not only targeting Muslims but also see the crushing of the most basic human rights as necessary in the name of defending liberal freedoms (Kundnani, 2008).

DEBATING INTELLECTUALS

Gramsci's formulation about everyone being an intellectual firmly locates the debate about intellectuals within a broader set of social relations that is central to Gramsci's argument about intellectual work, in which he stresses that everyone has an intellect and uses it but not all are intellectuals *by their social function*. Gramsci thus holds a very open notion of intellectual labour: 'there is no human activity from which every form of intellectual participation can be excluded', so that everyone 'carries on some form of intellectual activity … participates in a particular conception of the world, has a conscious line of moral conduct, and therefore contributes to sustain a conception of the world or to modify it, that is, to bring into being new modes of thought' (1971: 9).

Gramsci, however, identifies two types of intellectuals: traditional and organic. Traditional intellectuals are those who think of themselves as autonomous and independent of the dominant social group and are so regarded by the general population. Examples include the clergy, the professoriat and philosophers, all of whom seem to enjoy historical continuity and autonomy from the state. Gramsci notes that this autonomy is often illusory since, despite the ability of individuals to adopt more critical positions, the social location and institutionalisation of such groups is essentially conservative and supportive of the ruling group in society. Organic intellectuals, on the other hand, develop together with the dominant social group, the ruling class, and constitute their thinking and organising element. Such people are produced by the educational system to perform a function for the dominant social group and it is through this group that the ruling class maintains its hegemony over the rest of society.

Gramsci's class analysis thus required that, in order for any kind of counter-hegemonic position to grow and challenge the taken-for-granted common sense that prevailed, 'traditional' intellectuals needed to 'change sides' while the working-class movement had to produce its own 'organic intellectuals'. Any ideological struggle for social change required not only consciousness raising but also conscious transformation while the creation of a socialist consciousness would develop out of actual working lives. Theory and practice are not separate phenomena and therefore critical social theory emerges out of conscious struggle in and with the real world. So the intellectual sphere is thus not confined to a small elite, but rather is connected to something grounded in everyday life and indeed should 'speak' to and about that life in language that all can understand. According to Gramsci, 'the mode of being of the new intellectual can no longer consist in eloquence … but in active participation in practical life, as constructor, organiser, "permanent persuader" and not just a simple orator …' (1971: 10).

Insisting on the context and the purpose of Gramsci's concern with culture and politics, especially when many academics in many disciplines, including media and cultural studies, use his analysis of hegemony, is crucial. It would be futile to argue that 'un-Gramscian' scholars cannot have any claim on Gramsci, but the fact is that Gramsci remained a permanently active 'persuader'. His thinking about culture was inseparable from the biggest ever working-class revolutions that emerged during and in the aftermath of World War 1 (e.g. Ireland in 1916, Russia in1917, Hungary and Germany in 1919). It is not the insistence on this context that is 'vulgar', 'crude' and 'unscholarly', but the glossy attempt to divorce his contribution from any conception of working-class struggle (Thomas, 2009).

Other scholars concerned with categories of intellectuals have reworked and modified Gramsci's distinction between traditional and organic intellectuals. Foucault, for example, distinguished 'specific' from 'universal' intellectuals, where the former is a person who speaks 'in the name of those who were forbidden to speak the truth' while the latter speaks the truth 'to those who had yet to see it' (1977: 67–75). To this typology Bourdieu added the category of *collective intellectual* who is tasked with fulfilling both a *negative* and a *positive* function. Collective intellectuals through their research should produce and disseminate an 'instrument of defense against domination', critique dominant discourse with the aim of 'uncovering the social determinants that bear on the producers of them (starting with journalists, especially economic journalists)', and finally challenge the 'pseudoscientific authority of authorized experts'. These are *negative functions*. But Bourdieu insisted that the collective intellectual has a positive function as well, namely 'contributing to the collective work of political invention'. But to do so the collective intellectual has to break out of the '"small world" of academe, where it enchants itself with itself without ever being in position to really threaten anyone about anything' (2003: 20–21).

Drawing upon Gramsci's distinction between traditional and organic intellectuals, Edward Said divides intellectuals into the categories of amateur and professional, collusive and oppositional. Said was of course not only a cultural critic (as he is celebrated in academia), but also a Palestinian. His 'affiliation' to that origin and the political struggles for the emancipation of Palestine cannot be separated from his analysis of culture. In short, and as Aijaz Ahmad has pointed out:

> Much that is splendid in his work is connected with the fact that he has tried to do honour to that origin; and he has done so against all odds, to the full extent of his capacity, by stepping outside the boundaries of his academic discipline and original intellectual formation, under no compulsion of profession or fame, in no pursuit of personal gain – in fact, at frightening risk to himself. (1992: 160)

Said's critical project was about engagement with and commitment to the wretched of the earth, the context in which critical consciousness is allowed to emerge, and the relationship between culture and intellectuals. He set himself the task of investigating how 'common sense' was taking root and why the views of dominant social forces were not sufficiently resisted. In standing tall against the legions of professional intellectuals and experts who rent their services to the powerful, neither did he shy away from passionate attacks on a significant section of the intellectuals from the Middle East.

Said insisted that intellectuals should seek to intervene in the social world first by recognising the implications of power and then by telling the truth about those implications. Speaking truth to power involves 'carefully weighing the alternatives, picking the right one, and then intelligently representing it where it can do the most good and cause the right change' (Said, 1993b: 8). Intellectual thought, therefore, becomes especially meaningful when it is linked to the 'right change'. Of course, there will be huge debates about what constitutes such a change but Said reminded us that intellectual life ought to be based on more than simply participating in or engaging with the outside world. After all, the problems are likely to come not with engagement per se but with the methods and objectives of our engagement. Certainly, it takes some courage publicly to support an unpopular political position and therefore to invite flak, and there are of course numerous personal and professional reasons for avoiding conflict. Said, however, was unapologetic about the temptation to lead an easy life when the conflicts surrounding us demand a more robust response:

> Nothing in my view is more reprehensible than those habits of mind in the intellectual that induce avoidance, that characteristic turning away from a difficult and principled position which you know to be the right one, but which you decide not to take. You do not want to appear too political; you are afraid of seeming controversial; you need the approval of a boss or an authority figure; you want to keep a reputation for being balanced, objective, moderate; your hope is to be asked back, to consult, to be on a board or prestigious committee, and so, to remain within the responsible mainstream; someday you hope to get an honorary degree, a big prize, perhaps even an ambassadorship. For an intellectual these habits of mind are corrupting par excellence. If anything can denature, neutralise and finally kill a passionate intellectual life, it is those considerations, internalised and so to speak in the driver's seat. (1993b: 7–8)

Indeed, Said insisted that the intellectual's voice is all the more powerful when it connects to – or perhaps when it helps to amplify or crystallise – movements for progressive social change. The academic is most inspired and inspiring when she is part of an organic chain of events: 'One doesn't climb a mountain or pulpit and declaim from the heights. Obviously, you want to speak your piece where it can be heard best; and also you want it represented in such a way as to affiliate with an ongoing and actual process, for instance the cause of peace and justice' (Said, 1993b: 8).

'Affiliation', for Said, referred not simply to the institution mentioned on conference name badges – the most visible symbol of academic networking – but to a commitment to struggle: a commitment, as Said put it, to 'the common pursuit of a shared ideal' (1993b: 8). We can, of course, have an affinity with a set of normative ideas around ethics; we can recognise the affective dimension of the attempts to realise ethical positions; and we can show empathy with those who face the brunt of unequal social relations. However, all this counts for little if we do not connect ourselves to, and ideally take part along with others in, movements for change. What we need, therefore, is neither a pallid attachment to 'engagement' nor utilitarian calls to be 'impactful', but a commitment to equality, social justice and progressive social change.

The political ecomomist of the media, Nicolas Garnham, in his analysis of contemporary intellectual work in the West, reworks Gramsci's model and offers three broad definitions. He writes that intellectuals:

> ... may be defined as a class whose power, sometimes called symbolic power, derives from monopoly control over the production of knowledge and cultural legitimation through the possession of socially accredited

power to define what counts as either true, right and beautiful. Second, they may be defined functionally as information workers, those whose specialized position within the division of labour is the manipulation of symbolic forms. Third, they may be defined normatively as a vocation, as representatives of a critical, emancipatory tradition appealing to universal values. (1995: 360)

But if Gramsci, Said, Garnham and others help us theorise the socio-political locus of intellectuals, we still need to grapple with the nature of the spaces for intellectual work and better define what kinds of content, and indeed what kinds of people, might be worthy of such a designation, given the frequent exclusion of non-Western voices from the critical canon. For example, in her list of 25 thinkers for the twenty-first century, Mackenzie Wark (2017) could not think of any possible contributions to the 'general intellects' emanating from India, China, Latin America, the Middle East or Africa. Such provincial and narrow 'idolising' of intellectuals has prompted Hamid Dabashi (2015) to provocatively ask '*Can Non-Europeans Think?*'.

THE CHANGING NATURE AND SPHERE OF INTELLECTUAL WORK

The broad shifts in the nature and conceptualisation of intellectual work in contemporary modernity are not specific to a particular country. In many countries there is currently a debate about the changing face of education and the dislocation of intellectuals from their traditional ivory towers. One vigorous voice is Russell Jacoby (1989), who lambasts US academe as bureaucratised and corporatised, leading him to produce a mournful diatribe about living 'after the last intellectuals'. Shlomo Sand (2018) laments the degradation of a literary elite and the failure of French intellectuals to meet the ideal of the ethical lodestar of France. Clearly there is a general drift of knowledge workers away from educational institutions towards new bases in think tanks (the "thinktankerati" as Schlesinger has called them [2009a: 5]), government-supported R&D activities, and the mass media where information workers produce and disseminate information about matters of public life. The increased visibility of think tanks as 'media intellectuals', the current conditions of knowledge production in universities and the emphasis on 'impact'[1] together with the shift in research to meet

---

[1] In 2016 and in an attempt to entrench market forces within the university sector, the British government introduced a new regulatory structure that will increase competition for numbers and normalise an audit culture which serves as a proxy for meaningful quality of research. In this bill there is also an underlying assumption that what it calls 'impactful research' will be crucial to the future of a knowledge economy and prospects for growth (Department for Business Innovation & Skills, 2016: 16). Impact is precisely about how academic labour is measured by its application to non-academic settings. Research Councils UK (2014), for example, define research impact as 'the demonstrable contribution that excellent research makes to society and the economy'. To be 'impactful', therefore, is to be immediately relevant and to help generate informed citizenship as well as productivity and growth.

the needs of governments and business are all factors, rooted in neo-liberal public life, that have hindered the ability of academics, even when they are willing, to act as public intellectuals (Misztal, 2012).

A further shift in the nature of intellectual work has been triggered by the massive rolling out of digital information and communication technologies across the world (Castells, 2000) and the emergence of arguments about 'immaterial labour' in a 'knowledge society'. Throughout modern history, the democratic potential of communication technologies, variously 'new' in different historical epochs, for the expansion of the public sphere has been trumpeted (Kellner, 1995). The printing press revolutionised European intellectual life within fifty years of its development, and remains an epoch-defining technology (Eisenstein, 1979). Benjamin (1968) clearly saw the revolutionary potential of photography, film and the mechanical reproduction of works of art to produce new ways of seeing that decentred the dominant tradition of 'perspective'. Brecht argued for the possibility of making radio into something really democratic, arguing that this 'new' medium was more than an 'acoustical department store', and could be turned into a two-way communication that was 'capable not only of transmitting but of receiving, of making the listeners not only hear but also speak, not of isolating him but connecting him' (1979: 25). The relationship between media and intellectuals (traditional as well as organic) indeed goes back to the development of the first printing press and subsequent media. As Wright Mills suggested, these innovations had a serious implication:

> The independent artist and intellectual are among the few remaining personalities equipped to resist and to fight the stereotyping and consequent death of genuinely living things. Fresh perception now involves the capacity to continually unmask and to smash the stereotypes of vision and intellect with which modern communications swamp us. These worlds of mass-art and mass-thought are increasingly geared to the demands of politics. That is why it is in politics that intellectual solidarity and effort must be centred. If the thinker does not relate himself to the value of truth in political struggle, he cannot responsibly cope with the whole of live experience. (1963: 229)

It was precisely this passage that inspired Said to urge intellectuals to intervene in 'disputing the images, official narratives, justifications of power circulated by an increasingly powerful media – and not only media, but whole trends of thought that maintain the status quo, keep things within an acceptable and sanctioned perspective on actuality – by providing what Mills calls unmaskings or alternative versions in which, to the best of one's ability, the intellectual tries to tell the truth' (Said, 1993a: 7–8). That Said's eloquent presentations were given as part of the BBC's Reith Lectures was no accident. This not only put the narrative of intellectuals at the centre of public debate, but also offered a vision of the intellectual role and capacity of media (in this case of public service broadcasting).

Clearly there is a large step involved in going from a Gramscian model derived from the practices of factory workers in the neighborhoods of Turin to the practices of workers, activists and hackers in both face-to-face and online environments. But one of the central points of Gramsci's argument is that in the invitation to ordinary people to join in 'political' discussion, that is, their hailing or 'interpellation' as 'intellectuals', is part of the social process of actually producing intellectuals. It is in this context that the debate about an emergent public sphere is inevitably linked with intellectuals. Garnham suggests that the 'bourgeois public sphere was classically the creation of and ground for intellectuals. The project of the democratic generalization of the public sphere is a project to make everyone an intellectual' (1995: 376). Within such a narrative, the role of communication is central for it was not only through saloons and in coffee houses, but more significantly through ever-expanding journals and periodicals and printed texts, that the aspirations for social change and collective activities and identities were expressed.

How might this approach to commitment relate to current challenges in our field? We want to highlight four areas of concern, both dangers and opportunities, in relation to the agendas we pursue, the methods we use, the normative positions we adopt and the affiliations we make.

Firstly, it is vital that we do not passively accept the agendas that are given to us either in terms of research funding or our more general orientation. There is a strong temptation to wait for strategic calls from our national or transnational funders and then tailor our research to those areas that are flagged up to us as important. These will often favour short-term, instrumentalist 'solutions' to 'problems' defined by others. In the case of the United Kingdom, argues John Holmwood (2015): '[r]esearch councils like the ESRC [Economic and Social Research Council] are increasingly setting research priorities determined by the Department for Business, Innovation & Science that provides its block grant of funding—for example, on "big data" or the application of neuroscience to social problems'. Of course it is sometimes possible to tailor more critical research bids for strategic calls, but at a time of diminishing funds and greater centralisation of research funding this is by no means an easy task. We should avoid, to the extent that it is possible, research programmes that reflect the priorities and serve the interests of market and state exclusively. Instead we should aim to expand research agendas and to make visible themes and questions that have been all too often marginalised, either because they do not have an immediate solution (because they are complicated) or because they are not deemed to be significant (because they have not been defined as 'problems' as such). This involves challenging the current fetish for technological solutions and market imperatives and highlighting issues of, for example, class, inequality, discrimination, labour, power and control, both in relation to areas that already have salience (notably, big data, surveillance and the Internet of things) and in relation to emerging debates around rather more fluid concepts such as identity, diversity, power and democracy.

The discipline of media, culture and communications is blessed with pioneering research that challenges elite power and advocates for the marginal and the powerless. However, a funding system that increasingly privileges private and government beneficiaries together with managerial regimes that are overwhelmingly focused on rankings and audit culture is hardly conducive to a research environment that will protect, let alone nurture, independent and critical programmes of work. We need, therefore, both to challenge the encroachment of governmental and private-sector interests into research agendas and to press for more inclusive agendas that relate (and sometimes emerge as a response) to ongoing crises and conflicts. This might, for example, involve programmes of work exploring cultures of racism in contemporary Britain that are independent of the government's PREVENT regime or ones focusing on the media's vilification of refugees that seek to provide an evidential basis on which to confront news titles that break agreed codes of conduct. This would certainly mean more projects that comprehensively analyse coverage of key political events in order to hold broadcasters and editors to account, such as that produced by Berry (2016) on media coverage of economic debates, by academics in the Media Reform Coalition (2015) on press coverage of Labour leader Jeremy Corbyn, or the articles collected by Jackson, Thorsen, and Wring (2016) on the media's role in the referendum on EU membership. These are all interventions into, as well as reflections on, debates on media power and editorial independence.

Secondly, we should reject a methodology that relies purely on describing, enumerating, mapping and measuring. This is not at all to suggest that we avoid empirical research for fear of being tainted as crude positivists or voracious number-crunchers. Indeed, the examples provided in the previous paragraph depend in part on quantitative analysis that then forms the basis of a critical framework through which to understand media performance. There is, however, the temptation to believe that in a political landscape that privileges 'evidence-based policy', and at a time when we have so much data and so many ways of visualising and 'drilling down' into them, the data will speak for themselves. This ignores the difference between logics of 'calculation' and 'evaluation', where the latter depends on the adoption of particular moral or political positions. As Couldry and Powell (2014: 4) have argued in relation to the seductive allure of big data analysis, the ubiquity of data mining means that 'more insights are made available about more aspects of everyday life but no opportunity is provided for these insights to be folded back into the experience of everyday life'. This question of agency is crucial both in terms of our status as researchers and our relationship to living subjects and social processes that are not reducible to the data they generate. This relates to some rather old debates about the difference between 'administrative' and 'critical' research where the former is often seen as a rather unreflexive and narrowly empirical form of investigation while the latter is more methodologically promiscuous.

This is a salutary reminder that methods are neither innocent nor self-sufficient, and that what animate our methodological choices are our chosen theoretical frameworks and preferred political commitments, in particular our willingness to press for change or justify the status quo. This is particularly important in debates, for example, over media ownership where battles over metrics often seem to obscure a more profound discussion about what is being measured and for what purpose. We are inundated with figures – Herfindahl-Hirschman Indexes, market share, diversity indexes and consumption metrics – but these acquire meaning (and political efficacy) mostly in relation to one's definition of democracy or one's normative position on how resources should be most fairly distributed. As Freedman has previously argued, 'media ownership and levels of concentration are not … solely empirical matters, but ones that connect to more ideological questions about how, in neo-liberal circumstances, the market in particular is presented as the most desirable and efficient enabler of productive, symbolic activity' (2014: 52).

Thirdly, we should not attempt to hide, displace or pretend that we do not hold specific normative positions as researchers and scholars (neither does this mean that we should attempt to ram them down the throats of our audiences). Committed scholarship is motivated by a desire to investigate the social world in the hope that it can be understood and changed in the name of equality or social justice or democracy. Of course, the problem here is that these are very slippery terms and that one of our tasks is precisely to open up these normative positions to critical debate at the same time as attempting to realise them through research and advocacy. This means that we need to adopt normative positions that are sufficiently robust to address the conflicts we are dealing with, and sufficiently precise that they are not co-opted by groups with very different value systems. For example, in the United Kingdom, a commitment to press freedom is a pretty unremarkable phenomenon – after all, who will declare themselves to be against press freedom? Yet its most energetic proponents are billionaire proprietors who are resisting any form of meaningful and independent self-regulation, arguing that this would involve an unacceptable form of intervention into sovereign markets. Liberal theory, argues Simon Dawes, now 'conflates the freedom of the press with that of media owners' (2014: 22). If we are to continue using a discourse of freedom, then we will have constantly to distinguish between the freedoms that are exploited by the powerful and those that are sought by the poor and the vulnerable. Similarly, pluralism has largely been transformed from an aspiration to see a multitude of voices and outlets that resists centralised control into a measure to secure competition inside media markets. Its significance as a concept designed to challenge unaccountable build-ups of media power (that we discussed in Chapter 2) has been mostly eviscerated so that it may now be seen as a tool that keeps media markets fresh and dynamic instead of one that challenges their underlying logic of concentration and corporate control. We also should not be afraid to criticise institutions that are most closely predicated on some of these core values if we believe that they are falling short of realising them. We have been struck by the reluctance by some advocates of public service broadcasting to say anything negative about the BBC for fear of handing ammunition to its enemies in government and the press. Yet if we view concepts like universality and public service as fundamentally desirable, then surely we have a responsibility to act when audiences themselves have highlighted serious issues concerning diversity, representation and editorial bias. What is the point of adopting an uncritical defence of public service broadcasters if they themselves are internalising neoliberal agendas and organisational practices that undermine their ability to serve audiences of all backgrounds and from all locations and to hold power to account?

Fourthly, we should take the concept of 'affiliation' very seriously. As Said (1993b: 8) argued, we should affiliate 'with an ongoing and actual process, for instance the cause of peace and justice'. This is the crux of the matter. Affiliation should not be a bureaucratic symbol of institutional identity, but a marker of the willingness of scholars to participate in a process of social transformation. It would be far too crude to say that this means you cannot be a committed academic unless you march, protest, occupy and shout; there is, of course, a space for quiet scholarship that defamiliarises hegemonic structures and that challenges powerful orthodoxies. Contrary to Schlesinger's argument Said's position was not an 'all-or-nothing approach': 'the co-opted v the free, the clean v the corrupt, the principled opponent v the compliant bootlicker and the saint v the sinner', and the choice simply is not 'one of working inside the power structure or of being powerless' (Schlesinger, 2009b: 10). Said's point was not that intellectuals have to go on noisy demonstrations in order to be effective (or 'impactful'), but that the work of intellectuals should be intimately and explicitly linked to their normative positions and should be in solidarity with movements that seek to realise them. Said claimed that he always turned down consultancy work because he could never guarantee how his ideas might eventually be used. But he always, or at least to the best of his ability, accepted invitations to speak to campaign groups (notably pro-Palestinian and anti-Apartheid meetings) to which he was sympathetic. Siding with the oppressed is not the same as being powerless. 'In the end', he argued, 'one is moved by causes and ideas that one can actually choose to support because they conform to values and principles one believes in' (Said, 1993b: 2).

There are, of course, dangers associated with 'taking sides': it is especially tough if you want to be tenured or promoted; it endangers your chances of getting research funding; and, crucially, it can be seen as undermining your status as an independent scholar whose commitment ought to be to the 'truth' as opposed to a 'cause'. There is certainly 'flak' associated with being an activist academic. For example, academics in the Media Reform Coalition carried out some research in summer 2016 on broadcast coverage of the Labour leader Jeremy Corbyn and found that the BBC, in its main television news bulletins, gave twice as much airtime to critics as to supporters of Jeremy Corbyn. The BBC dismissed these findings as the work of a 'vested interest group', although interestingly they did not actually dispute the results (Ridley, 2016). Activist academics are regularly accused of undermining their scholarly credentials even though they use standard and accepted methodological tools not simply to theorise 'bias' but to seek to address it at the highest levels. Yet it is entirely legitimate for media scholars to see themselves not simply as 'independent academics', but as activists who take inspiration from and attempt to embed their scholarly work in wider movements. It is necessary also to step outside of our comfort zone and talk not just about but to the people we are urged to call 'stakeholders' or 'publics' – and in particular to those who are most excluded from centres of power. In practice, this might mean a commitment to work with anti-austerity groups if we want to address the very narrow consensus in economic coverage, to work with minority communities in order to seek better representation of all of the voices in this country, to work with refugee communities if we want to understand and change cultures of racism that are fostered through irresponsible media coverage, and to work with media unions in order most effectively to press for more safeguards for journalists in the face of bullying editors. There is a huge amount of work in media and communications scholarship that embraces this commitment, but there are also huge pressures not to do so and to rein in the activist dimension of this approach to scholarship. Embracing the concept of affiliation can be a crucial defence against these institutional and ideological pressures, and an instrument in generating relevant and high-quality political communications.

CONCLUSION: RECOGNISING THE IMPERATIVE OF BEING POLITICAL AND DOING CRITICAL SOCIAL SCIENCE RESEARCH

As we finish writing this book in autumn 2019, we are witnessing a series of astonishing political decisions by a number of governments: the *proroguing* of parliament in Britain by its Prime Minister Boris Johnson; the use of president's rule in India by Indian Prime Minister Narendra Modi to repeal Articles 370 and 35a of the Indian Constitution, which takes away a measure of autonomy of Kashmir; the Turkish president Recep Tayyip Erdoğan's decision to attack the autonomous administration of northern Syria known as Rojava; the revelation that US President Donald Trump urged the Ukrainian president to investigate his political rival Joe Biden; and the attempt in Hong Kong to introduce an extradition bill to make it easier to forcibly transfer 'law-breakers' to mainland China. Such developments bring to mind a famous poem by Bertolt Brecht, which poses an important question: When people lose confidence in government, 'would it not be simpler if the government simply dissolved the people and elected another?'. At a time of intense political polarisation, diminishing accountability and transparency, visible authoritarian turns in liberal democracy marked by exclusionary and violent practices directed against stigmatised minorities, at the same time as the rise of movements against austerity, poverty, war and environmental catastrophe, what is the role of the intellectual? To what extent is there space to think beyond the binary of 'the co-opted v the free, the clean v the corrupt, the principled opponent v the compliant bootlicker'? (Schlesinger, 2009b: 10).

It is tragic that the output of many intellectuals in the global south is often 'reviewed' and 'assessed' not in scholarly and literary journals, but in front of firing squads, torture chambers and prison, or in bitterly cold exile. These intellectuals are subjected to a different kind of 'metric system' and 'impact' study. Such physical and emotional tests that many 'symbolic producers' have to endure are as old as intellectual history across the globe. We know that Walter Benjamin committed suicide waiting to escape the Nazification of Europe; that Leon Trotsky was murdered while in exile; that Rosa Luxemburg was shot on the streets of Berlin; and that Antonio Gramsci wrote much of his best work in prison. While such brutal treatment of intellectuals in post-World War Two Europe has been rare, the continuing demonisation of intellectuals

(Chomsky and Said come to mind) and the prosecution of Edward Snowden, Chelsea Manning and Julian Assange and assassinations of a number of African American intellectuals including Medgar Evers, Malcom X and Martin Luther King, are just some examples that demonstrate the perils of raising a voice. What should we do when the principle of common humanity is denied and crushed?

We are under no illusion as to what academics, media academics included, can achieve on their own. Neither are we arguing for any measures that undermine the independence of scholars. In his contrasting analysis of Foucault's universal intellectual, Bourdieu argued that intellectuals can become the champions of the interest of the universal. The model for him, as was the case for other French intellectuals, was Emile Zola, and in particular, how Zola – through his intervention in the Dreyfus Affair – 'constituted, as a deliberate and legitimate choice, the stance of independence and dignity appropriate to a man of letters, by putting his own kind of authority at the service of political causes. To achieve this, Zola needed to produce a new figure, by inventing for the artist, a mission of prophetic subversion, inseparably intellectual and political' (Bourdieu, 1996: 130). Such interventions in public life do not subordinate the cultural to the political. On the contrary, Bourdieu asserts, such activity is essential for the full independence of the writer: 'paradoxically, it is the autonomy of the intellectual field that makes possible the inaugural act of a writer who, in the name of norms belonging to the literary field, intervenes in the political field, thus constituting himself as an intellectual' (1996: 130).

One does not have to subscribe to Bourdieu's assumption that intellectuals can play the role of a universal class. Academics and 'knowledge producers' are not by themselves revolutionary subjects and militant practitioners. We know that academia has all too often failed to predict significant uprisings, revolutions and social movements. In trying to catch history on the wing, however, media scholars still have an important role to play: to speak truth to power and to demonstrate empathy with the marginalised, demonised, oppressed, and all of those who face the brunt of unequal social relations. This is not an all or nothing position, but an aspiration to embrace a shared humanity and commit to the redistribution of material and intellectual resources. We should do this in order to navigate our way and not get lost. Prior to the invention of the compass, one technique that sailors used to navigate the Mediterranean was to stay in sight of land. The right and the humanity of ordinary people is a land that intellectuals should always have in sight.

BIBLIOGRAPHY

Abbott, A. (1988) *The System of Professions: An Essay on the Division of Expert Labor.* Chicago, IL: Chicago University Press.

Abrams, P. (1988 [1977]) Notes on the difficulty of studying the state, *Journal of Historical Sociology*, 1(1): 58–89.

Abramson, B.D. (2001) Media policy after regulation? *International Journal of Cultural Studies*, 4(3): 301–26.

Adorno, T. (1980) 'Commitment', in *Aesthetics and Politics*. London: Verso.

Agamben, G. (2005) *State of Exception.* Chicago, IL: University of Chicago Press.

Ahmad, A. (1992) *In Theory: Classes, Nations, Literatures.* London: Verso.

Albrow, M. and Glasius, M. (2008) 'Introduction: Democracy and the Possibility of a Global Public Sphere', in M. Albrow, H. Anheier, M. Glasius, M. Price and M. Kaldor (eds), *Global Civil Society 2007/08: Communicative Power and Democracy.* London: Sage.

Allan, K. (2018) '"Investment in Me": Uncertain Futures and Debt in the Intern Economy', in S. Taylor and S. Luckman (eds), *The New Normal of Working Lives: Critical Studies in Contemporary Work and Employment.* Basingstoke: Palgrave Macmillan, pp. 245–64.

Aljazeera (2019) 'State Department Rejects More Than 37,000 Visas Due to Travel Ban', 27 February. Available at: www.aljazeera.com/news/2019/02/state-department-rejects-37000-visas-due-travel-ban-190227210725292.html (accessed 24 February 2020).

Alperovitz, G. and Dubb, S. (2013) The possibility of a pluralist commonwealth and a community-sustaining economy, *The Good Society*, 22(1): 1–25.

Anderson, C., Bell, E. and Shirky, C. (2015) *Post Industrial Journalism: Adapting to the Present.* New York: Tow Centre for Digital Journalism.

Anderson, P. (2005) *Spectrum.* London: Verso.

Andrejevic, M. (2007) *iSpy: Surveillance and Power in the Interactive Era.* Lawrence: University of Kansas Press.

Andrejevic, M. (2014) Big data, big questions: the big data divide, *International Journal of Communication,* 8: 1673–89.

Angwin, J., Larson, J., Mattu, S. and Kirchner, L. (2016) 'Machine Bias: There's Software Used Across the Country to Predict Future Criminals. And It's Biased against Blacks'. *ProPublica,* 23 May. Available at: www.propublica.org/article/machine-bias-risk-assessments-in-criminal-sentencing (accessed 24 February 2020).

Arendt, H. (1951) *The Origins of Totalitarianism*. New York: Schocken Books.

Arendt, H. (1970) *On Violence*. New York: Harcourt.

Arendt, H. (1994) 'We Refugees', in M. Robinson (ed.), *Altogether Elsewhere: Writers on Exile*. Boston, MA and London: Faber and Faber.

Armingeon, K. and Schadel, L. (2015) Social inequality in political participation: the dark sides of individualisation, *West European Politics*, 38(1): 1–27.

Armstrong, S. (2018) *The New Poverty*. London: Verso.

Arora, P. (2018) *The Next.Billion Users: Digital Life Beyond the West*. Cambridge, MA: Harvard University Press.

Arora, P. and Thompson, L.H. (2018) Crowdsourcing as a platform for digital labour uions, *International Journal of Communications*, 12: 2314–32.

Atkinson, R., Parker, S. and Burrows, R. (2017) Elite formation, power and space in contemporary London, *Theory, Culture & Society*, 34(5–6): 179–200.

Babb, S. (2005) 'The Rise of the New Money Doctors in Mexico', in G. Epstein (ed.), *Financialization and the World Economy*. Cheltenham: Edward Elgar, pp. 243–59.

Bachrach, P. and Baratz, M. (1962) Two faces of power, *American Political Science Review*, 56(4): 947–52.

Bakir, V., Herring, E., Miller, D. and Robinson, P. (2018) Organized persuasive communication: a new conceptual framework for public relations and propaganda research, *Critical Sociology*. doi: 10.1177/0896920518764586

Balibar, E. (2008) Historical dilemmas of democracy and their contemporary relevance for citizenship, *Rethinking Marxism*, 20(4): 522–38.

Balibar, E. (2010) Marxism and war, *Radical Philosophy*, 160: 9–17.

Ball, T. and Dagger, R. (2013) *Ideals and Ideologies: A Reader* (9th edn). Abingdon: Routledge.

Barnett, A. (2017) *The Lure of Greatness: England's Brexit and America's Trump*. London: Unbound.

Barney, D. (2018) 'Infrastructure', *Krisis*, 2. Available at: https://krisis.eu/nl/infrastructure/ (accessed 24 February 2020).

Barrow, A. and Chia, J. (2016) *Gender, Violence and the State in Asia*, Abingdon: Routledge.

Bauman, Z. (2000) *Liquid Modernity*. Cambridge: Polity.

Bauman, Z. (2007) *Liquid Times: Living in an Age of Uncertainty*. Cambridge: Polity.

Bauman, Z. and Bordoni, C. (2014) *State of Crisis*. Cambridge: Polity.

Beck, U. (2006) *Cosmpolitan Vision*. Cambridge: Polity.

Benjamin, J. (May, 2015) 'PFI, the Banks and the People Uncovering the Biggest Threat to the NHS'. Available at: www.perc.org.uk/project_posts/

pfi-the-banks-and-the-people-uncovering-the-biggest-threat-to-the-nhs/ (accessed 24 February 2020).

Benjamin, W. (1968) *Illuminations*. New York: Schocken Books.

Benkler, Y. (2006) *The Wealth of Networks.* New Haven, CT: Yale University Press.

Bennett, W.L. and Livingston, S. (2018) The disinformation order: disruptive communication and the decline of democratic institutions, *European Journal of Communication*, 33(2): 122–39.

Bennett, W.L. and Pfetsch, B. (2018) Rethinking political communication in a time of disrupted public spheres, *Journal of Communication*, 68(2): 243–53.

Bennett, W.L. and Segerberg, A. (2013) *The Logic of Connective Action: Digital Media and the Personalization of Contentious Politics.* Cambridge: Cambridge University Press.

Bennett-Jones, O. (2018) Can't afford to tell the truth, *London Review of Books*, 40(24): 29–32.

Benson, R. (2014) 'Challenging the New Descriptivism', *Qualitative Political Communication Research.* Available at: https://qualpolicomm.wordpress.com/2014/06/05/challenging-the-new-descriptivism-rod-bensons-talk-from-qualpolcomm-preconference/ (accessed 20 February 2020).

Berry, M. (2016) No alternative to austerity: how BBC broadcast news reported the deficit debate, *Media, Culture & Society*, 38(6): 844–63.

Berry, M. (2019) *The Media, The Public and the Great Financial Crisis.* Basingstoke: Palgrave Macmillan.

Berry, M., Garcia-Blanco, I. and Moore, K. (2016) 'Press coverage of the refugee and migrant crisis in the EU: a content analysis of five European countries', project report. Geneva: United Nations High Commissioner for Refugees. Available at: www.unhcr.org/56bb369c9.html (accessed 21 February 2020).

Bevir, M. (2012) *Governance: A Very Short Introduction.* Oxford: Oxford University Press.

Birkinbine, B., Gomez, R. and Wasko, J. (eds) (2017) *Global Media Giants.* New York: Routledge.

Birkinbine, B.J. (2018) 'Commons praxis: towards a critical political economy of the digital commons, *tripleC*, 16(1): 290–305.

Birtchnell, J. and Caletrio, J. (eds) (2014) *Elite Mobilities.* Abingdon: Routledge.

Blanchflower, D.G. (2019) *Not Working: Where Have All the Good Jobs Gone?* Princeton, NJ: Princeton University Press.

Blau, U. (2017) 'Inside the Clandestine World of Israel's "BDS-busting" Ministry'. *Haaretz*, 26 March. Available at: www.haaretz.com/israel-news/MAGAZINE-inside-the-clandestine-world-of-israels-bds-busting-ministry-1.5453212 (accessed 20 February 2020).

Blumler, J. (2013) 'The Fourth Age of Political Communication'. Keynote address at Frei University, Berlin, 12 September. Available at: www.fgpk.de/en/2013/gastbeitrag-von-jay-g-blumler-the-fourth-age-of-political-communication-2/ (accessed 12 February 2020).

Blumler, J. and Coleman, S. (2015) 'Democracy and the media revisited', *Javnost: the Public*, 22(2): 118–28.

Blumler, J. and Gurevitch, M. (1995) *The Crisis of Public Communication*. Abingdon: Routledge.

Blumler, J. and Kavanagh, D. (1999) The third age of political communication: influences and features, *Political Communication*, 16(3): 209–30.

Bobbio, N. (1990) *Liberalism and Democracy*. London: Verso.

Bode, L. and Dalrymple, K. (2016) Politics in 140 characters or less: campaign communication, network interaction, and political participation on Twitter, *Journal of Political Marketing*, 15: 311–32.

Bolleyer, N. (2013) *New Parties in Old Party Systems: Persistence and Decline in 17 Democracies*. Oxford: Oxford University Press.

Borkin, S. (2019) *Platform Co-operatives: Solving the Capital Conundrum*. London: Nesta.

Bose, R. (2020) 'A Dangerous Fallout of Coronavirus Pandemic: Government Suspends Ban on Sex Determination Test', *NEWS18*, 8 April. Available at: https://www.news18.com/news/buzz/a-dangerous-fallout-of-coronavirus-pandemic-govt-suspends-ban-on-sex-determination-test-2569477.html (accessed 28 April 2020).

Botsman, R. (2017) 'Big Data meets Big Brother as China Moves to Rate its Citizens'. *Wire*, 21 October. Available at: www.wired.co.uk/article/chinese-government-social-credit-score-privacy-invasion (accessed 23 February 2020).

Bourdieu, P. (1984) *Distinction: A Social Critique of the Judgement of Taste*. Abingdon: Routledge.

Bourdieu, P. (2003) *Firing Back: Against the Tyranny of the Market 2*. London: Verso.

Bourdieu, P. (1988) *Homo Academicus*. Cambridge: Polity.

Bourdieu, P. (1996) *The Rules of Art*. Cambridge: Polity.

Bourdieu, P. (2014) *On the State*. Cambridge: Polity.

Boutang, Y.M. (2011) *Cognitive Capitalism*. Cambridge: Polity.

Bowman, A. et al. (2015) *What a Waste: Outsourcing and How It All Goes Wrong*. Manchester: Manchester University Press.

Braun, J. (2015) *This Programme is Brought to You By ... Distributing Television News Online*. New Haven, CT: Yale University Press.

Brecht, B. (1979) Radio as a means of communication: a talk on the function of radio, *Screen*, 20(3/4).

Brennen, J. et al. (2020) *Types, Sources and Claims of COVID-19 Misinformation.* Oxford: Reuters Institute for the Study of Journalism. Available at: https://www. ofcom.org.uk/__data/assets/pdf_file/0031/193747/covid-19-news-consumption-week-one-findings.pdf (accessed 15 April 2020)

Brevini, B. and Murdock, G. (2017) *Carbon Capitalism and Communications: Confronting Climate Crisis.* Basingstoke: Palgrave Macmillan.

Briant, E. (2015) *Propaganda and Counter-Terrorism: Strategies for Global Change.* Manchester: Manchester University Press.

Brie, M. (2008) 'Emancipation and the Left: The Issue of Violence', in L. Panitch and C. Leys (eds), *Socialist Register 2009: Violence Today: Actually-Existing Barbarism.* New York: Monthly Review Press, pp. 239–59.

Broumas, A. (2017) Social democratic and critical theories of the intellectual commons: a critical analysis, *tripleC: Communication, Capitalism & Critique. Open Access Journal for a Global Sustainable Information Society,* 15(1): 100–26.

Brown, W. (2005) *Edgework: Critical Essays on Knowledge and Power.* Princeton, NJ: Princeton University Press.

Brown, W. (2015) *Undoing the Demos: Neoliberalism's Stealth Revolution.* Cambridge, MA: MIT Press.

Brown, W. and Littler, J. (2018) 'Where the Fires Are'. *Soundings*, issue 68. Available at: www.lwbooks.co.uk/soundings/68/interview-where-the-fires-are (accessed 24 February 2020).

Butler, J. (1990) *Gender Trouble: Feminism and the Subversion of Identity.* Abingdon: Routledge.

Cable, V. (2009) *The Storm: The World Economic Crisis and What it Means.* London: Atlantic.

Cadwalladr, C. and Graham-Harrison, E. (2018) 'Revealed: 50 million Facebook Profiles Harvested for Cambridge Analytica in Major Data Breach'. *Guardian*, 17 March. Available at: www.theguardian.com/news/2018/mar/17/cambridge-analytica-facebook-influence-us-election (accessed 24 February 2020).

Cage, J. (2018) *Le Prix de la Démocratie.* Paris: Fayard.

Calhoun, C. (ed.) (1992) 'Introduction', in *Habermas and the Public Sphere.* Cambridge, MA: MIT Press.

Carlson, M. (2016) 'The Question of Objectivity in the 2016 Presidential Election', in D. Lilleker, E. Thorsen and D. Jackson (eds), *US Election Analysis 2016: Media, Voters and the Campaign.* Bournemouth: Center for the Study of Journalism, Culture and Community (CsJCC).

Carroll, R. (2018) 'Loughinisland Killings, Journalists Arrested Over Alleged Document Theft', *Guardian*, 31 August. Available at: www.theguardian.com/

uk-news/2018/aug/31/loughinisland-killings-journalists-arrested-over-stolen-docu-ments (accessed 20 February 2020).

Carroll, W. (2008) 'The Corporate Elite and the Transformation of Finance Capital: A View from Canada', in M. Savage and K. Williams (eds), *Remembering Elites*. Oxford: Wiley-Blackwell.

Castells, M. (1998) *End of Millennium*. Oxford: Blackwell.

Castells, M. (2000) *The Rise of the Network Society* (2nd edn). Cambridge, MA: Blackwell.

Castells, M. (2001) *The Internet Galaxy: Reflections on the Internet, Business and Society.* Oxford: Oxford University Press.

Castells, M. (2009) *Communication Power*. Oxford: Oxford University Press.

Castells, M. (2015) *Networks of Outrage and Hope: Movements in the Internet Age* (2nd edn). Cambridge: Polity Press.

Castoriadis, C. (1980) Socialism and autonomous society, *Telos*, 43: 91–105.

Cave, T. and Rowell, A. (2014) *A Quiet Word: Crony Capitalism and Broken Politics in Britain*. London: Bodley Head.

Cerny, P., Menz, G. and Soderberg, S. (2005) 'Different Roads to Globalization: Neo-Liberalism, the Competition State, and Politics in a More Open World', in S. Soderberg, G. Menz and G. Cerny (eds), *Internalizing Globalization: The Rise of Neo-Liberalism and the Decline of National Varieties of Capitalism*. Basingstoke: Palgrave Macmillan, pp. 1–30.

Chadwick, A. (2017) *The Hybrid Media System: Politics and Power* (2nd edn). Oxford: Oxford University Press.

Chadwick, A. and Howard, P.N. (eds) (2009) *Routledge Handbook of Internet Politics*. Abingdon: Routledge.

Chadwick, A. and Stromer-Galley, J. (2016) Digital media, power and democracy in parties and election campaigns: party decline or party renewal?', *Harvard Journal of Press/Politics*, 21(3): 283–93.

Chakravartty, P. and Da Silva, D.F. (2012) Accumulation, dispossession, and debt: the racial logic of global capitalism—an introduction, *American Quarterly*, 64(3): 361–85.

Chiaramonte, A. and Emanuele, V. (2017) Party system volatility, regeneration and de-institutionalisation in Western Europe (1945–2015), *Party Politics*, 23(4): 376–88.

Chugg, D. (2017) Winning the strategic communications war with Daesh, *Civil Service Quarterly*, 15(4–5).

Chun, W.H.K. (2017) *Updating to Remain the Same Habitual New Media*. Cambridge, MA: MIT Press.

Chun, W.H.K. (2019) 'Queerying Homophily', in C. Apprich, W.H.K. Chun, F. Cramer and H. Steyerl (eds), *Pattern Discrimination*. Minneapolis, MN: University of Minnesota and Meson Press.

CICOPA (2019) 'May the Cooperative Model Save the Local Media Industry?'. *Work Together,* winter 2018/2019. Available at: https://us2.campaign-archive.com/?u=3a 463471cd0a9c6cf744bf5f8&id=fa5bf03121 (accessed 23 February 2020).

Cobain, I. et al. (2016) 'Inside Ricu, the Shadowy Propaganda Unit Inspired by the Cold War', *Guardian*, 2 May. https://www.theguardian.com/politics/2016/may/02/inside-ricu-the-shadowy-propaganda-unit-inspired-by-the-cold-war

Cohn, T. (2016) *Global Political Economy: Theory and Practice*. New York: Routledge.

Coleman, S. and Blumler, J. (2009) *The Internet and Democratic Citizenship: Theory, Practice and Policy*. New York: Cambridge University Press.

Conti, N., Hutter, S. and Nanov, K. (2018) Party competition and political representation in crisis: introduction, *Party Politics*, 24(1): 3–9.

Coole, D. and Frost, S. (eds) (2012) *New Materialisms: Ontology, Agency, and Politics*. Durham, NC: Duke University Press.

Cordella, A. (2010) Information infrastructure: an actor network perspective, *Journal of Actor Network Theory and Technological Innovation*, 2(1): 27–53.

Corn, D. and Mahanta, S. (2011) 'From Libya With Love', *Mother Jones*, 3 March. Available at: www.motherjones.com/politics/2011/03/libya-qaddafi-monitor-group/ (accessed 20 February 2020).

Corner, J. (2018) 'Mediatization': media theory's word of the decade, *Media Theory Journal*, 2(2). Available at: http://mediatheoryjournal.org/john-corner-mediatization/ (accessed 24 February 2020).

Corner, J. and Pels, D. (2003) *Media and the Restyling of Politics*. London: Sage.

Couldry, N. and Hepp, A. (2013) Conceptualizing mediatization: contexts, traditions, arguments, *Communication Theory*, 23: 191–202.

Couldry, N. and Hepp, A. (2017) 'Call for Contributions to a Pre-Conference on "Data and the Future of Critical Social Research" for the 2017 ICA Conference in San Diego'. Available at: www.icahdq.org/mpage/PC27 (accessed 22 February 2020).

Couldry, N. and Powell, A. (2014) Big data from the bottom up, *Big Data & Society*, July–December: 1–5.

Cox, G. (2012) *Cox Review: Overcoming Short-Termism within British Business: The Key to Sustained Economic Growth*. London: Labour Party.

Coyle, D. (1999) *The Weightless World: Strategies for Managing the Digital Economy*. Oxford: Capstone.

Crawford, K. (2016) 'A.I.'s White Guy Problem', *New York Times,* 25 June. Available at: www.nytimes.com/2016/06/26/opinion/sunday/artificial-intelligences-white-guy-problem.html (accessed 21 February 2020).

Cribb, J., Keiller, A.N. and Waters, T. (2018) *Living Standards, Poverty and Inequality in the UK: 2018*. London: IFS.

Cronin, A. (2018) *Public Relations Capitalism: Promotional Culture, Publics and Commercial Democracy.* Basingstoke: Palgrave Macmillan.

Crouch, C. (2004) *Post-Democracy.* Cambridge: Polity.

Crouch, C. (2011) *The Strange Non-Death of Neo-Liberalism.* Cambridge: Polity.

CSF (2018) *Civil Society in England: Its Current State and Future Possibilities.* Available at: https://civilsocietyfutures.org/wp-content/uploads/sites/6/2018/11/Civil-Society-Futures__Civil-Society-in-England__small-1.pdf (accessed 20 February 2020).

Curran, J. (2002) *Media and Power.* Abingdon: Routledge.

Curran, J., Fenton, N. and Freedman, D. (2016) *Misunderstanding the Internet* (2nd edn). Abingdon: Routledge.

Curtis, L. (1998) *Ireland: The Propaganda War – The British Media and the Battle for Hearts and Minds.* London: Pluto.

Cushion, S. et al. (2018) Newspapers, impartiality and television news: intermedia agenda-setting during the 2015 UK General Election campaign, *Journalism Studies*, 19(2): 162–81.

Dabashi, H. (2015) *Can Non-Europeans Think?* London: Zed Books.

Dahl, R. (1961) *Who Governs? Democracy and Power in an American City.* New Haven, CT: Yale University Press.

Dahlgren, P. (1995) *Television and the Public Sphere: Citizenship, Democracy and the Media*. London: Sage.

Dahlgren, P. (2005) The internet, public spheres and political communication: dispersion and deliberation, *Political Communications*, 22(2): 147–62.

Dahlgren, P. (2012) Public intellectuals, online media, and public spheres: current realignments, *International Journal of Politics, Culture and Society*, 25(4): 95–110.

Dahlgren, P. and Sparks, C. (1992) *Communication and Citizenship: Journalism and the Public Sphere.* Abingdon: Routledge.

Dalton, R. (2004) *Democratic Challenges, Democratic Choices: The Erosion of Political Support in Advanced Industrial Democracies.* Oxford: Oxford University Press.

Dalton, R. (2017) Party representation across multiple issue dimensions, *Party Politics*, 23(6): 609–22.

Dalton, R. and Wattenberg, M. (eds) (2002) *Parties Without Partisans: Political Change in Advanced Industrial Democracies.* Oxford: Oxford University Press.

Danewid, I. (2019) The Fire this Time: Grenfell, racial capitalism and the urbanisation of empire, *European Journal of International Relations*, 26(1): 289–313.

Dasgupta, R. (2018) 'The Demise of the Nation State', *Guardian*, 5 April. Available at: www.theguardian.com/news/2018/apr/05/demise-of-the-nation-state-rana-dasgupta (accessed 18 January 2020).

Davies, N. (2008) *Flat Earth News*. London: Chatto and Windus.

Davies, R., Haldane, A., Nielsen, M. and Pezzini, S. (2014) Measuring the costs of short-termism, *Journal of Financial Stability*, 12: 16–25.

Davies, W. (2017) 'What Is 'Neo' about Neoliberalism?', in Abraham-Hamanoiel et al. (eds), *Liberalism in Neoliberal Times: Dimensions, Contradictions, Limits*. London: Goldsmiths.

Davis, A. (2002) *Public Relations Democracy: Public Relations, Politics and the Mass Media in Britain*. Manchester: Manchester University Press.

Davis, A. (2003) *Are Prisons Obsolete?* New York: Seven Stories.

Davis, A. (2013) *Promotional Cultures: The Rise and Spread of Advertising, Public Relations, Marketing and Branding*. Cambridge: Polity.

Davis, A. (2017a) The new professional econocracy and the maintenance of elite power, *Political Studies*, 65(3): 594–610.

Davis, A. (ed.) (2017b) *The Death of Public Knowledge?* Available at: gold.ac.uk/goldsmiths-press/the-death-of-public-knowledge/

Davis, A. (2018) *Reckless Opportunists: Elites at the End of the Establishment*. Manchester: Manchester University Press.

Davis, A. (2019) *Political Communication: A New Introduction for Crisis Times*. Cambridge: Polity.

Davis, A. and Walsh, C. (2017) The role of the state in the financialisation of the UK economy, *Political Studies*, 64(3): 666–2.

Davis, A. and Williams, K. (2017) Introduction: elites and power after financialization, *Theory, Culture & Society*, 34(5–6): 27–51.

Dawes, S. (2014) Press freedom, privacy and the public sphere, *Journalism Studies*, 15(1): 17–32.

Day, J. (2003) 'Murdoch Praises Blair's Courage', *Guardian,* 12 February. Available at: www.theguardian.com/politics/2003/feb/12/uk.iraqandthemedia (accessed 24 February 2020).

De Angelis, M. (2017) *Omnia Sunt Communia*. London: Zed Books.

De Beauvoir, S. (1971) *The Second Sex*. New York: Knopf.

De Peuter, G. and Dyer-Witheford, N. (2010) Commons and cooperatives, *Affinities: A Journal of Radical Theory, Culture, and Action*, 4(1): 30–56.

Deacon, D. and Stanyer, J. (2014) Mediatization: key concept or conceptual bandwagon? *Media, Culture & Society*, 36(7): 1032–44.

Dean, J. (2009) *Democracy and Other Neoliberal Fantasies: Communicative Capitalism and Left Politics*. Durham, NC and London: Duke University Press.

Delaney, C. (2019) 'How to use the internet to change the world – and win elections'. Epolitics.com.

Delli Carpini, M.S. and Williams, B.A. (2001) 'Let Us Infotain You: Politics in the New Media Environment', in W.L. Bennett and R.M. Entman (eds), *Mediated Politics: Communication in the Future of Democracy*. Cambridge: Cambridge University Press.

Department for Business Innovation & Skills (2016) 'Success as a Knowledge Economy: Teaching Excellence, Social Mobility and Student Choice', white paper. Available at: https://fee.org/articles/academics-write-rubbish-nobody-reads/?utm_source=zapier&utm_medium=facebook (accessed 24 February 2020).

Domhoff, G. (1967) *Who Rules America?* Englewood Cliffs, NJ: Prentice Hall.

Dore, L. (2016) '*The Sun* has Deleted its List of "Iraq war traitors" from 2003', *Independent*, 7 July. Available at: www.indy100.com/article/the-sun-has-deleted-its-list-of-iraq-war-traitors-from- 2003–WJYTGafvHW (accessed 19 February 2020).

Dorling, D. (2014) *Inequality and the 1%.* London: Verso.

Downie, L. (2013) 'The Obama Administration and the Press', *Committee to Protect Journalists*. Available at: https://cpj.org/x/5729 (accessed 24 February 2020).

Durkheim, E. (1992 [1904]) *Professional Ethics and Civil Morals.* Abingdon: Routledge.

Eatwell, R. and Goodwin, M. (2018) *National Populism: The Revolt Against Liberal Democracy.* London: Pelican.

Edelman (2020) *Edelman Trust Barometer. Special Report: Trust and the Coronavirus*. Available at https://www.edelman.com/sites/g/files/aatuss191/files/2020-03/2020%20Edelman%20Trust%20Barometer%20Coronavirus%20Special%20Report_0.pdf (accessed 15 April 2020).

Edwards, D. and Cromwell. D. (2003) 'How Andrew Marr got carried away', *New Statesman*, 21 April. Available at: www.newstatesman.com/node/194710?page=24 (accessed 24 February 2020).

Edwards, P. (2003) 'Infrastructure and Modernity: Force, Time, and Social Organization in the History of Sociotechnical Systems', in T. Misa, P. Brey and A. Feenberg (eds), *Modernity and Technology.* Cambridge, MA: MIT Press, pp. 185–226.

Eisenstein, E. (1979) *The Printing Press as an Agent of Change*. Cambridge: Cambridge University Press.

EIU (2016) *Democracy Index 2016* (8th edn). London: Economist Intelligence Unit.

EIU (2017/18) *Democracy Index 2016/2017* (9th/10th edns). London: Economist Intelligence Unit.

Ekström, M., Fornäs, J., Jansson, A. and Jerslev, A. (2016) Three tasks for mediatization research: contributions to an open agenda, *Media, Culture & Society*, 38(7): 1090–8.

Elder, L., Emdon, H., Fuchs, R. and Petrazzini, B. (eds) (2013) *Connecting ICTs to Development: The IDRC Experience*. London: Anthem.

Electoral Commission (2018) *Digital Campaigning – Increasing Transparency for Voters*. Available at: www.electoralcommission.org.uk/who-we-are-and-what-we-do/changing-electoral-law/transparent-digital-campaigning/report-digital-campaigning-increasing-transparency-voters.

Elliott, A. (2014) 'Tracking the Mobile Lives of Globals', in J. Birtchnell and J. Caletrio (eds), *Elite Mobilities*. Abingdon: Routledge, pp. 21–39.

Elliott, L. and Atkinson, D. (2009) *The Gods that Failed: How the Financial Elite Have Gambled Away Our Futures*. London: Vintage.

Eltantawy, N. and Wiest, J. (2011) The Arab Spring: social media in the Egyptian revolution: reconsidering resource mobilization theory, *International Journal of Communication*, 5: 1207–24.

Elvestad, E. and Phillips, A. (2018) *Misunderstanding News Audiences: Seven Myths of the Social Media Era*. Abingdon: Routledge.

eMarketer (2019) 'Digital Ad Spending 2019'. https://www.emarketer.com/content/global-digital-ad-spending-2019

En comu (2019) *Fearless Cities – A Guide to the Global Municipalist Movement*. London: New Internationalist Publications.

Engelen, E. et al. (2011) *After the Great Complacence: Financial Crisis and the Politics of Reform*. Oxford: Oxford University Press.

Engels, F. (1947 [1878]) *Anti-Duhring*. Moscow: Progress.

Entman, R. and Usher, N. (2018) Framing in a fractured democracy: impacts of digital technology on ideology, power and cascading network activation, *Journal of Communication* 68(2): 309–17.

European Federation of Journalists (2018) 'Hungary: Demonstrators Demand Independence of Public Service Media', 19 December. Available at: https://europeanjournalists.org/blog/2018/12/19/hungary-demonstrators-demand-independence-of-public-service-media/ (accessed 12 February 2020).

Fairvote (2008) 'Presidential Election Inequality: The Electoral College in the 21st Century', The Center for Voting and Democracy. Available at: http://archive.fairvote.org/media/perp/presidentialinequality.pdf (accessed 24 February 2020).

Fairvote (2013) 'Fairvote Maps the 2012 Presidential Campaign'. Available at: www.fairvote.org/fairvote-maps-the-2012-presidential-campaign (accessed 24 February 2020).

Farah, W. (2020) 'Institutional Racism in the NHS Intensifies in Times of Crisis', *Institute of Race Relations*, 23 April. Available at: http://www.irr.org.uk/news/institutional-racism-in-the-nhs-intensifies-in-times-of-crisis/ (accessed 28 April 2020).

Featherstone, M. (2014) 'Super-rich Lifestyles', in J. Birtchnell and J. Caletrio (eds), *Elite Mobilities*. Abingdon: Routledge, pp. 99–135.

Fekete, L. (2016) 'Flying the flag for neoliberalism', *Race & Class*, 58(3): 3–22.

Fekete, L. (2020) 'Is the "War on COVID-19" Morphing into a War on the Poor?', *Institute of Race Relations*, 9 April. Available at: http://www.irr.org.uk/news/is-the-war-on-covid-19-morphing-into-a-war-on-the-poor/ (accessed 28 April 2020).

Fenton, N. (2010) 'Drowning or Waving? New Media, Journalism and Democracy', in N. Fenton (ed.), *New Media, Old News: Journalism and Democracy in the Digital Age*. London: Sage, pp. 3–16.

Fenton, N. (2016) *Digital, Political, Radical*. Cambridge: Polity.

Fenton, N. (2018) Regulation is freedom: phone hacking, press regulation and the Leveson Inquiry – the story so far, *Communications Law,* 23(3).

Fenton, N. and Titley, G. (2015) Mourning and longing: media studies learning to let go of liberal democracy, *European Journal of Communication*, 30(5): 1–17.

Ferguson, C. (2012) *Inside Job: The Financiers Who Pulled Off the Heist of the Century*. Oxford: Oneworld.

Ferguson, J. (2018) 'Tory Minister "misled Parliament" over Government Funded Infowars Attack on Jeremy Corbyn', *Daily Record*, 16 December. www.dailyrecord.co.uk/news/scottish-news/tory-minister-mislead-parliament-over-13738951

Fisk, R. (2016) 'I'm already tired of the "lessons" of Chilcot: What can we learn from a report that ignores Iraqis?', *Independent*, 7 July. www.independent.co.uk/voices/chilcot- inquiry-report-iraq-war-robert-fisk-tired-of-lessons-ignores-iraqis-a7124841.html

Flew, T. (2007) *Understanding Global Media*. Basingstoke: Palgrave Macmillan.

Flew, T., Iosifidis, P. and Steemers, J. (eds) (2016) *Global Media and National Policies: The Return of the State*. Basingstoke: Palgrave Macmillan.

Flinders, M. and Buller, J. (2006) 'Depoliticization, Democracy and Arena Shifting', in T. Christensen and P. Laegreid (eds), *Autonomy and Regulation*. Cheltenham: Edward Elgar.

Forbes (2016) *The World's Largest Companies*. Available at: www.forbes.com/sites/steveschaefer/2016/05/25/the-worlds-largest-companies-2016/#5a472fa137eb (accessed 21 February 2020).

Foucault, M. (1977) *Language, Counter-memory, Practice: Selected Essays and Interviews*. Ithaca, NY: Cornell University Press.

Frank, T. (2016) *Listen Liberal: Or, Whatever Happened to the Party of the People?* London: Scribe UK.

Franklin, B. (1997) *Newzak and News Media.* London: Arnold.

Franklin, B. (2004) *Packaging Politics: Political Communications in Britain's Media Democracy* (2nd edn). London: Arnold.

Fraser, N. (1997) 'Rethinking the Public Sphere: A Contribution to the Critique of Actually Existing Democracies', in N. Fraser (ed.), *Justice Interuptus: Critical Reflections on the "Postsocialist" Condition.* Abingdon: Routledge.

Fraser, N. (2019) *The Old Is Dying and the New Cannot Be Born.* London: Verso.

Fraser, N. and Jaeggi, R. (2018) *Capitalism: A Conversation in Critical Theory.* Cambridge: Polity.

Freedman, D. (2009) 'The Political Economy of the "New" News Environment', in N. Fenton (ed.), *New Media, Old News: Journalism and Democracy in a Digital Age.* London: Sage.

Freedman, D. (2014) *The Contradictions of Media Power.* London: Bloomsbury.

Freedman, D. (2016) Media policy norms for a Europe in crisis, *Javnost*, 23(2): 120–34.

Freedman, D. (2016) 'The Internet of Rules', in J. Curran, N. Fenton and D. Freedman (eds), *Misunderstanding the Internet* (2nd edn). Abingdon: Routledge, pp. 117–44.

Freedman, D. (2018) 'Populism and media policy failure', *European Journal of Communication*, 33(6): 604–18.

Freedman, D. (2019) 'Public service' and the journalism crisis: is the BBC the answer? *Television & New Media*, 20(3): 203–18.

Freedom House (2017) *Freedom in the World 2017.* Washington, DC: Freedom House.

Freeland, C. (2012) *Plutocrats: The Rise of the New Global Super-Rich.* London: Penguin.

Frum, D. (2018) *Trumpocracy: The Corruption of the American Republic.* New York: HarperCollins.

Fuchs, C. (2014a) *Social Media: A Critical Introduction* (2nd edn). London: Sage.

Fuchs, C. (2014b) *Digital Labour and Karl Marx.* Abingdon: Routledge.

Gandy, O. (1982) *Beyond Agenda Setting: Information Subsidies and Public Policy.* Norwood, NJ: Ablex.

Garnham, N. (1995) The media and narratives of the intellectual, *Media, Culture & Society*, 17(3): 359–84.

Gerbaudo, P. (2012) *Tweets and Streets: Social Media and Contemporary Activism.* London: Pluto.

Gerbaudo, P. (2017) *The Mask and the Flag: Populism, Citizenship and Global Protest.* London: Hurst and Co.

Gerbaudo, P. (2018) *The Digital Party: Political Organisation and Online Democracy.* London: Pluto.

Gibson, R.K. (2015) Party change, social media and the rise of 'citizen-initiated' campaigning, *Party Politics*, 21(2): 183–97.

Gibson-Graham, J.K. (2006) *A Postcapitalist Politics*. Minneapolis, MN: University of Minnesota Press.

Giddens, A. (2006) 'The Colonel and His Third Way', *New Statesman*, 28 August. Available at: www.newstatesman.com/politics/politics/2014/04/colonel-and-his-third-way (accessed 24 February 2020).

Giddens, A. (2007) 'My Chat with the Colonel', *Guardian*, 9 March. Available at: www.theguardian.com/commentisfree/2007/mar/09/comment.libya (accessed 20 February 2020).

Gitlbert, J. (2014) *Common Ground: Democracy and Collectivity in an Age of Individualism.* London: Pluto.

Giltin, T. (2011) 'Perils of Public Intellectualizing', *The Chronicle of Higher Education*, 24 February. Available at: www.chronicle.com/blogs/brainstorm/perils-of-public-intellectualizing/32610 (accessed 24 February 2020).

Gitlin, T. (2011) 'The Left Declares Its Independence', *New York Times*, 8 October. Available at: www.nytimes.com/2011/10/09/opinion/sunday/occupy-wall-street-and-the-tea-party.html (accessed 24 February 2020).

Goclowski (2016) 'Public Media Independence Undermined in Poland – OSCE', *Reuters*, 22 September. https://uk.reuters.com/article/uk-poland-media-osce-idUKKCN11S18W

Golding, P. (2017) Citizen detriment: communications, inequality, and social order, *International Journal of Communication*, 11: 4305–23.

Golding, P. and Elliot, P. (1979) *Making the News*. London and New York: Longman.

Golding, P. and Murdock, G. (2000) 'Culture, Communications and Political Economy', in J. Curran and M. Gurevitch (eds), *Mass Media and Society* (3rd edn). London: Arnold.

Goodhart, D. (2017) *The Road to Somewhere: The Populist Revolt and the Future of Politics.* London: Hurst and Co.

Gorz, A. (2010) *The Immaterial: Knowledge, Value and Capital.* London: Seagull.

Gramsci, A. (1971) *Selections from the Prison Notebooks.* London: Lawrence & Wishart.

Graves, L. (2016) *Deciding What's True: The Rise of Political Fact-Checking in American Journalism*. New York: Columbia University Press.

Greenwald, G. (2014) *No Place to Hide: Edward Snowden, the NSA & The Surveillance State.* London: Penguin.

Grunig, J. and Hunt, T. (1984) *Managing Public Relations.* New York: Holt, Rinehart and Winston.

Habermas, J. (1989 [1962]) *The Structural Transformation of the Public Sphere: An Inquiry into a Category of Bourgeois Society* (trans. T. Burger). Cambridge: Polity.

Habermas, J. (2002) 'Letter to America: Resentment of US policies is growing', *The Nation*, 26 November. Available from https://www.thenation.com/article/archive/letter-america-0/

Hahnel, R. (2005) *Economic Justice and Democracy: From Competition to Cooperation*. Abingdon: Routledge.

Haiven, M. and Khasnabish, A. (2014) *The Radical Imagination*. London: Zed Books.

Haldane, A. (2010) 'The Contribution of the Financial Sector: Miracle or Mirage?' Speech at the Future of Finance Conference, LSE, 14 July. www.bankofengland.co.uk/speech/2010/the-contribution-of-the-financial-sector-miracle-or-mirage-speech-by-andy-haldane

Hall, S., Critcher, C., Jefferson, T., Clarke, J. and Roberts, B. (1978) *Policing the Crisis: Mugging, the State, and Law and Order*. London: Macmillan.

Hall Jamieson, K. (1996) *Packaging the Presidency: A History and Criticism of Presidential Campaign Advertising* (3rd edn). Oxford: Oxford University Press.

Hansard (2015/2018) *An Audit of Political Engagement*, 12th/15th *Reports*. London: Hansard Society and Electoral Commission.

Hardt, M. and Negri, A. (2011) *Commonwealth*. Cambridge, MA: Harvard University Press.

Harvey, D. (2005) *A Brief History of Neoliberalism*. Oxford: Oxford University Press.

Haskel, J. and Westlake, S. (2018) *Capitalism Without Capital: The Rise of the Intangible Economy*. Princeton, NJ: Princeton University Press.

Hay, C. (2007) *Why We Hate Politics*. Cambridge: Polity.

Held, D. (1983) *States and Societies*. Oxford: Martin Robertson.

Held, D. (2002) Laws of states, laws of peoples, *Legal Theory*, 8: 1–44.

Held, D. (2006) *Models of Democracy* (3rd edn). Cambridge: Polity.

Herman, E. and Chomsky, N. (2002 [1988]) *Manufacturing Consent* (2nd edn). New York: Pantheon.

Hershey, M. (2017) *Party Politics in America* (17th edn). New York: Routledge.

Hess, C. (2008) 'Mapping the New Commons', SSRN. Available at: https://ssrn.com/abstract=1356835 or http://dx.doi.org/10.2139/ssrn.1356835

Hess, C. and Ostrom, E. (2003) Ideas, artifacts, and facilities: information as a common-pool resource, *Law and Contemporary Problems*, 66(1/2): 111–45.

Hess, C. and Ostrom, E. (2007) *Understanding Knowledge as a Commons: From Theory to Practice*. Cambridge, MA: MIT Press.

Heywood, A. (2017) *Political Ideologies: An Introduction* (6th edn). Basingstoke: Palgrave.

Hibbings, J. and Theiss-Morse, E. (2002) *Stealth Democracy: Americans' Beliefs About How Government Should Work.* Cambridge: Cambridge University Press.

High Pay Centre (2015) *Cheques and the City.* London: High Pay Centre.

High Pay Commission (Dec. 2012) *The State of Play: One Year On from the High Pay Commission.* London: High Pay Commission.

Hintz, A., Dencik, L. and Wahl-Jorgenson, K. (2019) *Digital Citizenship in a Datafied Society*. Cambridge: Polity.

Hjarvard, S. (2011) The mediatisation of religion: theorising religion, media and social change, *Culture and Religion*, 12(2): 119–35.

Ho, K. (2009) *Liquidated: An Ethnography of Wall Street.* Durham, NC: Duke University Press.

Holmwood, J. (2015) 'Social Science Inc.', *openDemocracy*, 23 March. Available at: www.opendemocracy.net/en/opendemocracyuk/social-science-inc/ (accessed 20 February 2020).

Holt, J. and Vonderau, P. (2015) '"Where the Internet Lives": Data Centers as Cloud Infrastructure', in L. Parks and N. Starosielski (eds), *Signal Traffic: Critical Studies of Media Infrastructures*. Urbana, IL: University of Illinois Press, pp. 71–93.

Holtz Bacha, C., Langer, A. and Merkle, S. (2014) The personalization of politics in comparative perspective, *European Journal of Communication*, 29(2): 153–70.

Hood, C. (1995) The 'New Public Management' in the 1980s: variations on a theme, *Accounting, Organizations and Society*, 20(2/3): 93–109.

Horkheimer, M. (1982) *Critical Theory*. New York: Seabury.

Horwitz, R. (1989) *The Irony of Regulatory Reform.* Oxford: Oxford University Press.

House of Commons Library (2018) 'All Party Parliamentary Group on Inclusive Growth' 6 April 2018. Available at: https://www.inclusivegrowth.co.uk/house-commons-library-research/

Howard, P., et al. (2011) 'Opening Closed Regimes: What was the Role of Social Media During the Arab Spring?', Working Paper 2011.1, ITPI. Washington, DC: Centre for Communication and Civic Engagement.

Huws, U. (2014) *Labor in the Global Digital Economy.* New York: Monthly Review.

IDEA (2016/2017) *The Global State of Democracy.* Stockholm: Institute for Democracy and Electoral Assistance.

Information Commissioner's Office (2018) *Investigation into the Use of Data Analytics in Political Campaigns: A Report to Parliament.* London: ICO.

Inglehart, R. (1977) *The Silent Revolution: Changing Values and Political Styles Amongst Western Publics.* Princeton, NJ: Princeton University Press.

Inglehart, R. (1990) *Culture Shift.* Princeton, NJ: Princeton University Press.

Inglehart, R. (1997) *Modernization and Postmodernization: Cultural, Economic and Political Change in 43 Countries*, Princeton, NJ: Princeton University Press.

Inglehart, R. and Norris, P. (2016) 'Trump, Brexit, and the Rise of Populism: Economic Have-Nots and Cultural Backlash', Harvard Working Paper No. RWP16-026. Cambridge, MA: Harvard University.

Innis, H. (1964) *The Bias of Communication.* Toronto: University of Toronto Press.

Iosifidis, P. (2016) 'Globalisation and the Re-emergence of the Regulatory State', in T. Flew, P. Iosifidis and J. Steemers (eds), *Global Media and National Policies: The Return of the State.* Basingstoke: Palgrave Macmillan, pp. 16–31.

IPCC (Intergovernmental Panel on Climate Change) (2018) 'Global Warming of 1.5°C', IPCC Report, Korea: IPCC. Available at: http://www.ipcc.ch/report/sr15/

IPPR (Institute for Public Policy Research) (2018) *Prosperity and Justice: A Plan for the New Economy.* London: Polity.

Jackson, D., Thorsen, E. and Lilleker, D. (2016) *EU Referendum Analysis 2016: Media, Voters and the Campaign.* Bournemouth: Centre for the Study of Journalism, Culture and Community (CsJCC).

Jackson, D., Thorsen, E. and Wring, D. (eds) (2016) *EU Referendum Analysis 2016: Media, Voters and the Campaign.* Bournemouth: Centre for the Study of Journalism, Culture and Community (CsJCC).

Jackson, R. (1993) *Quasi-states: Sovereignty, International Relations and the Third World.* Cambridge: Cambridge University Press.

Jacoby, R. (1989) *The Last Intellectuals.* New York: Basic Books.

Jakubowski, F. (1976) *Ideology and Superstructure in Historical Materialism.* London: Allison & Busby.

Jessop, B. (1982) *The Capitalist State: Marxist Theories and Methods.* Oxford: Martin Robertson.

Jessop, B. (2002) *The Future of the Capitalist State.* Cambridge: Polity.

Jo Cox Commission on Loneliness (2017) 'Combatting Loneliness One Conversation at a Time'. www.jocoxloneliness.org/pdf/a_call_to_action.pdf

Jones, O. (2015) *The Establishment: And How They Get Away With It.* London: Penguin.

Judis, J. (2016) *The Populist Explosion: How the Great Recession Transformed American and European Politics.* New York: Columbia Global Reports.

Kakar, A. (2018) 'Parts of "Snoopers Charter" ruled "unlawful" by High Court judges', *Press Gazette*, 1 February. Available at: www.pressgazette.co.uk/parts-of-snoopers-charter-ruled-unlawful-by-high-court-judges/ (accessed 21 February 2020).

Kalogeropoulos, A. and Nielsen, R. (2018) 'Social Inequalities in News Consumption', Reuters Institute for the Study of Journalism. Available at: https://reutersinstitute.

politics.ox.ac.uk/risj-review/social-inequalities-news-consumption (accessed 24 February 2020).

Katz, R. and Mair, P. (1995) Changing models of party organization and party democracy: the emergence of the cartel party, *Party Politics*, 1(1): 5–28.

Kay, J. (2013) *The Kay Review of UK Equity Markets and Long-Term Decision-Making*. London: Department of Business, Innovation and Skills.

Kaye, J., et al. (2015) 'Dynamic Consent: A patient interface for twenty-first century research networks.' *European Journal od Human Genetics* 23: 141–6.

Kazmin, A. (2018) 'Narendra Modi Accused of Turning India into a Surveillance State', *ft.com*, 21 December. Available at: www.ft.com/content/395b59ba-04fe-11e9-99df-6183d3002ee1 (accessed 24 February 2020).

Keane, J. (1991) *The Media and Democracy*. Cambridge: Polity.

Kekst CNC (2020) *COVID-19 Opinion Tracker*, 14 April. Available at: https://www.kekstcnc.com/media/2568/kekst-report-16apr2020.pdf (accessed 15 April 2020).

Kellner, D. (1995) Intellectuals and new technologies, *Media, Culture & Society*, 17(3): 427–48.

Kellner, D. (2000) 'Habermas, the Public Sphere, and Democracy: A Critical Intervention', in L. Hahn (ed.), *Perspectives on Habermas*. Chicago, IL: Open Court.

Kelly, M. and Howard, T. (2019) *The Making of a Democratic Economy: Building Prosperity for the Many Not Just the Few*. San Francisco, CA: Berrett-Koehler.

Kennard, M. (2019) 'How the UK Military and Intelligence Establishment is Working to Stop Jeremy Corbyn Becoming Prime Minister', *Daily Maverick*, 4 December. www.dailymaverick.co.za/article/2019-12-04-how-the-uk-military-and-intelligence-establishment-is-working-to-stop-jeremy-corbyn-from-becoming-prime-minister/

Khan, S. (2011) *Privilege: The Making of an Adolescent Elite at St Paul's School*. Princeton, NJ: Princeton University Press.

King, N. (2016) *No Borders: The Politics of Immigration Control and Resistance*. London: Zed Books.

King, S. (2017) *Grave New World: The End of Globalization, the Return of History*. New Haven, CT: Yale University Press.

Kirchheimer, O. (1966) 'The Transformation of the Western European Party Systems', in M. Weiner and J. LaPalombara (eds), *Political Parties and Political Development*. Princeton, NJ: Princeton University Press, pp. 177–200.

Kovach, B., Rosentiel, T. and Mitchell, A. (2004) *A Crisis of Confidence: A Commentary on the Findings*. Washington, DC: Pew Research Centre.

Kreiss, D. (2016) *Prototype Politics: Technology-intensive Campaigning and the Data of Democracy*. New York: Oxford University Press.

Kristensen, P. (2015) 'Fighting the Financial Crisis: The Social Construction and Deconstruction of the Financial Crisis in Denmark', in G. Morgan, P. Hirsch and S. Quack (eds), *Elites on Trial Special Issue in Research in the Sociology of Organizations*, 43: 371–98.

Krugman, P. (2008) *The Return of Depression Economics and the Crisis of 2008.* London: Penguin.

Kundnani, A. (2008) Islamism and the roots of liberal rage, *Race & Class*, 50(2): 40–68.

Kuttner, R. (2018) *Can Democracy Survive Global Capitalism?* New York: Norton.

Larkin, B. (2013) The politics and poetics of infrastructure, *Annual Review of Anthropology*, 42: 327–43.

Lawrence, M. and Laybourn-Langton, L. (2019) 'Building a Digital Commonwealth', *openDemocracy*, 13 March. Available at: www.opendemocracy.net/en/oureconomy/building-digital-commonwealth/ (accessed 25 February 2020).

Lawrence, R. and Boydstun, A. (2017) 'Celebrities as Political Actors and Entertainment as Political Media', in P. Van Aelst and S. Walgrave (eds), *How Political Actors Use the Media*. Cham: Palgrave Macmillan.

Leadbeater, C. (1999) *Living on Thin Air: The New Economy.* London: Viking.

Lees-Marshment, J. (2008) *Political Marketing and British Political Parties: The Party's Just Begun* (2nd edn). Manchester: Manchester University Press.

Lees-Marshment, J. (2011) *The Political Marketing Game.* Basingstoke: Palgrave Macmillan.

Lees-Marshment, J. (2015) *The Political Marketing Handbook*. Abingdon: Routledge.

Lenin, V. (1977 [1917]) *The State and Revolution.* Moscow: Progress.

Leveson, The Right Honourable Lord Justice (2012) *The Leveson Inquiry: The Report into the Culture, Practices and Ethics of the Press.* London: The Stationery Office.

Lewis, H. (2020) 'The Coronavirus Is a Disaster for Feminism', *Atlantic*, 19 March. Available at: https://www.theatlantic.com/international/archive/2020/03/feminism-womens-rights-coronavirus-covid19/608302/ (accessed 28 April 2020).

Lewis, S. and Carlson, M. (2016) 'The Dissolution of News: Selective Exposure, Filter Bubbles, and the Boundaries of Journalism', in D. Lilleker, E. Thorsen and D. Jackson (eds), *US Election Analysis 2016: Media, Voters and the Campaign.* Bournemouth: Centre for the Study of Journalism, Culture and Community (CsJCC).

Liberty (2020) 'New Law is Biggest Restriction on Our Freedom in a Generation', 26 March. Available at: https://www.libertyhumanrights.org.uk/issue/new-law-is-biggest-restriction-on-our-freedom-in-a-generation/ (accessed 28 April 2020).

Lilleker, D. and Lees Marshment, J. (2005) *Political Marketing: A Comparative Perspective.* Manchester: Manchester University Press.

Lilleker, D., Thorsen, E. and Jackson, D. (2016) *US Election Analysis 2016: Media, Voters and the Campaign.* Bournemouth: Centre for Journalism, Culture and Community (CsJCC).

Lipman, P. (2020) 'The Reassertion of Ruling Class Power in Education: Tales from a Global City', in C. McCarthy, et al. (eds), *Spaces of New Colonialism: Reading Schools, Museums and Cities in the Tumult of Globalisation.* New York: Peter Lang.

Loader, B., Vromen, A. and Xenos, M. (2016) Performing for the young networked citizen? Celebrity politics, social networking and the political engagement of young people, *Media, Culture & Society*, 38(3): 400–19.

Losurdo, D. (2011) *Liberalism: A Counter History*. London: Verso.

Losurdo, D. (2015) *War and Revolution: Rethinking the 20th Century*. London: Verso.

Loughborough (2015) *The UK General Election of 2015.* http://blog.lboro.ac.uk/crcc

Lowe, L. (2015) *The Intimacies of Four Continents.* Durham, NC: Duke University Press.

Luce, E. (2017) *The Retreat of Western Liberalism.* London: Little and Brown.

Lukes, S. (2005) *Power: A Radical View* (2nd edn). Basingstoke: Palgrave Macmillan.

Lunt, P. and Livingstone, S. (2016) Is 'mediatization' the new paradigm for our field? A commentary on Deacon and Stanyer (2014, 2015) and Hepp, Hjarvard and Lundby (2015), *Media, Culture & Society*, 30(3): 462–70.

Luxemburg, R. (1951) *The Accumulation of Capital* (trans. A. Schwarzschild). Abingdon: Routledge & Kegan Paul.

Luyendijk, J. (2015) *Swimming with Sharks: My Journey into the World of Bankers.* London: Guardian/Faber.

Maarek, P. (1995) *Political Marketing and Communication.* Eastleigh: John Libby.

Maclean, M., Harvey, C. and Kling, G. (2014) Pathways to power: class, hyper-agency and the French corporate elite, *Organization Studies*, 35(6): 825–55.

Maclean, M., Harvey, C. and Kling G. (2017) Elite business networks and the field of power: a matter of class? *Theory, Culture & Society*, 34(5–6): 127–51.

Madianou, M. (2015) Digital inequality and second-order disasters: social media in the Typhoon Haiyan recovery, *Social Media + Society*, 1(2): 1–11.

Madianou, M., Ong, J., Longboan, L. and Cornelio, J. (2016) The appearance of accountability: communication technologies and power asymmetries in humanitarian aid and disaster recovery, *Journal of Communication*, 66(6): 960–81.

Magleby, D. (2011) 'Adaption and Innovation in the Financing of the 2008 Election', in D. Magleby and A. Corrado (eds), *Financing the 2008 Election.* Washington, DC: Brookings Institute.

Mair, P. (2013) *Ruling the Void: The Hollowing of Western Democracy.* London: Verso.

Mansell, R. (2010) The information society and ICT policy: a critique of the mainstream vision and an alternative research framework, *Journal of Information, Communication and Ethics in Society*, 8(1): 22–41.

Marsh, D. (ed.) (1998) *Comparing Policy Networks.* Buckingham: Open University Press.

Marty, R. (2020) 'How Anti-Abortion Activists Are Taking Advantage of the Coronavirus Crisis', *Time*, 24 March. Available at: https://time.com/5808471/coronavirus-abortion-access/ (accessed 28 April 2020).

Marx, K. (1977 [1859]) *Preface to A Contribution to the Critique of Political Economy.* Moscow: Progress. www.marxists.org/archive/marx/works/1859/critique-pol-economy/preface.htm

Marx, K. (1978) 'On the Jewish Question', in R. Tucker (ed.), *The Marx-Engels Reader*. New York: Norton.

Marx, K. (1992) *The First International and After: Political Writings,* Vol. 3. London: Penguin.

Mason, P. (2012) *Why It's Kicking Off Everywhere: The New Global Revolutions.* London: Verso.

Massoumi, N., Mills, T. and Miller, D. (2017) *What is Islamophobia? Racism, Social Movements and the State.* London: Pluto.

Maxwell, R. and Miller, T. (2012) *Greening the Media.* Oxford: Oxford University Press.

Mayer-Schönberger, V. and Cukier, K. (2013) *Big Data: A Revolution That Will Transform How We Live, Work and Think*. London: John Murray.

Mazzucato, M. (2013) *The Entrepreneurial State: Debunking Public vs Private Sector Myths.* London: Anthem.

McChesney, R. (2012) This isn't what democracy looks like, *Monthly Review*, 64(6).

McChesney, R. (2013) *Digital Disconnect: How Capitalism is Turning the Internet Against Democracy.* New York: New Press.

McChesney, R. and Nichols, J. (2010) *The Death and Life of American Journalism.* New York: Nation Books.

McChesney, R. and Nichols J. (2016) *People Get Ready: The Fight Against a Jobless Economy and a Citizenless Democracy.* New York: Nation Books.

McGregor, S., Lawrence, R. and Cardona, A. (2016) Personalization, gender and social media, *Information, Communication and Society*, 20(1): 264–83.

McKie, R. (2017) 'Biologists think 50% of species will be facing extinction by the end of the century', *Observer*, 25 February. Available at: www.theguardian.com/environment/2017/feb/25/half-all-species-extinct-end-century-vatican-conference (accessed 25 February 2020).

McLachlin, S. and Golding, P. (2000) in C. Sparks and J. Tulloch (eds), *Tabloid Tales: Global Debates Over Media Standards*. Oxford: Rowman and Littlefield.

McLuhan, M. (1964) *Understanding Media: The Extensions of Man*. London: Routledge & Kegan Paul.

McNair, B. (2003) *News and Journalism in the UK*. Abingdon: Routledge.

McNair, B. (2006) *Cultural Chaos*. New York: Routledge.

McNair, B. (2015) 'Islam and the media – let's not fear open debate', *Conversation*, 20 April. https://theconversation.com/islam-and-the-media-lets-not-fear-open-debate-40468

McNair, B. (2017) *An Introduction to Political Communication* (6th edn). Abingdon: Routledge.

McPherson, T. (2018) 'Digital Platforms and Hate Speech'. Paper presented at the Society for Cinema and Media Studies Conference, Toronto.

McQuillan, D. (2015) Algorithmic States of Exception, *European Journal of Cultural Studies*, 18(4/5): 564–76.

Media Ownership Monitor (2019) *Who Owns the Media in Argentina?* http://argentina.mom-rsf.org/en/

Media Reform Coalition (2015) 'Corbyn's First Week: Negative Agenda Setting in the Press'. Available at: www.mediareform.org.uk/wp-content/uploads/2015/11/ (accessed 24 February 2020).

Media Reform Coalition (2018) 'Submission to Cairncross Review' Available at: www.mediareform.org.uk/get-involved/mrc-submission-to-cairncross-review (accessed 24 February 2020).

Media Reform Coalition (2019a) 'Media Manifesto 2019'. Available at: www.mediareform.org.uk/blog/media-manifesto-2019 (accessed 24 February 2020).

Media Reform Coalition (2019b) 'Who owns the UK media?' Available at: www.mediareform.org.uk/wp-content/uploads/2019/03/FINALonline2.pdf (accessed 24 February 2020).

Meek, J. (2014) *Private Island: Why Britain Now Belongs to Someone Else*. London: Verso.

Mehta, U.S. (1999) *Liberalism and Empire: A Study in Nineteenth-Century British Liberal Thought*. Chicago, IL: Chicago University Press.

Melamed, J. (2015) 'Racial Capitalism'. *Critical Ethnic Studies* 1(1): 76–85.

Miliband, R. (1969) *The State in Capitalist Society*. London: Camelot.

Mill, J.S. (2005) *On Liberty*. New York: Cosimo.

Miller, D. (1994) *Don't Mention the War: Northern Ireland, Propaganda and the Media*. London: Pluto.

Miller, D. (2003) *Tell Me Lies: Propaganda and Media Distortion in the Attack on Iraq*. London: Pluto.

Miller, D. and Dinan, W. (2008) *A Century of Spin: How Public Relations Became the Cutting Edge of Corporate Power.* London: Pluto.

Miller, D. and Sabir, R. (2012) 'Propaganda and Terrorism', in D. Freedman and D. Thussu (eds), *Media and Terrorism: Global Perspectives.* London: Sage, pp. 77–94.

Mills, T. (2016) *The BBC: Myth of a Public Service.* London: Verso.

Minder, R. (2017) 'Spain Looks to Seize Catalonia Radio and TV as Crisis Mounts', *New York Times*, 25 October. Available at: www.nytimes.com/2017/10/25/world/europe/the-catalonia-crisis-has-not-divided-spain-just-its-media.html (accessed 24 February 2020).

Mirowski, P. and Plehwe, D. (eds) (2009) *The Road from Mont Pèlerin: The Making of the Neoliberal Thought Collective.* Cambridge, MA: Harvard University Press.

Misztal, B. (2012) Public intellectuals and think tanks: a free market in ideas? *International Journal of Politics, Culture and Society*, 25(4): 127–41.

Mitchell, B. and Fazi, T. (2017) *Reclaiming the State: A Progressive Vision of Sovereignty for a Post-Neoliberal World.* London: Pluto.

Mitchell, N. (1997) *The Conspicuous Corporation: Business, Publicity, and Representative Democracy.* Ann Arbor, MI: University of Michigan Press.

Mizruchi, M. (2013) *The Fracturing of the American Corporate Elite*. Cambridge, MA: Harvard University Press.

Monbiot, G. (2000) *The Captive State.* London: Pan.

Moore, M. (2018) *Democracy Hacked: Political Turmoil and Information Warfare in the Digital Age*. London: Oneworld.

Moran, M. (2003) *The British Regulatory State: High Modernism and Hyper-Innovation.* Oxford: Oxford University Press.

Morozov, E. (2015) 'The Taming of Tech Criticism', *The Baffler*, No. 27, March.

Morozov, E. (2019) 'Capitalism's New Clothes', *The Baffler*, 4 February.

Mosco, V. (2009) *The Political Economy of Communication.* London: Sage.

Motta, M. (2016) 'Air War? Campaign Advertising in the 2016 Presidential Election', in D. Lilleker, E. Thorsen and D. Jackson (eds), *US Election Analysis 2016: Media, Voters and the Campaign.* Bournemouth: Centre for the Study of Journalism, Culture and Community (CsJCC).

Mouffe, C. (2005) *On the Political.* Abingdon: Routledge.

Mudde, C. and Rovira Kaltwasser, C. (2017) *Populism: A Very Short Introduction.* Oxford: Oxford University Press.

Mudge, S. and Chen, A. (2014) Political parties and the sociological imagination: past, present and future directions, *Annual Review of Sociology*, 40: 305–30.

Muller, D. (2016) 'Trump, Truth and the Media', in D. Lilleker, E. Thorsen and D. Jackson (eds), *US Election Analysis 2016: Media, Voters and the Campaign.* Bournemouth: Centre for the Study of Journalism, Culture and Community (CsJCC).

Murdock, G. (2017) Mediatisation and the transformation of capitalism: the elephant in the room, *Javnost – The Public*, 24(2): 119–35.

Murdock, G. (2018) Media materialities: for a moral economy of machines, *International Journal of Communication*, 68: 359–68.

Murdock, G. and Golding, P. (1989) Information poverty and political inequality: citizenship in the age of privatized communications, *Journal of Communication*, 39(3): 180–95.

Naím, M. (2013) *The End of Power: From Boardrooms to Battlefields and Churches to States: Why Being in Charge Isn't What it Used to Be*. New York: Basic Books.

Narayanan, V. et al. (2018) *Polarization, Partisanship and Junk News Consumption Over Social Media in the US*. Oxford: Oxford Internet Institute.

Näser-Lather, M. and Neubert, C. (2015) *Traffic: Media as Infrastructures and Cultural Practices*. Leiden: Brill.

Nelson, A. (2016) *Social Life of DNA: Race, Reparations, and Reconciliation after the Genome*. Boston, MA: Beacon.

Nessman, K. (1995) Public relations in Europe: a comparison with the United States, *Public Relations Review*, 21: 151–60.

Neuman, W.R. (1996) Political communications infrastructure, *Annals of the American Academy of Political and Social Science*, 546: 9–21.

Newman, B. (ed.) (1999) *The Handbook of Political Marketing*. Thousand Oaks, CA: Sage.

Newman, N. (2019) 'Executive Summary and Key Findings', *Digital News Report 2019*, Reuters Institute for the Study of Journalism. https://reutersinstitute.politics.ox.ac.uk/sites/default/files/2019-06/DNR_2019_FINAL_0.pdf

Nichols, J. and McChesney, R. (2013) *Dollarocracy: How the Money and Media Election Complex is Destroying America*. New York: Nation.

Nineham, C. (2019) *State Power: A Warning*. London: Zer0 Books.

Noble, S.U. (2018) *Algorithms of Oppression: How Search Engines Reinforce Racism*. New York: New York University Press.

Norris, P. (1999) 'Changes in Party Competition at Westminster', in G. Evans and P. Norris (eds), *Critical Elections: British Parties and Voters in Long-term Perspective*. London: Sage.

Norris, P. (2000) *A Virtuous Circle: Political Communications in Postindustrial Societies*. Cambridge: Cambridge University Press.

Norris, P. (2002) *Democratic Phoenix: Political Activism World Wide*. New York: Cambridge University Press.

Norris, P. (2004) 'Global Political Communication: Good Governance, Human Development, and Mass Communication', in F. Esser and B. Pfetsch (eds), *Comparing Political Communication: Theories, Cases and Challenges*. Cambridge: Cambridge University Press.

Norris, P. (2011) *Democratic Deficit: Critical Citizens Revisited.* Cambridge: Cambridge University Press.

Norton, A. (2013) *On the Muslim Question*. Princeton, NJ and Oxford: Princeton University Press.

Nye, J. (1990) Soft power, *Foreign Policy*, 80: 153–71.

Nye, J. (2011) *The Future of Power*. New York: Public Affairs.

Nyhan, B. (2013) 'Fast and Wrong Beats Slow and Right', *Columbia Journalism Review*, 22 April. Available at: https://archives.cjr.org/united_states_project/speed-induced_misinformation_boston_bombings_coverage.php (accessed 25 February 2020).

Ofcom (2018a) *Communications Market Report*, 2 August. www.ofcom.org.uk/__data/assets/pdf_file/0022/117256/CMR-2018-narrative-report.pdf

Ofcom (2018b) *News Consumption in the UK,* 25 July. www.ofcom.org.uk/research-and-data/tv-radio-and-on-demand/news-media/news-consumption

Ofcom (2019a) *Ofcom Media Literacy Tracker 2018 – Adults.* www.ofcom.org.uk/__data/assets/pdf_file/0012/130008/Adults-media-literacy-data-tables.pdf

Ofcom (2019b) *Adults: Media Use and Attitudes Report 2019*, 30 May. www.ofcom.org.uk/__data/assets/pdf_file/0021/149124/adults-media-use-and-attitudes-report.pdf.

Ofcom (2020) *COVID-19 News and Information: Consumption and attitudes*. London: Ofcom. Available at: https://www.ofcom.org.uk/__data/assets/pdf_file/0031/193747/covid-19-news-consumption-week-one-findings.pdf (accesssed 15 April 2020).

Office for National Statistics (2018) 'Loneliness – What characteristics and circumstances are associated with feeling lonely?'. London: ONS. Available at: www.ons.gov.uk/peoplepopulationandcommunity/wellbeing/articles/lonelinesswhatcharacteristicsandcircumstancesareassociatedwithfeelinglonely/2018-04-10 (accessed 25 February 2020).

Office for National Statistics (2019) 'Detailed household expenditure by equivalised disposable income decile group: Table 3.1E'. www.ons.gov.uk/peoplepopulationandcommunity/personalandhouseholdfinances/expenditure/bulletins/familyspendingintheuk/financialyearending2018.

Ohmae, K. (1995) *The End of the Nation State: The Rise of Regional Economies.* New York: Free Press.

Omi, M. and Winant, H. (1994) *Racial Formation in the United States: From the 1960s to the 1990s* (2nd edn). New York: Routledge.

O'Neil, C. (2016) *Weapons of Math Destruction: How Big Data Increases Inequality and Threatens Democracy.* London: Penguin.

OpenSecrets (2017) www.opensecrets.org/news/2017/04/election-2016-trump-fewer-donors-provided-more-of-the-cash/

Oreglia, E. (2014) ICT and (personal) development in rural China, *Information Technologies and International Development*, 10(3): 19–30.

Örnebring, H. (2010) Technology and journalism-as-labour: historical perspectives, *Journalism*, 11(1): 57–74.

Ostrom, E. (1990) *Governing the Commons: The Evolution of Institutions for Collective Action*. Cambridge: Cambridge University Press.

Owen, J. (2018) '"Comms Helped Defeat Isis in Iraq", Claims Government Counter-propaganda Unit', *PR Week*, 17 January. Available at: www.prweek.com/article/1454653/comms-helped-defeat-isis-iraq-claims-government-counter-propaganda-unit (accessed 25 February 2020).

Owens, P. (2017) Racism in the theory canon: Hannah Arendt and 'the one great crime in which America was never involved', *Millennium*, 45(3): 403–24.

Oxfam (2017) *An Economy for the 99%*. Oxford: Oxfam GB.

Oxfam (2019) *Public Good or Private Wealth?* London: Oxfam GB.

PAC (2013) *Tax Avoidance: The Role of Large Accountancy Firms*. London: Public Accounts Committee, HC 870.

Packer, J. and Crofts Wiley, S. (2012) 'Introduction: The Materiality of Communication', in J. Packer and S. Crofts Wiley (eds), *Communication Matters: Materialist Approaches to Media, Mobility and Networks*. Abingdon: Routledge, pp. 3–16.

Palley, T. (2007) 'Financialization: What It Is and Why It Matters', Political Economy Research Institute Working Paper 153. Amherst, MA: University of Massachusettes.

Panebianco, A. (1988) *Political Parties: Organisation and Power*. Cambridge: Cambridge University Press.

Parks, L. and Starosielski, N. (2015) 'Introduction', in L. Parks and N. Starosielski (eds), *Signal Traffic: Critical Studies of Media Infrastructures*. Urbana, IL: University of Illinois Press, pp. 1–27.

Pasquale, F. (2015) *The Black Box Society*. Cambridge, MA: Harvard University Press.

Patterson, T. (2016) *News Coverage of the 2016 Election: How the Press Failed Us*. Cambridge, MA: Shorenstein Centre, Harvard-Kennedy School.

Paulussen, S. (2012) 'Technology and the Transformation of News Work: Are Labor Conditions in (Online) Journalism Changing?', in E. Siapera and A. Veglis (eds), *The Handbook of Global Online Journalism*. Oxford: Wiley, pp. 192–208.

Peters, J.D. (2012) 'Becoming Mollusk: A Conversation with John Durham Peters about Media, Materiality, and Matters of History', in J. Packer and S. Crofts Wiley (eds), *Communication Matters: Materialist Approaches to Media, Mobility and Networks*. Abingdon: Routledge, pp. 35–50.

Peters, J.D. (2015) *The Marvelous Clouds: Towards a Philosophy of Elemental Media*. Chicago, IL: University of Chicago Press.

Pew Research Center (2009) *The State of the News Media 2009.* Washington, DC: Pew/The Project for Excellence in Journalism.

Pew Research Center (2016a) *State of the News Media 2016.* Washington, DC: Pew/The Project for Excellence in Journalism.

Pew Research Center (2016b) *Many Americans Believe Fake News is Sowing Confusion.* Washington, DC: Pew/The Project for Excellence in Journalism.

Pew Research Center (2017) *Covering President Trump in a Polarized Media Environment.* Washington, DC: Pew/The Project for Excellence in Journalism.

Pew Research Center (2018) *Political Engagement, Knowledge and the Midterms.* Washington, DC: Pew/The Project for Excellence in Journalism.

Pew Research Center (2019) 'Digital divide persists even as lower-income Americans make gains in tech adoption', *Fact Tank*, 7 May. https://www.pewresearch.org/fact-tank/2019/05/07/digital-divide-persists-even-as-lower-income-americans-make-gains-in-tech-adoption/

Pickard, V. (2014) *Media Democracy: The Triumph of Corporate Libertarianism and the Future of Media Reform.* New York: Cambridge University Press.

Piketty, T. (2014) *Capital in the 21ˢᵗ Century.* Cambridge, MA: Harvard University Press.

Plantin, J.-C. and Punathambekar, A. (2019) Digital media infrastructures: pipes, platforms and politics, *Media, Culture & Society,* 41(2): 163–74.

Platform Cooperativism Consortium (2019) 'Vision and Advantages'. https://platform.coop/about/vision-and-advantages/

Polat, R. (2005) The internet and political participation, *European Journal of Communication*, 20(4): 435–59.

Poulantzas, N. (1978) *State, Power, Socialism.* London: New Left Books.

Power, M. (1997) *The Audit Society: Rituals of Verification.* Oxford: Oxford University Press.

Priansack, B. (2019) Logged out: ownership, exclusion and public value in the digital data and information commons, *Big Data & Society*, 6 (1): npn.

Price, V. and Cappella, J.N. (2002) Online deliberation and its influence: the electronic dialogue project in Campaign 2000, *IT & Society*, 1(1): 303–29.

Provost, C., Archer, N. and Nambiru, L. (2020) 'Alarm as 2 Billion People have Parliaments Shut or Limited by COVID-19'. Available at: https://www.opendemocracy.net/en/5050/alarm-two-billion-people-have-parliaments-suspended-or-limited-covid-19/ (accessed 29 April 2020).

Putnam, R. (2000) *Bowling Alone: The Collapse and Revival of American Community.* New York: Simon and Schuster.

Putnam, R. (ed.) (2002) *Democracies in Flux: The Evolution of Social Capital in Contemporary Societies.* Oxford: Oxford University Press.

Puttnam, Lord (chair) (2016) 'An Inquiry into the Future of Public Service Television', final report. Available at: www.futureoftv.org.uk/report (accessed 25 February 2020).

Rancière, J. (2007) *Hatred of Democracy*. London: Verso.

Rancière, J. (2010) *Dissensus: On Politics and Aesthetics*. London: Bloomsbury.

Ratcliffe, R. (2020) 'Teargas, Beatings and Bleach: The most extreme COVID-19 lockdown controls around the world', *Guardian*, 1 April. Available at: https://www.theguardian.com/global-development/2020/apr/01/extreme-coronavirus-lock-down-controls-raise-fears-for-worlds-poorest" (accessed 28 April 2020)

Raworth, K. (2017) *Doughnut Economics: 7 Ways to Think Like a 21st Century Economist.* White River Junction, VT: Chelsea Green.

Reed, M. (2012) Masters of the Universe: power and elites in organization studies, *Organization Studies*, 33(2): 203–21.

Reeves, R. (2007, February 19) 'We Love Capitalism', *The New Statesman*. www.newstatesman.com/200702190026

Rennie Short, J. (2016) 'The Politics of De-legitimacy', in D. Lilleker, E. Thorsen and D. Jackson (eds), *US Election Analysis 2016: Media, Voters and the Campaign.* Bournemouth: Centre for the Study of Journalism, Culture and Community (CsJCC).

Research Councils UK (2014) 'Pathways to Impact'. Available at: http://impact.ref.ac.uk/CaseStudies/ (accessed 25 February 2020).

Reuters Institute (2017) *Reuters Institute Digital News Report.* Oxford: Reuters Institute for the Study of Journalism.

Ricci, A. (2018) 'French Opposition Parties are taking Macron's Anti-misinformation Law to Court', *Poynter*, 4 December. Available at: www.poynter.org/fact-checking/2018/french-opposition-parties-are-taking-macrons-anti-misinformation-law-to-court/ (accessed 25 February 2020).

Ridley, L. (2016) 'Jeremy Corbyn Study Claims TV and Online News "Persistently" Biased Against Labour Leader', *Huffington Post*, 30 July. www.huffingtonpost.co.uk/entry/jeremy-corbyn-media-bias-bbc_uk_579a3cd7e4b06d7c426edff0

Risen, J. (2016) 'If Donald Trump Targets Journalists, Thank Obama', *New York Times*, 30 December. https://www.nytimes.com/2016/12/30/opinion/sunday/if-donald-trump-targets-journalists-thank-obama.html (accessed 1 April 2020).

Rossiter, N. (2017) *Software Infrastructure Labor: A Media Theory of Logistical Nightmares.* Abingdon: Routledge.

RSA (2017) 'Citizenship 4.0: An invitation to power change'. Available at: https://medium.com/citizens-and-inclusive-growth/citizenship-4-0-an-invitation-to-power-change-910bf07d319c (accessed 25 February 2020).

Runciman, D. (2018) *How Democracy Ends.* London: Profile.

Sabadish, N. and Mishel, L. (2013) 'CEO Pay in 2012 Was Extraordinarily High Relative to Typical Workers and Other High Earners' Economic Policy Institute'. Available at: www.epi.org/publication/ceo-pay-2012-extraordinarily-high/ (accessed 25 February 2020).

Said, E. (1993a) 'Representations of an Intellectual.' *Reith Lecture 1: Representation of Intellectuals, transmitted 23 June*, BBC. http://downloads.bbc.co.uk/rmhttp/radio4/transcripts/1993_reith1.pdf

Said, E. (1993b) 'Representations of an Intellectual.' *Reith Lecture 5: Speaking Truth to Power, transmitted 9 August*, BBC. http://downloads.bbc.co.uk/rmhttp/radio4/transcripts/1993_reith5.pdf

Sampson, A. (1962) *Anatomy of Britain.* London: Hodder and Stoughton.

Sand, S. (2018) *The End of the French Intellectual.* London: Verso.

Sanders, K. and Canel, M. (2013) 'Introduction: Mapping the Field of Government Communication', in K. Sanders and M. Canel (eds), *Government Communication: Cases and Challenges.* London: Bloomsbury, pp. 1–26.

Sartre, J. (1950) *What is Literature?* London: Methuen.

Savage, M. (2015) *Social Class in the Twenty-First Century.* London: Penguin.

Scammell, M. (1995) *Designer Politics: How Elections are Won.* London: Macmillan.

Scammell, M. (2003) 'Citizen Consumers: Towards a New Marketing of Politics?', in J. Corner and D. Pels (eds), *Media and the Restyling of Politics: Consumerism, Celebrity and Cyncism.* London: Sage.

Scammell, M. (2014) *Consumer Democracy: The Marketing of Politics.* Cambridge: Cambridge University Press.

Scharenberg, A. (2020) 'Transeuropa: Transnational activism in a changing Europe'. PhD thesis, Goldsmiths University of London.

Schattschneider, E. (1942) *Party Government.* New Brunswick: Transaction.

Scheufele, D.A. (2000) Agenda-setting, priming and framing revisited: another look at cognitive effects of political communication, *Mass Communication and Society*, 3(2–3): 297–316.

Schiffrin, A. (2017) *In the Service of Power: Media Capture and the Threat to Democracy*, Washington, DC: National Endowment for Democracy. www.cima.ned.org/wp-content/uploads/2017/08/CIMA_MediaCaptureBook_F1.pdf

Schiller, H. (1969) *Mass Communications and American Empire.* Boston, MA: Beacon.

Schlesinger, P. (2009a) Creativity and the experts: New Labour, think tanks, and the policy process, *International Journal of Press/Politics*, 14(1): 3–20.

Schlesinger, P. (2009b) 'The Politics of Media and Cultural Policy', *Media@LSE Working Papers*, 17. Available at: www.lse.ac.uk/media-and-communications/assets/documents/research/working-paper-series/EWP17.pdf (accessed 25 February 2020).

Schlosberg, J. (2018) 'Digital Agenda Setting: Reexamining the Role of Platform Monopolies', in M. Moore and D. Tambini (eds), *Digital Dominance: The Power of Google, Amazon Facebook, and Apple*. Oxford: Oxford University Press, pp. 202–18.

Scholz, T. and Schneider, N. (2016) *Ours to Hack and to Own: The Rise of Platform Cooperativism*. New York: OR Books.

Scott, J. (1991) *Who Rules Britain?* Cambridge: Polity.

Sennett, R. (2012) *Together: The Rituals, Pleasures and Politics of Cooperation*. London: Penguin.

Seymour, R. (2019) *The Twittering Machine*. London: Indigo.

Shaxson, N. (2011) *Treasure Islands: Tax Havens and the Men Who Stole the World*. London: Vintage.

Siegel, E. (2013) *Predictive Analytics: The Power to Predict Who Will Click, Buy, Lie or Die*. Hoboken, NJ: Wiley.

Silva, L. and Westrup, C. (2009) Development and the promise of technological change, *Information Technology for Development*, 14(1): 13–23.

Skeggs, B. (2014) Values beyond value? Is anything beyond the logic of capital? *British Journal of Sociology*, 65(1): 1–20.

Skeggs, B. (2019) The forces that shape us: the entangled vine of gender, race and class, *Sociological Review*, 67(1): 28–35.

Skocpol, T. (1979) *States and Social Revolutions*. Cambridge: Cambridge University Press.

Sowemimo, A. (2020) 'Coronavirus is Being Used to Roll Back Abortion Rights by Stealth', *Independent*, 25 March. Available at: https://www.independent.co.uk/voices/coronavirus-abortion-clinic-doctor-nurse-mental-health-a9424236.html (accessed 28 April 2020).

Sparks, C. (1986) 'The Media and the State', in J. Curran et al. (eds), *Bending Reality: The State of the Media*. London: Pluto, pp. 76–86.

Sparks, C. (2000) 'From Dead Trees to Live Wires: The Internet's Challenge to the Traditional Newspaper', in J. Curran and M. Gurevitch (eds), *Mass Media and Society* (3rd edn). London: Edward Arnold.

Sparks, C. (2016) 'Global Integration, State Policy and the Media', in T. Flew, P. Iosifidis and J. Steemers (eds), *Global Media and National Policies: The Return of the State*. London: Palgrave.

Sparks, C. (2018) Changing concepts for a changing world, *Journal of Communication,* 68(2): 390–98.

Srnicek, N. (2016) *Platform Capitalism*. Cambridge: Polity.

Srnicek, N. (2017) 'We Need to Nationalise Google, Facebook and Amazon. Here's Why', *Guardian*, 30 August. Available at: www.theguardian.com/commentisfree/

2017/aug/30/nationalise-google-facebook-amazon-data-monopoly-platform-public-interest (accessed 26 February 2020).

Stanistreet, M. (2016) 'The Government is Using Terrorism as an Excuse to Spy on Journalists', *Guardian*, 14 March. Available at: www.theguardian.com/media/2016/mar/14/government-terrorism-journalists-investigatory-powers-bill-snooper-charter (accessed 25 February 2020).

Stanyer, J. (2007) *Modern Political Communication: Mediated Politics in Uncertain Times*. Cambridge: Polity.

Stanyer, J. (2013) *Intimate Politics*. Cambridge: Polity.

Starosielski, N. (2015) 'Fixed Flow: Undersea Cables as Media Infrastructure', in L. Parks and N. Starosielski (eds), *Signal Traffic: Critical Studies of Media Infrastructures*. Urbana, IL: University of Illinois Press, pp. 53–70.

Stauber, J. and Rampton, S. (1995) *Toxic Sludge is Good for You! Lies, Damn Lies and the Public Relations Industry.* Monroe, ME: Common Courage.

Stefan, R. and Mounk, Y. (2016) The danger of deconsolidation, *Journal of Democracy*, 27(3): 5–17.

Steyerl, H. (2019) 'A Sea of Data: Pattern Recognition and Corporate Animism', in C. Apprich, W.H.K. Chun, F. Cramer and H. Steyerl (eds), *Pattern Discrimination*. Minneapolis, MN: University of Minnesota and Meson Press.

Stiglitz, J. (2013) *The Price of Inequality*. London: Penguin.

Stiglitz, J. (2017) *Globalization and its Discontents Revisited: Anti-Globalization in the Era of Trump.* London: Penguin.

Stockholm International Peace Research Institute (2018) 'Trends in international arms transfer'. Available at: www.sipri.org/publications/2018/sipri-fact-sheets/trends-international-arms-transfers-2017 (accessed 26 February 2020).

Stoetzler, M. and Yuval-Davis, N. (2002) Standpoint theory, situated knowledge and the situated imagination, *Feminist Theory*, 3 (December): 315–33.

Strange, S. (1996) *The Retreat of the State*. Cambridge: Cambridge University Press.

Streeck, W. (2011) 'The Crisis of Democratic Capitalism', *New Left Review* 73, September–October.

Streeck, W. (2016) *How Will Capitalism End? Essays on a Failing System.* London: Verso.

Streeck, W. (2017) *Buying Time: The Delayed Crisis of Democratic Capitalism* (2nd edn). London: Verso.

Stromer-Galley, J. (2014) *Presidential Campaigning in the Internet Age.* Oxford: Oxford University Press.

Sunstein, C. (2018) *#Republic: Divided Democracy in the Age of Social Media.* Princeton, NJ: Princeton University Press.

Sussman, G. (2011) *The Propaganda Society: Promotional Culture and Politics in Global Context.* New York: Peter Lang.

Sutton Trust (2019) *Elitist Britain 2019.* www.suttontrust.com/research-paper/elitist-britain-2019/

Svendsen, A.D. (2009) *Intelligence Cooperation and the War on Terror: Anglo-American Security Relations After 9/11.* Abingdon: Routledge.

Swanson, D. and Mancini, P. (eds) (1996) *Politics, Media and Modern Democracy: An International Study of Innovations in Electoral Campaigning and Their Consequences.* New York: Praeger.

Swenson, H. (2015) 'Anti-Immigration as austerity policy: the rejection of maternalist governance in Arizona's SB 1070 Immigration Law', *Feminist Formation*, 27(2): 98–120.

Swenson, M. (2004) *Democracy Under Assault: Theopolitics, Incivility and Violence on the Right.* Denver, CO: Sol Ventures.

Syvertsen, T. , Enli, G., Mjøs, O.J. and Moe, H. (2014) *The Media Welfare State: Nordic Media in the Digital Era.* Ann Arbor, MI: University of Michigan Press.

Tambini, D. (2018) 'Social Media Power and Election Legitimacy', in M. Moore and D. Tambini (eds), *Digital Dominance: The Power of Google, Amazon, Facebook and Apple.* Oxford: Oxford University Press.

Tapscott, D. and Williams, A. (2007) *Wikinomics: How Mass Collaboration Changes Everything.* New York: Penguin.

Tawil-Souri, H. (2015) 'Cellular Borders: Dis/Connecting Phone Calls in Israel/Palestine', in L. Parks and N. Starosielski (eds), *Signal Traffic: Critical Studies of Media Infrastructures.* Urbana, IL: University of Illinois Press, pp. 157–80.

Terranova, T. (2004) *Network Culture: Politics for the Information Age.* London: Pluto.

Therborn, G. (2009) The killing fields of inequality, *Soundings*, 42: 20–32.

Thomas, P. (2009) *The Gramscian Moment: Philosophy, Hegemony and Marxism.* Leiden: Brill.

Thompson, E.P. (1959) Commitment in politics, *Universities & Left Review*, 6: 50–55.

Thompson, M. (2008) ICT and development studies: towards development 2.0., *Journal of International Development*, 20(6): 821–35.

Thorsen, E., Jackson, D. and Lilleker, D. (eds) (2017) *UK Election Analysis 2017: Media, Voters and the Campaign.* Bournemouth: Centre for the Study of Journalism, Culture and Community (CsJCC).

Thussu, D. (2008) *News as Entertainment: The Rise of Global Infotainment.* London: Sage.

Timm, T. (2016) 'The US Needs its own Chilcot Report', *Guardian*, 6 July. Available at: www.theguardian.com/commentisfree/2016/jul/06/us-george-bush-needs-chilcot- report-iraq-war (accessed 25 February 2020).

TJN (2015) *The Greatest Invention: Tax and the Campaign for a Just Society*, Tax Justice Network. Padstow, Cornwall: Commonwealth Publishing.

Tooze, A. (2018) *Crashed: How a Decade of Financial Crises Changed the World.* London: Allen Lane.

Trappel, J. (2019) 'Inequality, (New) Media and Communications', in J. Trappel (ed.), *Digital Media Inequalities: Policies Against Divides, Distrust and Discrimination.* Göteborg: Nordicom, pp. 9–30.

Trottier, D. and Fuchs, C. (2015) 'Theorising Social Media, Politics and the State: An Introduction', in D. Trottier and C. Fuchs (eds), *Social Media, Politics and the State.* Abingdon: Routledge, pp. 3–38.

Tsingou, E. (2015) Club governance and the making of global financial rules, *Review of International Political Economy*, 22(2): 225–56.

TUC (Trades Union Congress) (2018) 'Two million self-employed adults earn less than the minimum wage'. www.tuc.org.uk/news/two-million-self-employed-adults-earn-less-minimum-wage

Tufekci, Z. (2014) Engineering the public: big data, surveillance and computational politics, *First Monday*, 19(7). Available at: http://firstmonday.org/article/view/4901/4097 (accessed 26 February 2020).

Tully, M. and Ekdale, B. (2014) Sites of playful engagement: Twitter hashtags as spaces of leisure and development in Kenya, *Information Technologies and International Development*, 10(3): 67–82.

Turkle, S. (2011) *Alone Together: Why We Expect More From Technology and Less From Each Other*. New York: Basic Books.

Turner, G., Bonner, F. and Marshall, P. (2000) *Fame Games: The Production of Celebrity in Australia.* Cambridge: Cambridge University Press.

Turow, J. and Couldry, N. (2018) Media as data extraction: towards a new map of a transformed communications field, *Journal of Communication*, 68(2): 415–23.

Tutty, J. (2017) 'London terror attacks: QUT lecturer says Islam a "cancer", *The Courier-Mail*, 5 June. Available at: www.couriermail.com.au/news/queensland/london-terror-attacks-qut-lecturer-says-islam-a-cancer/news-story/b8b98a9aaa4bf08d7640d62c0500a431 (accessed 26 February 2020).

Unwin, P.T.H (2009) *ICT4D: Information and Communication Technology for Development*. Cambridge: Cambridge University Press.

Urry, J. (2014) 'The Super-rich and Offshore Worlds', in J. Birtchnell and J. Caletrio (eds), *Elite Mobilities.* Abingdon: Routledge, pp. 226–40.

Useem, M. (1984) *The Inner Circle: Large Corporations and the Rise of Political Activity in the US and UK.* Oxford: Oxford University Press.

Useem, M. (2015) From classwide coherence to company-focused management and director engagement, *Research in the Sociology of Organizations*, 43: 399–421.

Vaidhyanathan, S. (2011) *The Googlization of Everything (And Why We Should Worry).* Berkeley, CA: University of California Press.

Vaidhyanathan, S. (2018) *Anti-Social Media: How Facebook Disconnects Us and Undermines Democracy.* New York: Oxford University Press.

van Biezen, I. and Poguntke, T. (2014) The decline of membership-based politics, *Party Politics*, 20(2): 205–16.

Vargo, C. and Guo, L. (2017) Networks, big data, and intermedia agenda-setting: an analysis of traditional, partisan and emerging online US news, *Journalism and Mass Communication Quarterly*, 94(4): 1031–55.

Varoufakis, Y. (2016) *And the Weak Suffer What They Must? Europe, Austerity and the Threat to Global Stability.* London: Vintage.

Vartanova, E. and Gladkova, A. (2019) 'New Forms of the Digital Divide', in J. Trappel (ed.), *Digital Media Inequalities: Policies Against Divides, Distrust and Discrimination.* Göteborg: Nordicom, pp. 193–213.

Walker, S. (2020) 'Concerns over Polish Government Tightening Abortion Laws During COVID-19 Crisis', *Guardian*, 14 April. Available at: https://www.theguardian.com/world/2020/apr/14/concerns-over-polish-government-tightening-abortion-laws-during-covid-19-crisis (accessed 28 April 2020).

Wall Street Journal (2017) 'Google and Facebook Drive 2017 Digital Ad Surge', 14 March. www.wsj.com/articles/cmo-today-google-and-facebook-drive-2017-digital-ad-surge-1489491871

Wark, M. (2017) *General Intellects: Twenty-five Thinkers for the Twenty-first Century.* London: Verso.

Wayne, M. (2018) *England's Discontents: Political Cultures and National Identities.* London: Pluto.

We are Flint (2018) *Social Media Demographics 2018.* https://weareflint.co.uk/main-findings-social-media-demographics-uk-usa-2018

Webb, P. (2007) 'Political Parties and the Democratic Disconnect: A Call for Research', in P. Webb (ed.), *Democracy and Political Parties.* London: Hansard.

Weber, M. (1948) *From Max Weber: Essays in Sociology*, H. Gerth and C. Wright Mills (eds). Abingdon: Routledge.

Weber, M. (1978) *Economy and Society: An Outline of Interpretive Sociology.* Berkeley, CA: University of California Press.

Wedel, J. (2009) *Shadow Elite: How the World's New Power Brokers Undermine Democracy, Government and the Free Market.* New York: Basic Books.

Wedel, J. (2014) *Unaccountable.* New York: Pegasus.

Weeks, B., Ardevol-Abrew, A. and Gil de Zuniga, H. (2017) Online influence? Social media use, opinion leadership and political persuasion, *International Journal of Public Opinion Research*, 29(2): 214–39.

Wells, C. et al. (2016) How Trump drove coverage of the nomination: hybrid media campaigning, *Political Communication*, 33: 669–76.

Werbell, A. (2005) Terror, war and democracy: an interview with Stephen Eric Bronner, *New Political Science*, 27(4): 521–27.

Wernick, A. (1991) *Promotional Culture.* London: Sage.

West, D. and Orman, J. (2003) *Celebrity Politics.* Upper Saddle River, NJ: Prentice Hall.

Wheeler, M. (2014) *Celebrity Politics.* Cambridge: Polity.

Whyte, D. and Muttitt, G. (2016) 'Chilcot's Blind Spot: Iraq War Report Buries Oil Evidence, Fails to Address Motive', *Open Democracy*, 6 July. Available at: www. opendemocracy.net/david- whyte/chilcot-s-oil-blind-spot-in-iraq-war-report (accessed 26 February 2020).

Wilkinson, R. and Pickett, K. (2009) *The Spirit Level: Why Equality is Better for Everyone.* London: Penguin.

Wilkinson, R. and Pickett, K. (2018) *The Inner Level: How More Equal Societies Reduce Stress, Restore Sanity and Improve Everyone's Well-being.* London: Allen Lane.

Wilks, S. (2015) *The Revolving Door and the Corporate Colonisation of UK Politics.* London: High Pay.

Williams, R. (1961) *The Long Revolution.* London: Penguin.

Williams, R. (1981a) Marxism, structuralism and literary analysis, *New Left Review*, September–October, No. 129: 51–66.

Williams, R. (1981b) 'Communication Technologies and Social Institutions', in R. Williams (ed.), *Contact: Human Communication and its History.* London: Thames & Hudson.

Williams, R. (2014) *Keywords: A Vocabulary of Culture and Society.* London: Fourth Estate.

Winseck, D. and Pike, R. (2007) *Communication and Empire: Media, Markets and Globalization, 1860–1930.* Durham, NC: Duke University Press.

Woolley, S. and Howard, P. (2017) 'Computational Propaganda Worldwide', Working Paper No 2017.11. Oxford: Oxford Internet Institute.

Woolley, S. and Howard, P. (eds) (2018) *Computational Propaganda: Political Parties, Politicians and Political Manipulation on Social Media.* Oxford: Oxford University Press.

World Values Survey (2010–2014) 'World Values Survey 6th Wave'. Available at: www.worldvaluessurvey.org (accessed 26 February 2020).

Worlds of Journalism (2012–2016) www.worldsofjournalism.org/

Wright, E.O. (2010) *Envisioning Real Utopias.* New York: Verso.

Wright, K. (2019) 'Journalists and the boundaries of state-funded international news', forthcoming.

Wright Mills, C. (1956) *The Power Elite.* Oxford: Oxford University Press.

Wright Mills, C. (1963) *Power, Politics and People: The Collected Essays of C. Wright Mills.* New York: Oxford University Press.

Wright Mills, C. (1970) *The Sociological Imagination.* Middlesex: Penguin.

Wring, D. (2005) *The Politics of Marketing the Labour Party.* Basingstoke: Palgrave.

Yip, H. (2018) 'China's $6 Billion Propaganda Blitz in a Snooze', *Foreign Policy*, 23 April. Available at: https://foreignpolicy.com/2018/04/23/the-voice-of-china-will-be-a-squeak/ (accessed 26 February 2020).

Zald, M. and Lansbury, M. (2010) The Wizards of Oz: towards an institutional approach to elites, expertise and command posts, *Organization Studies*, 31(7).

Zuboff, S. (2019) *The Age of Surveillance Capitalism: The Fight for a Human Future and the New Frontier of Power.* Oxford: Oxford University Press.

INDEX

Lightning Source UK Ltd.
Milton Keynes UK
UKHW022106161020
371717UK00002B/5